CHURCH FINANCE HANDBOOK

Edited by

KEVIN E. MCKENNA
LAWRENCE A. DINARDO
JOSEPH W. POKUSA

CANON LAW SOCIETY OF AMERICA
The Catholic University of America
Washington, D.C. 20064

Canon Law Society of America
The Catholic University of America
Washington, D.C. 20064

1999

TABLE OF CONTENTS

Basic Principles

Acquiring Ecclesiastical Goods

Administering Temporal Goods

Conveyance of Ecclesiastical Goods

PREFACE

THE FORMAT OF THIS HANDBOOK

This text is intended to be useful to a broad range of persons involved in administration of church property and resources. This *Church Finance Handbook*, therefore, offers a description of fundamental concepts and principles of church property law and provides background to assist practitioners. An introductory chapter reviews historical circumstances in which church law regarding property has evolved through the centuries. Beyond history, it is likewise important to understand technical terms of law such as "ecclesiastical goods" or "juridic persons." Administrators, moreover, must appreciate the various levels of consultation, which ought to take place in more complicated transactions as well as those permissions, which may be required for administration of church property. It is also critical for administrators to be clear about the relationship between civil law and church law so that the civil law interest of a given church community is adequately protected. Such topics are discussed, therefore, in a preliminary chapter. Then, chapter by chapter, the *Church Finance Handbook* presents a variety of topics in property law.

For each topic most chapters as appropriate follow a similar format which will help the reader to understand the principles and to recognize how norms and procedures can be applied in particular cases. Chapters are usually developed in the following sections:

Cases

The first section of the chapter presents "a case" (or "cases") which can serve as a "fact model" or "fact models" to illustrate the topic under consideration. The cases illustrated are only hypothetical models. Some of the cases, however, may be quite parallel to current instances with which a parish or diocese is dealing. At other times particular circumstances will be at most vaguely similar to an actual case. The reader, therefore, must make the appropriate adjustments in recognizing how a particular instance for a diocese or parish differs from the fact model. Nonetheless the model should be helpful. Cases are labeled with Arabic numbers and follow consecutively, e.g., "Case 1" is the first case in chapter two.

Canonical Principles

The second section of the chapter discusses the canonical principle or principles, which apply to the particular topic under consideration. Relevant canons will also be cited and commented on in terms of their application.

Application

The third section of the chapter reviews the application or procedures involved for the particular topic. For instance, what offices, councils or authorities need to be involved on the local level? Must any superiors be consulted? Who are the proper agents to act on each level? Is the consent of any person or group necessary? What civil law considerations may apply?

Sample Documents

The fourth section of many chapters provides some sample documents, under the generic title "formulary" which could be used in the type of case(s) treated for the particular topic, for instance:

1. sample letters;

2. forms;

3. decrees; and

4. a check list which may be helpful to review steps.

Some authors have chosen to vary the order of the presentation due to the complexity of the topic or for some other reason.

The experience and advice of others who have been active in church finances can also be very helpful. In 1995, a document offering a sound perspective on the organization of church administration was provided by the Committee on Budget and Finance of the National Conference of Catholic Bishops, entitled *Diocesan Internal Controls, A Framework*. It may be obtained from the United States Catholic Conference.

Some chapters of this *Church Finance Handbook* likewise provide samples of diocesan guidelines and statutes. Such samples may be helpful to dioceses or parishes, which must address similar concerns.

The last part of the *Church Finance Handbook* includes a glossary of canonical and civil law terms, which provides some definitions found in this *Church Finance Handbook*. This part of the *Church Finance Handbook* can make it, hopefully, even more useful for many readers.

PURPOSE OF THIS HANDBOOK

This text is a handbook. It is intended as a concise, ready reference for clergy, religious and lay personnel who work in the day to day administration of the Church's temporal goods. It can be helpful for the people who must allocate the resources of our Catholic Church community for fulfillment of our mission in today's world. The text, however, is not a commentary on the canons of the Code of Canon Law, Book V, "The Temporal Goods of the Church."

This *Church Finance Handbook* should be useful both for church professionals involved from day to day with church activities and for lay people engaged in more limited circumstances with the work of the Church. Church administrators, members of diocesan staffs or a bishop's various consultors, pastors or members of a parish finance council, no doubt, approach the topics treated from the perspective of their own particular responsibilities. Hopefully many can benefit from the various presentations made in this text.

Since the Second Vatican Council, our Church has increasingly called upon the aid and expertise of lay people who participate actively in various aspects of the Church's life and mission. In a significant way, at the diocesan and at the parochial level, many lay persons have taken an ever more active role in caring for and in the administration of ecclesiastical property and the resources of parishes and institutions. They may not all be experts in the field of church law. They should, nevertheless, understand how church property law functions. They should know how responsibility for proper administration is shared among various offices and, at times, among various consultative bodies, for the good of all. The right administration of church property is never the prerogative of isolated individuals. Cooperation is essential. The purpose of this handbook is to enhance the participation of both professional church personnel and other Christians in such important endeavors.

In addition to the many authors who have contributed to this text, the editors wish to express gratitude to many who have guided and assisted in this effort. We are especially grateful to Prof. Michael Carragher, O.P. of the Pontifical University of St. Thomas, Rome who reviewed the manuscript and made many helpful suggestions. We are also grateful to Dr. Marvin Mich who provided much editorial assistance. We also wish to thank the Board of Governors of the Canon Law Society of America who first assigned this task and provided helpful encouragement as well as many useful corrections, additions and recommendations. To all who either directly or indirectly assisted in this effort, we are truly grateful.

Kevin E. McKenna, Chief Editor
Lawrence A. DiNardo, Editor
Joseph W. Pokusa, Editor

ABBREVIATIONS

AAS	*Acta Apostolicae Sedis*, Vatican City, 1909-
AICPA	American Institute of Certified Public Accountants
c.	canon
cc.	canons
CCEO	Code of Canons of the Eastern Churches (*Codex Canonum Ecclesiarum Orientalium*)
CD	Vatican II, decree, Christus Dominus
CLD	Canon Law Digest
CLSA	Canon Law Society of America
CIC	1983 Code of Canon Law (*Codex Iuris Canonici*)
1917CIC	1917 Code of Canon Law (*Codex Iuris Canonici*)
CICLSAL	Congregation for Institutes of Consecrated Life and Societies of Apostolic Life
ERISA	Employee Retirement Income Security Act
FASB	Financial Accounting Standards Board
FLSA	Fair Labor Standards Act
GAAP	Generally Accepted Accounting Procedures
GS	Vatican II, pastoral constitution, *Gaudium et spes*
LG	Vatican II, dogmatic constitution, *Lumen Gentium*
NCCB	National Conference of Catholic Bishops
USCC	United States Catholic Conference

Introduction to a Church Finance Handbook

Joseph W. Pokusa

Background for the Law on Temporal Goods

The Church's use of the goods of this world is coterminous with the Christian community's own existence. Jesus and his own disciples kept a "common purse" (John 13:29). The Lord, moreover, indicated that the disciples whom he sent out could expect people's support: "Stay in the one house eating and drinking what they have, for the laborer is worth his wage" (Luke 10:7). From the start of church life, the Acts of the Apostles manifests concerns about the use and distribution of the resources of the Christian community. Income from sale of personal property could be rightfully donated to the Church (Acts 4:37). Some Christians failed, however, to be completely forthright in the appearance of contributing to the work of the Church (Acts 5:2). A choice of the seven men who are often considered to be the first deacons was occasioned by concern on the part of Greek-speaking Christian Jews who "complained that their widows were being neglected in the daily distribution of food, as compared with the widows of those who spoke Hebrew" (Acts 6:1). Likewise, to prepare for a collection which he had organized to be taken up in Galatia, Macedonia and at Corinth to help with the needs of the Jerusalem community, St. Paul stipulated that on Sundays, "everyone should put aside whatever he has been able to save" (1 Cor 16:1-3). St. Paul commented about this effort and the freewill nature of these contributions when he wrote: "Everyone must give according to what he inwardly decided; not sadly, not grudgingly, for God loves a cheerful giver" (2 Cor 9:7). The Christian scriptures such as these make it clear that administration of the temporal goods of the Church is nothing new and that a proper administration is a genuine part of the Gospel way.

In fact, a proper attitude for religious people about economic resources relates, in part, to the conditions that surround them. Velasio DePaolis notes how the Hebrew scripture recognize an ambiguity in the blessings, which come with the goods of the world. Great material blessings, on the one hand, may be seen as signs of God's favor for Abraham (Gen 13:2) and Isaac (Gen 26:12). Yet, because economic conditions are uncertain at best, among God's holy people there was to be "a relaxation of debts" every seven years; "since the Lord ... will bless you abundantly ... there should be no one of you in need" (Deut 15:4). Still aware of real injustices, which persist in the distribution of this world's goods, the Psalmist, on the other hand, declares God "shall govern ... with judgment" and "defend the afflicted among the people, save the children of the poor and crush the oppressor" (Ps 72:1-3). Such contradictory aspects of material blessings are seen to be rooted in the disordered human state after original sin: "Cursed be the ground because of you! In toil shall you eat its yield .... Thorns and thistles shall it bring forth" (Gen 3:17-18). The Psalmist acknowledges the prosperity of the wicked: "they are free from the burdens of mortals, and are not afflicted like the rest of men" (Ps 73:5-6) but reflects that God has set these rich "on a slippery road ... to ruin" (Ps 73:18). Even while there is respect for material blessings, the prophets, for instance, Amos and Hosea, can make a strong plea for the need of justice to be done on behalf of the oppressed poor.

DePaolis insists on how Jesus, in his own ministry, expressed emphatically a genuine danger in having too much wealth.[1] Jesus said to the crowd: "Avoid greed in all its forms. A man may be wealthy, but his possessions do not guarantee him life" (Luke 12:15). Jesus urged his followers: "Do not lay up for yourselves an earthly treasure" because "you cannot give yourself to God and money" (Matt 6:19, 24). Christ, indeed, commends voluntary evangelical poverty. To a man who already kept the Commandments but sought to share in everlasting life, "Jesus looked at him with love" and said: "There is one thing more ... Go and sell what you have and give to the poor; you will then have treasure in heaven" (Mark 10:21). But, Jesus did not require renunciation of wealth. Joseph of Arimathea who provided his own tomb for Jesus' body was described as "a wealthy man" and "another of Jesus' disciples" (Matt 27:57). Likewise, in his ministry, "Joanna, the wife of Herod's steward Chuza, Susanna and many others ... were assisting them out of their means" (Luke 8:3). Such faithful disciples must have remained people with some good measure of temporal resources.

The Christian scriptures, therefore, exhibit a cautious and balanced approach to the goods of the world. Christians have responsibility to fulfill the Hebrew scriptures' concern about the needs of the poor. The Epistle of James asks: "If a brother or sister has nothing to wear and no food for the day, and you ... do not meet their bodily needs, what good is that?" (Jas 2:15-16); and the Epistle of John asks: "How can God's love survive in a man who has enough of this world's goods yet closes his heart to his brother when he sees him in need?" (1 John 3:17). St. Paul insists, nevertheless, that "the willingness to give should accord with one's means, not go beyond them. The relief of others ought not to impoverish you; there should be a certain equality" (2 Cor 8:12-13).

---

[1] Velasio DePaolis, *I beni temporali della Chiesa* (Bologna: Centro Edizioni Dehoniane, 1995) 245-247.

In the course of almost 2,000 years, the Church has witnessed transitions from the ancient imperial economy through the chaos of the Dark Ages, the feudal land based economy of the Middle Ages, the development of capitalism, the advent of socialism and the coming of the international free enterprise system which dominates so much of today's world. Also in all ages, some local churches existed in those isolated areas where barter types of commerce were dominant.

The military strength of the Roman Empire provided a stability in society which Pliny described as the *Pax Romana*, a situation of prevailing peace from Britain to the Euphrates and across much of North Africa which lasted for centuries. The Church grew in that atmosphere even though at various times and places Christians faced fierce persecutions. In the ancient world, Christian communities acquired property and dealt with finances. In his *First Apology in Defense of Christians* (no. 67), St. Justin, who was martyred about 165, described Sunday Mass in Rome: "The collection is placed in the custody of the president [that is, the bishop] who uses it to help the orphans and widows and all who for any reason are in distress, whether because they are sick, in prison, or away from home." Legal mechanisms by which the early church communities held property are not clear. Opinion varied about whether Churches organized themselves as *collegia tenuiorum* or burial associations, which assured their members of a decent funeral through collection of monthly fees. In his *Apologeticum* (29, 5), written in 197, the African Christian scholar, Tertullian, described the Church as "a society with a common religious feeling, unity of discipline, a common bond of hope" and said about bishops that "our presidents are elders of proved character ... for nothing that is God's goes for a price." In the same text, moreover, he offered some insight into the financial organization of the Church when he wrote that the "chest ... is not made up of money paid in entrance fees as if religion were a matter of contract" but that "every man once a month brings some coin, – or whatever he likes ... a voluntary offering ... the trust funds of piety." Writing about 222 in Rome, St. Hippolytus noted that Pope Zephyrinus named Callistus, his chief deacon (who later succeeded him as Bishop of Rome), to be the manager of the clergy and the superintendent of the cemetery (*Refutation of All Heresies*, IX, 7). Observations such as these may support the cemetery association hypothesis. In those early centuries, whatever properties the Churches held were likely modest. In any case, church leaders did administer the goods of the Christian community in order to fulfill the Church's mission.

As the persecutions ended, the patrimony of the Church began to increase. Very generous donations came from emperors, wealthy converts and the growing numbers of the faithful. They made the Church a real economic factor in society. Churches came to be recognized as corporate persons able to acquire property. Church holdings often were protected by special privileges. At the same time, however, some conflicts arose over particular dispositions of property. As a result, secular regulations and canonical norms were enacted to assure use of ecclesiastical property for proper purposes. Regulations precluded use for church property to enrich private persons and sought to prevent the despoiling of a family's fortunes by overly generous contributions made to the Church. The churches throughout the Christian Roman Empire developed various specialized roles for the administration of church property such as the offices of the archdeacon, the finance officer, an advocate for the Church and lay counselors who represented churches in lawsuits. In those centuries, the administration of church property was most certainly carried out in terms of classical Roman property law.

As the centuries passed, however, the Empire began to collapse throughout the West. Successive invasions by the Vandals, the Visigoths, the Franks, the Alamanni, the Burgundi and later Asiatic and Slavic invasions entirely reshaped both the political and the economic face of Europe and North Africa. In such terrible times, the local churches were often the only institutions available to handle all sorts of community needs. Hamman writes: "The economic crisis, the social conditions of the West and the various waves of invasions forced the bishops to organize relief, distribute grain, receive refugees, watch over the city like a sentinel, meet with the invaders and, at times, even to organize the defense."[2] No universal norms as yet existed about use of church revenues. But in a 494 letter to the bishops of Lucania, Pope Gelasius I judged that a fourfold division of the income as well as the offerings from the faithful would be a suitable arrangement; namely, that a quarter of it was to be given to the bishop, another quarter was for the clergy's use, a third quarter should provide for the needs of the poor and the last quarter was to be dedicated to the care of church property. Such a distribution reflects traditional concerns (e.g., support for the clergy, assistance to the needy and maintenance of church facilities) as well as the broader duty of bishops, as chief shepherds, who cared for concerns of a more far reaching community. An ancient formula in allocation of church funds – *clerus, caritas, cultus* – indicates social service and charity were acknowledged as very significant purposes in the use of church revenues.

By the end of the fourth and beginning of the fifth century, numbers of outlying churches had parochial holdings of their own that were distinct from the property and treasury of the bishop's church. Speaking of such churches, Imbart

---

[2] Adalbert Hamman, "The Turnabout of the Fourth Century," *Patrology*, Angelo Di Berardino, ed., trans. Placid Solari, O.S.B. (Westminster, MD: Christian Classics, Inc., 1986), *The Golden Age of Latin Patristic Literature*, Angelo Di Berardino and others, 4:13.

de la Tour says that deacons "assist the pastor in the administration of ecclesiastical patrimony ... visit the sick [and] take care of the schools."[3] A sixth century canonical letter of Italian origin, for instance, reflects, with limitations, the involvement of deacons in property administration when it insists that deacons had "no authority to sell, transfer, or in any way alienate church real estate; to breach trusts; to appoint agents ... under penalty of restitution ... those who receive churches do so for administering them, not for despoiling them."[4]

During those centuries called the Dark Ages which lasted until about 1,000, local bishops or their synods sought guidance as best they could by matching received traditions to the changing economic realities of their regions. But the transition from commerce to a largely land based economy had serious implications in evolution of church property law. The agrarian situation of sharecroppers and tenant farmers in the late empire gradually evolved into a condition called serfdom. Serfs, as members of a servile class, were "bound to the soil" and required to work the land in return for their subsistence from its fruits. They were subject to the will of their landlords. A real decline in peaceful trade and the subsequent scarcity of money eliminated the older system of cash compensations and salaries. Agriculture alone remained the stable business of the day. The powerful landholders granted the use of lands, or fiefs, to vassals in various descending layers of service. Thus, a system known as feudalism came to prevail throughout Europe into the 1400s. Within the new economic system, the Church found itself constrained by the same economic practices. A system known as benefices became the ordinary means for support of church ministers and to assure ecclesiastical services. Yet just as they dominated other subjects, society's powerful men sometimes tried to appoint clergy for their own village churches or private chapel. But even those clerics who were appointed by bishops, or a bishop's official, were recompensed "in land" and their rights to the produce of the land. The Middle Ages saw conflicts between bishops as leaders of the Church and economically powerful lay people who sought to control the Church in the way that they controlled their lands.

In such changing economic situations, the traditions of church law had to be rethought. Medieval church writers employed the heritage of classical Roman law, which they meshed, with historic decisions of church councils, synods and papal decrees to forge the *Corpus iuris canonici* (Body of canon law) of the Western Church. Gratian compiled what became the first book of the *Corpus iuris canoni-*

---

[3]Pierre Imbart de la Tour, *De Ecclesiis rusticanis Aetate Carolingica* (Burdegalae: G. Gounouilhou, 1890) 127.
[4]Epistola Canonica, J.P. Migne, ed. *Patrologiae Cursus completus, Series secunda, in qua prodeunt Patres, Doctores, Scriptores Ecclesiae Latinae* (Paris, 1844-64) 56:892.

ci, his *Decretum* of 1140. Noting he reflected the tradition of the Church Fathers about care for those in need, DePaolis says that Gratian summarized how "it belongs to the Church to care for the weak and to take care of pilgrims" and points to norms in the *Decretum* "to protect less fortunate persons [*miserabiles personae*], to uphold their rights and their dignity: they have a right to receive assistance from the 'surplus' in a community and there exists, moreover, a corresponding obligation on the part of whoever possesses or is in charge of the surplus."[5] But, while it was one thing to repeat those traditions of the past, it was another thing to make such principles effective in practice.

As the Middle Ages advanced, ecclesiastical property became an important factor in the overall development of society. Beside the property that belonged to the bishop and his clergy, other church properties belonged to monasteries or to religious communities of men and women. Some religious property even belonged to dedicated lay Catholics who created various kinds of charitable associations. This economic base in no small measure financed the building of the great cathedrals, an advancement in hospitals and orphanages as well as the growth of those centers of learning from which evolved Europe's great universities. Unfortunately, with a growth in church property and with the inadequacies of the system for support of the local clergy, abuses generated criticism of church personnel and of the Church in general. The feudal structures of society were also beginning to be transformed by growth of city life, development of banking, and advance of a free capitalism system. DePaolis states: "Institutions that functioned during the thirteenth century were no longer adequate to meet the needs of the fourteenth century."[6]

But the Church was not always readily able to respond to such changes. The benefice system itself was resistant to reform. Benefices had the effect of isolating office holders extensively, even from the authority of bishops who might have wished to reform things. Ecclesiastics who were thereby assured of some income could be insulated personally from economic struggles that arose, especially in the later era of industrialization. Churches might try to give assistance to individuals in desperate straits. Some church leaders were critically aware of the emerging economic patterns. Fifteenth century archbishop of Florence, St. Antoninus, both aided the poor with the revenues from his archdiocese and – being an astute analyst of the times – wrote as a sociologist and an economist as well as a theologian.[7] Under a feudal system, serfs bound to the soil could look for help from their own landlords when hard times pressed them. But workers in the growing cities, not

---

[5] DePaolis, 256.
[6] Ibid., 257.
[7] *New Catholic Encyclopedia*, s.v. "Antoninus," by James B. Walker.

bound to particular landlords, enjoyed no such patronage or protection from those capitalistic enterprises that employed them and might let them go at will. Thus churchmen were often not clear on how to evaluate such business practices and their effects on workers.

One innovation was the development of *montes pietatis*, of nonprofit credit charities that allowed poor people to pawn objects at low interest rates to protect themselves against exploitation by usuers in economic hardships.[8] In 1361, Michael Nothburg, Bishop of London, willed money for such a purpose. In the same century, Durandus of Saint-Pourcain and later Philip of Maizieres promoted similar approaches for helping the impoverished. More than sixty (60) Franciscan friars founded *montes pietatis* between 1462 and 1515. "But the friar whose name will always be associated with the *montes pietatis* is Blessed Bernardino da Feltre (1439–1494), who between 1484 and 1494 was tireless in founding and reforming the *montes* (over thirty of them) which he placed on a solid basis."[9] Yet theological battles over the lawfulness of charging even small interest rates – as opposed to usury – were not settled until the papal intervention of Leo X in 1515. Nevertheless, McFadden observes, such *montes* did "prepare the way for acceptance of credit business as a means of livliehood, and for the legitmacy of investment in lending organization."[10] Furthermore, as time went on, various aspects of charity and assistance to the sick which had traditionally been "church work" were to become more the responsibility of various secular authorities in the new cities and states that emerged.

In church property procedure, processes of administration that became practices in subsequent ecclesiastical law had foundations in the transformation of ownership developed within feudal society. Subsequent church property law, for instance, was highly orientated to protection of property holdings since "the land" was perceived as so important a patrimony, the key for future stability of church ministry. It finally took the Second Vatican Council to call for elimination of the benefice system. In their Decree on the Ministry and Life of Priests, the Council Fathers said: "the so-called system of benefices is to be abandoned or else reformed in such a way that the part that has to do with the benefice – that is, the right to revenues attached to the endowment of the office – shall be regarded as secondary and the principal emphasis in law given to the ecclesiastical office itself" (no. 20).

[8] *New Catholic Encyclopedia*, s.v. "Montes Pietatis," by Agnes B. McFadden.
[9] Raphael M. Huber, O.F.M. Conv., *A Documented History of the Franciscan Order (1182–1517)* (Milwaukee, WI: The Nowiny Publishing Apostolate, Inc., 1944) 926.
[10] *New Catholic Encyclopedia*, s.v. "Montes Pietatis," by Agnes B. McFadden.

The 1917 codification of canon law attempted to set church administration more securely within the developed capitalism of the Western world. While many of its structures still reflected a feudal prejudice and its property mentality, the first Code of Canon Law in 1917 took into account new structures. One instance deals with a consultative body of particular significance in the more important decisions of property administration in the local church. Instead of cathedral chapters intimately connected to the benefice system, the 1917 code recognized also an institution developed first in the United States, diocesan consultors. The 1917 code ascribed those powers of government, which the code attributed to a cathedral chapter also to boards of diocesan consultors. Later, in the Decree on the Pastoral Office of Bishops in the Church, the Council Fathers at Vatican II wrote: "Among the cooperators of the bishop in the governing of the diocese are included the priests who constitute his senate or council, such as the cathedral chapter, the council of consultors, or other committees. ... These councils, and especially the cathedral chapters, should be reorganized, as far as necessary, to suit contemporary needs" (no. 27). In still further innovation, moreover, the 1983 Code of Canon Law gave preeminent position in the universal church to a board of diocesan consultors and reduced cathedral chapters largely to their liturgical duties. Both the 1917 code and the 1983 code sought to "canonize" aspects of contemporary economics, which were thought to protect rightful use of church property, for example, the civil laws on contracts. Yet even the 1983 code struggles with aspects of the international enterprise which dominate the twentieth century world.

Because people who make up the Church live in a world of time and space, the things of the world, or "temporal goods," must be used by the church community just to carry out the spiritual dimensions of religious life. We worship in sacred spaces called churches or chapels. We bury our dead in consecrated cemeteries. We house our programs of education and charity within institutions and offices. We provide living space for clergy and religious. We also dedicate facilities such as hospitals and homes for people in special need of assistance. Still, for instance, how do we who enjoy abundance and prosperity unknown in prior human history and proportionately consume more resources of the earth than others living today in different parts of the world judge religiously what it means to have enough or to have too much? In their Decree on the Apostolate of Lay People the bishops at the Second Vatican Council stated:

> In the early days the Church linked the "agape" [the love feast offered the poor] to the Eucharistic supper, and by doing so showed itself as one body around Christ united by the bond of charity. ... That is why mercy to the poor and the sick, and charitable works and works of mutual aid

for the alleviation of all kinds of human needs, are held in special honor in the Church.

... Wherever men are to be found who are in want of food and drink, of clothing, housing, medicine, work, education, the means necessary for leading a truly human life, wherever there are men racked by misfortune or illness, men suffering exile or imprisonment, Christian charity should go in search of them and find them out, comfort them with devoted care and give them the helps that will relieve their needs. This obligation binds first and foremost the more affluent individuals and nations (no. 8).

In context of this historical overview, a contemporary approach to the purposes and utilization of church property may be easier to understand or, at least, seen within an authentic perspective.

PURPOSES OF TEMPORAL GOODS IN CHURCH

The Church holds and administers temporal goods to serve the mission that the Lord has entrusted to the Church. The first point, which should be kept in mind, therefore, is that church property never belongs to an individual person as if it were his or her own personal property. Church property always belongs to some juridic person and is the concern of the Christian community. The canonical norms, therefore, structure the Church's administration of property to facilitate the Church's mission, to protect the rights of various Christian communities to the proper use of property entrusted to them and to promote the welfare of those persons and groups who should benefit from the wise use of the goods which are made available to the Church.

Canon law states four broad purposes for church property:

1. pursuit of divine worship;

2. support for clerics and other ministers;

3. performance of the apostolic works proper to the Church; and

4. works of charity, especially concern for the needy (c. 1254, §2).

Christian worship involves more than just church services such as Mass and the sacraments. Canon law states: "Christian worship ... is a work which proceeds from faith and is based on it;" and, therefore, "sacred ministers are to strive diligently to arouse and enlighten that faith, especially through the ministry of the word by which faith is born and nourished" (c. 836). The scope of divine worship, therefore, can be seen to be related also to the whole broad range of preaching and of teaching activities that are associated with communication of the Gospel as a way of living.

Support of the Church's ministers certainly means the support of the clergy. But support for the Church's ministers is broader than simply caring for the needs of bishops, priests and deacons. Women and men religious, for instance, have traditionally been included among persons whom the Church ought to support in one way or another. Today many other lay persons are likewise associated with the Church's ministry. The 1973 *Directory on the Pastoral Ministry of Bishops* notes that a diocesan bishop "requires and willingly employs suitable, chosen collaborators – clerics, religious, or lay people – whom he makes his associates in some areas of his charge … with them he shares the apostolic mission and to them he entrusts responsibilities, according to the norms of prudent pastoral cooperation" (no. 198). Thus the appropriate support necessary for such other ministers to serve the mission of the Church in the world may also be included among those rightful purposes for which Church resources are utilized.

Church apostolates involve a limitless range of endeavors and different types of undertakings: schools, religious instruction programs, social organizations, family life activities, justice concerns, etc. Whatever processes and tasks touch on a genuine human development of persons and communities are important to the Church and are potentially legitimate apostolates.

Charitable outreach, especially for the pressing concerns of the needy, also typifies many activities of the church community. A wide variety of social service programs, legitimately apostolic in purpose, may rightfully lay claim to funding from the temporal goods of the Church.

The Second Vatican Council called for a preferential option for the poor. In their Decree on the Pastoral Office of Bishops in the Church, the council fathers wrote: "Bishops should present the doctrine of Christ in a manner suited to the needs of the times … in presenting this doctrine they should proclaim the maternal solicitude of the Church for all men, whether they be Catholics or not, and should be especially solicitous for the poor and weaker brethren whom the Lord has commissioned them to evangelize" (no. 13).[11] Hamman states of the ancient

---

[11] James Provost notes: "The Council considered poverty from several angles, including the preaching of the gospel to the poor (*LG* 8), following Christ in poverty of spirit (*AA* 4), and the practical needs of poor people today (*LG* 27) that even call for the transformation of the international social order (*GS* 63, 90). It did not specify a dominical precept as such, but it implied one when addressing the practical consequences of human dignity (*LG* 27)." James H. Provost, "Social Justice," in *The Code of Canon Law: A Text and Commentary*, ed. James A. Coriden, et al. (New York/Mahwah: Paulist Press, 1985) 379.

Church that "Fathers and councils repeated that the offerings made to the church, except for what was necessary for its ministers, belonged to the poor."[12] The tradition of church care for those in need became expanded in the late Roman Empire. Comparing the bishops with "the Swedish ombudsman," Hamman explains that "in the face of the failures of the civil authority, the bishop was obliged to concern himself with the city, defend the interests of the citizens, intervene in the secular courts, soften the rigors of the laws, ameliorate the condition of prisoners, and obtain a reduction or a postponement of taxes."[13] Many such duties were later assumed by dedicated lay Christians, by religious societies and by religious orders. Civil authorities in modern nation states, however, eventually began to assume responsibility for such social welfare issues. The Church, nevertheless, continues to have a special concern for the needs of the poor, to encourage initiatives for the betterment of their condition and to offer both symbolic and effectual demonstrations of assistance to the needy. Indeed, with the contemporary American movement to retrench welfare programs, increasingly those in need are turning to churches for assistance.

Obviously multiple claims will be made on the resources of the Church. At the same time, no church has unlimited sources to fund its activities. Churches will always face the question of choices as a crucial dimension in the administration of church property. What is to be funded, from which sources and for how long? Thus one of the major goals of the canonical norms on temporal goods is to assist all engaged in church administration in such a decision making process. The canons make stipulations about consultation, give principles for the stability of resources and assign various levels of authority for the allocation of church funds.

The topics treated in the following chapters present various questions and the relevant canonical norms about consultative groups, required procedures and particular considerations regarding use of the temporal goods of the Catholic Church as they apply in the decision making process addressing those many claims which today compete for funding from the temporal goods of churches.

[12]Hamman, 12.
[13]Ibid., 13.

BASIC PRINCIPLES

CHAPTER ONE

BASIC CONCEPTS AND PRINCIPLES

FRANCIS G. MORRISEY, O.M.I.

In order to understand the legislation relating to the ownership and administration of temporal goods, and to be able to apply it correctly, it would be
important to make certain that a number of basic underlying concepts which are
found throughout Book V are properly understood. We shall try to examine some
of these in turn, giving practical contemporary applications where possible.

This first chapter will review basic concepts and principles, which are utilized by
the *Code of Canon Law* when discussing the church's temporal goods. In reviewing
these concepts we will be establishing a common vocabulary and basic orientation
in dealing with the proper administration of the church's physical resources.

WHAT ARE JURIDIC PERSONS?

Types of Juridic Persons

The Church is a community of believers. However, in addition to those individuals who have been baptized and who constitute the vital force of the community, there are also other legal institutes, which surpass the capacity of individuals, and which have been duly set up to enable the Church to carry out its
mission of salvation.

For this reason, the *Code of Canon Law* speaks of three types of "persons" who
are entrusted in various ways with carrying out this mission.

First of all, there are *physical persons*, that is individuals who have, through baptism, acquired a number of rights (and corresponding obligations) in the Church
(see c. 96). These rights and obligations of physical persons may be exercised
according to their status; for instance, depending on whether or not they are

infants, minors, or adults; whether they are subject to ecclesiastical penalties; whether they have, through religious profession or some other type of commitment, renounced the exercise of certain rights.

The second category comprises *moral* persons, who come into existence without the intervention of any legal authority. The code recognizes two such moral persons: the Catholic Church, and the Apostolic See (c. 113, §1). In similar fashion, the secular world recognizes "nations" and "families" which come into existence without outside formal intervention.

The third category comprises *juridic* persons, that is, those "artificial" persons who, in canon law, are subjects of rights and obligations, which are in accord with their nature (c. 113, §2). Like a corporation in the secular world, a juridic person is a fiction of law. It is established to carry out works which transcend the purposes and capacities of individuals (c. 114, §1), and, by its nature is perpetual (c. 120, §1). The competent legislator intervenes to bring it into existence, and, if necessary, to modify or even to suppress it.

The code could not have used a secular term such as "corporation" to describe juridic persons, because this term is not universal. In some countries, indeed, these artificial groupings are called "*sociétés anonymes*," "trusts," "moral persons," "associations," and so forth. So, as is so often the case with canon law, a neutral term was employed.

Public and Private Juridic Persons

The Latin code speaks of two types of juridic persons: public and private.[1] Public juridic persons function in the name of the Church, with the full moral authority of the Church behind their undertakings, within the limits allotted to them; private juridic persons, on the other hand, while having due recognition, carry out their activities simply in the name of the members (c. 116, §1).

The code provides that juridic persons come into existence either in virtue of a provision of the law itself, or by a decree of the competent authority (c. 114, §1). While the code is quite clear in mentioning those instances where the law itself provides for such recognition (see, among many others, c. 238, §1 – seminaries; c. 363 – particular churches; c. 515, §3 – parishes; c. 634, §1 – religious institutes, provinces, and established houses), it is not as clear when it comes to determining who is the "competent authority" to grant juridical personality. By analogy

---

[1] The *Code of Canon Law* affects the Latin Church, that is the "Western" Roman Catholic Church. The twenty-one Churches of the "Eastern" Catholic Church are governed by the *Code of Canons of the Eastern Churches*, which was promulgated by Pope John Paul II on October 18, 1990. See chapter three for a fuller discussion of the canons of the Eastern Churches.

with canon 312, it is recognized that the Holy See, the conference of bishops, or the diocesan bishop can grant juridical personality for ecclesiastical institutes immediately subject to their authority (for instance, associations, special works). But, the code does not determine whether major superiors in religious institutes can grant such, even though some major superiors are also ordinaries.

The situation arises quite frequently today in dioceses where religious who have assumed responsibility for a school or a healthcare institution, now have to withdraw from it. While in most cases the institution simply shared in the juridic personality of the sponsoring institute, when it is left standing on its own, it is not easy to state clearly whether, in fact, it received formal juridical recognition, especially if there is no documentation to support the claim. This obviously has implications for such issues as the distribution of funds allocated to the institution. It might be possible to consider that the rights (and obligations) deriving from juridical personality could be acquired by prescription[2] (see c. 1270), although this is not frequently mentioned in the writings of canonists. Because of the uncertainty of the situation, a number of church organizations are now taking steps to have their juridical situation clarified through the office of the diocesan bishop, just as they made provision for separate incorporation in the secular sphere. This should be encouraged so as to avoid unnecessary difficulties down the road.

There is a specific reason for this concern and a practical consequence flowing from the acquisition of juridical personality in canon law. For instance, canon 1256 states that: "Under the supreme authority of the Roman Pontiff, ownership of goods belongs to that juridic person which has acquired them legitimately." Obviously, we are speaking of canonical "ownership," and not of the civil registration of titles. Thus, if a hospital or a school has been given canonical juridical personality, in church law the goods it acquires through the years belong to it and not to the sponsoring institute. Therefore, if at some later date the institute needs to withdraw, the hospital or school retains its property. A similar unclear situation can exist with regard to parishes and the diocese, which are juridical persons by law, but where canonical ownership does not always correspond with civil ownership. This would be the case, for example, in those instances where the diocese is a corporation sole and all the property is thereby vested in the person of the diocesan bishop and his successors in office.

---

[2]By "prescription," we usually mean the manner of acquiring the ownership of property, or discharging debts, by the effect of time, and under the conditions regulated by law. Usually, prescription has close connections with what is known as a "statute of limitations."

The Statutes Governing Juridic Persons

Every juridic person must have statutes approved by the competent authority (this is determined in canon 117). According to canons 94, §1 and 1279, §1, these statutes are to provide, among other things, for the proper governance of the juridic person and for the administration of its temporal goods.

When the statutes have been carefully prepared, they provide practical answers to a number of potentially contentious issues. Indeed, on many occasions, the *Code of Canon Law* simply defers to the statutes which are recognized as constituting the "proper law" of the juridic person, as distinct from the "common law" governing the entire Church, or the "particular law" which is applicable to territory.

WHAT ARE ECCLESIASTICAL GOODS?

Types of Temporal Goods

According to the *Code of Canon Law* (c. 1257), ecclesiastical goods are those temporal possessions which belong either to a *moral person* (the Catholic Church, the Apostolic See) or to a *public juridic person* which functions in the name of the church (such as a diocese, a parish, a religious institute). On the other hand, goods belonging to *individuals* or to *private juridic persons* are not considered to be ecclesiastical goods to which the canons of Book V apply, unless otherwise stated. In passing, it could be mentioned that in the Eastern Catholic Churches, there is a slightly different understanding of what constitutes ecclesiastical goods, since the Eastern code makes no distinction between public and private juridic persons (see CCEO c. 1009, §2).

Temporal possessions can include not only money, stocks, foundations, trusts, land, buildings, and so forth, but also rights arising from intellectual labor (for instance, copyrights, and/or patent rights), and from natural increase (for instance, a herd of cattle, crops, fruit, and so forth). In some instances, a juridic person's "name" is also a significant temporal possession, because, like a brand name on a product, it signifies a specific quality, history, or some other important element of its identity. At times, when juridic persons are being reorganized, people insist on being able to retain the name under which a given institution originally carried on its business, because this is what prospective clients identify with. To lose a name often entails losing identity. To lose one's good name is even worse (see c. 220). Changes in identity arise frequently in the case of mergers of parishes, hospitals, foundations, and similar undertakings and the potential increase or loss of value should be taken into consideration when the transaction is being negotiated.

The Administration of Ecclesiastical Goods

Ecclesiastical goods, although they must be administered by physical persons, do not belong to any individual. Rather, they are considered to be part of the common possessions of the Church, to be used to further those purposes for which the Church may acquire, retain, administer and alienate temporal goods (c. 1254, §1). The principal purposes of ecclesiastical goods are fourfold: divine worship, the support of the clergy and of other persons who work for the Church, the works of the apostolate, and works of charity. This division was set out in the Vatican II document, *Presbyterorum ordinis*, 17 and was retained in canon 1254, §2 of the 1983 *Code of Canon Law*.

Because ecclesiastical goods are not the goods of private individuals, but are considered to be part of the common heritage of the church community, it is not surprising to see that extensive norms are given in the code to cover the ways they can be acquired and retained. In particular, the law prescribes that for all such goods, an administrator is to be designated, with specific terms of reference. The code, in canon 1273, when speaking directly of the Roman Pontiff, uses the general concept of "stewardship" when referring to this responsibility; the term can also be applied to other administrators. This implies a twofold duty: to administer the entrusted goods as a prudent householder would do (as mentioned in c. 1284, §1) and to give an account to the faithful of the goods received and the uses to which these were put (as prescribed in c. 1287, §2). For this reason, it is not surprising to note that canon 1283 has stringent norms relating both to the preparation and updating of inventories, so that a clear record may be kept of the goods that are held, and, more particularly, to the necessity of observing the intentions of donors (see c. 1267, §3).

The prescriptions relating to the observance of the intentions of donors are not exclusive to the canonical system. We find them also, and rightly so, enshrined in other legal systems. It is commonly held that this principle derives from natural law. Of course, at times, it is difficult to know with certainty what were the specific intentions of the donor, particularly if the gift was made long ago, or if vague or general conditions were attached to the donation. Canons 1308-1310 provide some practical principles to be used in resolving these dilemmas.

When Are Goods "Ecclesiastical Goods"?

At times, it is not always easy to determine whether goods are indeed ecclesiastical goods. For instance, when parishioners embark on fund-raising activities under the auspices of a parish, but for purposes not directly related to it (for instance, to support a parish baseball or hockey team), do the goods received become the property of the parish or do they remain the property of those who donated them for a specific purpose? Because of the numerous difficulties which arise from unclear fund-raising activities, canon 1265, §1 prescribes that certain permissions are required before such activities are undertaken.[3] This permission could, and indeed should, include norms relating to the eventual ownership and administration of any goods so acquired. This becomes especially important later on when a work is closed or substantially modified and its assets are to be distributed according to the norms of law (see c. 123).

In the Latin code, the goods of associations, which have not been given juridical recognition, are, according to canon 310, not considered to be ecclesiastical goods, but are the joint possessions of the members of the group. Nevertheless, because of the close connection of such associations with the Church, it is appropriate to have clear norms drawn up in the statutes of the group governing the use and administration of its goods.

A well-publicized decision of the Holy See, November 13, 1920,[4] (discussed in chapter two) determined that the goods owned by the St. Vincent de Paul Society are not ecclesiastical goods, and, consequently, they are not governed by the general prescriptions of canon law, but rather by their own statutes. The same would apply to the goods of the Knights of Columbus and similar associations, which do not have public juridical personality in the Church. As an interesting aside, it could be noted that because such organizations are not recognized as being public or private associations as such, they generally cannot take up collections during church services; however, a common practice has been to allow for collections for the St. Vincent de Paul Society to be taken up at the door of the Church after the religious services are completed.

---

[3] Guidelines for fund-raising were issued by the National Conference of Catholic Bishops on November 1977, and have been reprinted in James I. O'Connor, ed., *Canon Law Digest*, (Mundelein, IL: St. Mary of the Lake Seminary, 1978) 8:415-421. These are still considered to be in effect after the promulgation of the 1983 code, since they have not been replaced by subsequent legislation.

[4] *AAS* 13 (1921) 135-144.

WHO ADMINISTERS ECCLESIASTICAL GOODS?

The Person In Charge Of Administration

Canon 1279 provides a general principle: the administration of ecclesiastical goods pertains to the one with direct power of governance over the moral or juridical person to whom the goods belong.

In other words, canons 393, 532 and 636 provide that the diocesan bishop is responsible for administering the goods belonging to the diocese, the parish priest for those belonging to the parish, and the religious superior for those belonging to the institute or to its appropriate part.

This does not mean that the diocesan bishop, the parish priest, or the religious superior must personally intervene in all transactions. Rather, these persons establish the applicable policies and others may be designated to assist in implementing them. Thus, in each religious institute, according to canon 636, a treasurer is to be appointed to carry out, under the authority of the superior, the various acts of administration. The diocesan bishop is to appoint a finance officer (see c. 494, §1). Likewise, qualified persons can assist a parish priest.

Types Of Administration

The code distinguishes between those acts that the canonical administrator may carry out personally, without having to refer continually to others – these are usually called acts of *ordinary administration* (c. 1281, §1) – and those acts which call, among other things, for a special faculty in writing in order to be carried out – these are usually called acts of *extraordinary administration* (discussed more thoroughly in chapter sixteen). In the case of dioceses, there is also a third category of acts: acts of *major importance*, which require special advice before being carried out (c. 1277).

Acts of *ordinary* administration are usually routine acts which occur on a repetitive basis; they include payment of bills, distribution of salaries and stipends, banking of receipts, ordinary repairs to property, and so forth. Acts of *extraordinary* administration are to be determined by the conference of bishops, and usually refer either to specific acts (such as the purchasing of real estate, involvement in court action, major repairs, and so forth) or to acts whose cost exceeds a certain sum of money (for example, acts that entail the spending of money beyond a given percentage of the $3,000,000 maximum amount presently allowed by the Holy See for acts of alienation of stable property in the United States). Acts of *major importance* are determined by the diocesan bishop, and, again, are often based on a given sum of money (for example, acts that are between five and ten percent of the maximum allowed).

In most instances, advisers who are specially designated for this purpose assist the person who is responsible for the administration of ecclesiastical goods.

What Consultative Groups Are Involved?

The Finance Committee

Canon 1280 offers a general principle: "Each juridic person is to have its own finance counsel or at least two counselors who, according to norm of the statutes, are to assist the administrator in fulfilling his or her function."

The canon does not go into detail; the specifics are found in other parts of the code, when dealing with various juridic persons. However, the principle is clear: since it would be unfair to expect that all canonical administrators have the qualifications necessary to ensure the optimum form of financial governance, because they are often chosen for their other qualities, these persons must be assisted in various ways by those who are specially competent in this area. Indeed, bishops, parish priests, and major superiors are not generally appointed or elected to their offices simply because they are good administrators. Rather, other qualities might be more opportune.

Furthermore, because the world of finance is becoming so complicated, it would be unrealistic to expect that all canonical administrators would have the time and the capacity to keep abreast of changes occurring in secular society. Government regulations in relation to employment, taxation, and so forth, are continually changing. In this context, canon 1286 reminds us that administrators are to observe the applicable civil legislation relating to employment contracts, and canon 1284, §2, 3° prescribes that administrators are to take special care that the Church will not suffer damage through the non-observance of the civil law.

Canon 537 mandates a finance council in every parish to help the parish priest carry out his administrative duties (discussed in chapter twelve). The diocesan bishop is to draw up norms governing the functioning of this council, and to provide criteria for membership.

Canon 492 states that there is to be a finance council in each diocese, composed of at least three baptized persons, expert in financial affairs and civil law, of outstanding integrity, and appointed by the bishop. Their appointment is for five years, renewable. In addition to its other duties, the diocesan finance council is to intervene in all cases where an act of major importance or an act of extraordinary administration is to take place (see c. 1277).

The code is not as categorical when it comes to religious institutes (see chapter four). A general, provincial, or local council, as the case may be, is mandated by canon 627. While, generally speaking, this council intervenes on a number of matters relating to the internal governance of the institute, there is nothing in the law preventing its acting also as the finance council. Indeed, this has been the case in canonical tradition. The commission preparing the new code recognized this possibility,[5] and the original decree of the Holy See establishing such councils[6] provided that the ordinary council could fulfill this dual role. Of course, there is nothing preventing the setting up of a separate finance council, distinct from the ordinary council, if such expertise is readily available.

The College Of Consultors

In addition to the finance council, the code, in canon 502, mandates another body which is to intervene at the diocesan level when certain transactions are to be carried out: this is known as the college of consultors, and is composed of priests chosen from among the members of the presbyteral council.

Like the finance council, the college of consultors must intervene when there is question of acts of major importance or of acts of extraordinary administration at the diocesan level. For the first type of acts, both councils must be consulted; for the latter, they must give their consent beforehand if the transaction is to be considered valid (see c. 1277). It should be noted, however, that even if the councils are in favor of the act, the diocesan bishop is not obliged to go ahead with the act (see c. 127, §2, 2°). He could, for example, have second thoughts about the appropriateness of a given transaction, even though his advisers would be in favor of it. If either or both boards withhold their consent (in cases where such is required), he cannot act.

No such general prescription exists at the parish level.

In Religious Institutes

For religious institutes the code adopts a broader approach: it is up to the institute's own law, within the limits of the universal law, first of all to define the acts which exceed the purpose and the manner of ordinary administration, and then to establish what is needed for the validity of an act of extraordinary administration (c. 638, §1). The usual practice is to require the consent of the appropriate

---

[5] *Communicationes* 27 (1995) 102.

[6] See Congregation for Religious, *Inter ea*, *AAS* 1 (September 15, 1909) 695-699.

council before the superior can authorize such acts, but a religious institute could also bind itself to seek the intervention of its finance council before making the decision. The code does not prescribe that such decisions also be approved by the diocesan bishop (with his consultors and finance council intervening), but in some diocesan institutes, especially at the beginning, provision might possibly be made for this special intervention (see c. 637).

WHAT KINDS OF PERMISSIONS MAY BE NEEDED?

Certain acts relating to temporal goods are more complicated than others; in such instances, a more elaborate system of authorizations is required.

The code, for instance, clearly distinguishes between acts of *administration* (whether ordinary or extraordinary), and acts of *alienation* of property whereby a juridic person divests itself of all or part of its stable patrimony, or poses acts that could jeopardize this patrimony.

In the case of acts of administration relating to a parish, a diocesan work, or the diocese itself, no permissions from outside the diocese are required. However, in cases where the alienation of stable property is at stake, permission from the Holy See might also be required, depending on the amount of money involved in the transaction. The Holy See sets the maximum amounts authorized, either in the case of goods subject to a diocesan bishop's authority (see c. 1292), or for those subject to religious superiors (see c. 638, §3). It often happens that the maximum amount is the same for both categories (for instance, presently it is fixed at $3,000,000 in the USA).[7]

Thus, in the case of goods subject to the authority of the diocesan bishop, it is the Congregation for the Clergy which grants the required permission; while in the case of religious, it is the Congregation for Institutes of Consecrated Life and Societies of Apostolic Life.[8] In other instances, other offices of the Holy See could be involved such as the Congregation for the Oriental Churches or the Congregation for the Evangelization of Peoples.

Permission is relatively easy to obtain if the request is properly motivated and the required supporting documents are in order. However, given the changing social situations, the focus these days is placed much more on the effects of the action rather than simply on the amount of money involved. This is particularly

[7]See National Conference of Catholic Bishops, *Implementation of the 1983 Code of Canon Law*, (Washington, DC: NCCB, 1991) 24 (letter from the Holy See, April 16, 1991).
[8]See John Paul II, *Pastor bonus*, AAS 80 (June 28, 1988) art. 98 and art. 108, §1.

true when a Catholic healthcare institution is being reorganized, but wishes to retain its "Catholic" identity. In such instances, it will be important also to show how the Ethical and Religious Directives for Catholic Health Care Services[9] (or a similar document) are being applied, and who has ultimate responsibility for the designation of members of the Board of Directors (see chapter twenty-two).

Religious institutes of pontifical right do not, according to the letter of the law, require the permission of the diocesan bishop of the place where the goods are situated before alienation can take place. However, the practice of the Holy See is to request a *nihil obstat* from him to make certain that there are no major objections on his part to the transfer.

What Is the Relationship of Canon and Civil Law?

The Church operates in two spheres, both in the ecclesiastical and in the secular. Both spheres have their own legislation. At times, their laws are concordant; but, on other occasions, there are significant differences between the two. Which set has priority? In a secularized society, the tendency would probably be to privilege the secular legislation, since it is the one than can be enforced. Indeed, it must be recognized that many of the canons in the code contain prescriptions for which there are no corresponding penalties for non-observance. Furthermore, the canons themselves insist on the observance of the applicable civil legislation (see cc. 1268; 1284, §2, 2°; 1284, §2, 3°; 1286, 1°; 1296 and so forth). Nevertheless, we must recognize that the canons also call for observance of the canonical legislation, perhaps not under pain of punishment, but rather as an expression of an attitude of mind and of a true sense of responsible stewardship.

Although the canons call for observance of the secular law, the converse is not always true – while secular legislation may not call for observance of canon laws, secular courts may, in their decisions, consider whether or not applicable ecclesiastical laws were observed. For this reason, in the secular world, the corporate documents governing ecclesiastical undertakings (such as institutions, foundations, etc.) are considered to be the operative norms, and recourse to canon law is not required. However, in order to remedy this situation, the civil charters of incorporation or the accompanying by-laws now often contain what are called

[9] The *Ethical and Religious Directives for Catholic Health Care Services* were approved by the NCCB on November 17, 1994, for use in the USA. See *Origins* 24: 27 (December 15, 1994) 449, 451-462. Other Conferences of Bishops have issued similar documents; for instance, in Canada, *Healthcare Ethics Guide*, (Ottawa: Catholic Health Association of Canada, February 1991) 1-91.

"reserved powers." The notion of "reservation" is found in canon 87, §1, and in other canons throughout the code. The reserved powers are such that the secular corporation binds itself in its by-laws, or possibly even in its charter, not to act until the required canonical authorizations have been obtained for those specific instances which have been reserved.

Although there is, to date, no formally approved list of reserved powers, it is generally held and recognized that it would be essential to retain at least the following ones if the canonical steward (administrator) is to be able to carry out the duties inherent in the office:

1) to change the philosophy and mission of the work;

2) to have the corporate documents – charter and by-laws – approved, amended, or abrogated;

3) to establish subsidiary corporations;

4) to amalgamate the corporation with other corporations, or to suppress it;

5) to encumber the real estate and the funds of the juridic person with indebtedness. Others could be added, such as;

6) designating the chief executive officer and some or all of the members of the board;

7) appointing the auditor; and

8) approving operating or capital budgets, or both. As new situations arise, the listing of reserved powers can change.

Generally speaking, the secular courts will base their decisions on the applicable secular legislation. In some instances, though, the courts have deferred the matter to the canon law, considering it to be equivalent to the internal rules and regulations of a voluntary association. Usually, in such instances the court uses the services of an expert in canon law who is able to explain the applicable legislation and place it in its proper context.

Nevertheless, in spite of the eventual presence of canonical experts, there is a reluctance on the part of many canonists and secular lawyers to integrate the canon law as such into civil documents since it would then, in final analysis, be subject to interpretation and evaluation by the secular judges. These canonists would prefer that certain specific items be integrated into the governing documents of the corporation, whether in the form of reserved powers or not. However, on the other hand, we note that in spite of this reluctance, many civil documents have simply integrated the Ethical and Religious Directives, without any special qualification. The jury is still out at this point in time as to which approach is preferable.

Since in many instances today, agreements are being made between a Catholic institution and a public one that is non-denominational, arrangements are included for the resolution of disputes which might eventually arise. We often see today a clause to the effect that if the dispute centers on the interpretation of the Ethical and Religious Directives, it is the local bishop who shall decide the proper meaning of these directives. In this way, we avoid going to secular court over the interpretation of what is essentially a religious document.

As noted above, there are other occasions when both legal systems are apparently in conflict, particularly when it comes to the ownership of ecclesiastical goods. The secular law will presume that the goods belong to the corporation, while canon law will consider that they are ecclesiastical goods, using secular law mechanisms purely as a protection. In addition, it often happens that a number of juridic persons have the same secular recognition (as when all parishes are registered civilly under a corporation sole which is either the diocese or the bishop). On the other hand, a juridic person could have more than one civil corporation under which it operates (as is the case when certain diocesan funds are incorporated separately from the general operating ones).

These general canonical principles and concepts will find their expression throughout all of Book V of the code and in the coming chapters of this handbook. They are not absolutes as such, because the modalities can vary from place to place. However, they provide common benchmarks against which certain administrative acts can be measured.

CHAPTER TWO

INDIVIDUALS OR ASSOCIATIONS WITHOUT JURIDIC STATUS

JOHN R. AMOS

CASE 1

As the threat of a global war rises on the horizon, the Holy See grows steadily more nervous that branches of a lay agency in one European country will refuse to raises funds for missions shepherded by citizens from its enemy. Eventually, the funds belonging to the agencies in both countries are seized by church authorities and "pontificalized" or placed under the management of an agency directly responsible to the pope.

CASE 2

With the war over but having witnessed the Holy See's successful expropriation of the funds of a lay agency, a bishop poses the question whether the funds belonging to another lay agency belong to the diocese. An agency of the Holy See rules in no uncertain terms that they belong to the lay agency.

CASE 3

Many years later, after both another world war and an ecumenical council, lay agencies proliferate in light of provisions from a revised *Code of Canon Law*. One which is recognized by the Church but does not have juridic personality acquires property by reason of its popularity among Catholics favoring charismatic spirituality. Bishops, without questioning the group's practices in any way, want to know how to exercise vigilance and jurisdiction over these goods so obviously dedicated to the spread of the gospel.

Cases 1 and 2 actually happened. The first arose before the 1917 *Code of Canon Law* had been formulated. The second was occasioned partly by that code's silence on lay associations. The third case is imaginary but quite possible.

Without in depth study of pre-code law it is impossible to decide what canonical principles governed the Holy See's consolidation of the funds of the Society for the Propagation of the Faith. The lay society had ignored the Holy See's directive to consolidate its leadership. Perhaps the dangers of war time made the move imperative.

Despite the title of this chapter, it is hard to imagine individuals within the Church without juridic status which comes with baptism. However, it is not hard to imagine individual Catholics engaged in apostolic activity without an official connection to hierarchical authority since the charge to Christianize the world comes not from orders or from hierarchical authority, as we supposed in the days of Catholic Action, but from the sacraments of initiation – especially baptism and confirmation.

For a variety of reasons apostolic individuals and groups or associations may operate without juridic status. The group may wish to keep its distance from hierarchical authority or the apostolic activity may be too new to warrant the approval inherent in juridic status.

Technically, groups without any juridic status can be called unrecognized associations. Canon law provides other possibilities. An association of the Christian faithful may be recognized (and thus allowed to operate) but not have juridic status in the sense of enjoying juridic personality, which is roughly the canonical equivalent of incorporation. Not even approval of an association, a step above recognition, confers juridic personality.

These possibilities raise significant canonical questions. Who owns or administers the property belonging to individuals or associations without juridic personality? To whom and when must reports on such property be rendered?

THE PRINCIPLES

The Holy See's appropriation of the goods belonging to the Society for the Propagation of the Faith remains an anomaly unless one reads the action of Pope Gregory XVI as a withdrawal of its lay status. In 1840, he grouped the society among "the universal Catholic institutions" – a rank just below that of the Propaganda Congregation.[1] The action occurred less than twenty years after the organization was founded, and as noted above, lay persons continued to administer it for nearly another eighty-two years. Pope Gregory's ranking was simply another way of promoting the Society for the Propagation of the Faith as had his predecessor Pius VII and as did his successors Leo XIII and Benedict XV.

Ecclesiastical authority's recommendation that the laity join and foster an association is a level beyond mere recognition of an association. It constitutes as closer link between the association and the authority, a kind of mid-point between an association's right to exist and its governance by the hierarchy.

These distinctions are found in the revised *Code of Canon Law*, which terms associations founded and governed by lay persons – whether recommended or not – "private associations of the Christian faithful"[2] and associations founded or governed by ecclesiastical authority as "public associations of the Christian faithful."[3] The distinction between private and public associations of the Christian faithful is also found in the history of associations, which can be traced almost to the earliest days of the Church – but especially after its spread to Rome.[4] Thus, one might observe that the 1917 code's silence on associations of lay origin and governance is about as much of an anomaly as the take over of the goods belonging to the Society for the Propagation of the Faith.

The principle that ecclesiastical authority can intervene in the financial and other internal matters of associations cannot be denied. This almost goes without saying for a public association, which in an emergency can have a trustee appointed to direct its affairs (c. 318) and which administers its temporal goods under the higher direction of ecclesiastical authority (c. 319). Ecclesiastical authority can

---

[1] See Edward John Hickey, *The Society for the Propagation of the Faith: Its Foundation, Organization and Success (1822-1922)*, (Washington, DC: Catholic University of America Press, 1922) 4.

[2] Canon 299 makes the distinction between private associations which are merely recognized and those which are "praised or recommended by ecclesiastical authority."

[3] Canon 301 describes public associations as those which ecclesiastical authority alone has the right to erect.

[4] For a concise history see John Amos, *Associations of the Christian Faithful in the Revised Code of Canon Law: A Canonical Analysis and Evaluation*, Canon Law Studies no. 516, (Washington, DC: The Catholic University of America, 1986; Ann Arbor, Michigan: University Microfilms International, 1986) 6-21. See also idem, *Studia Canonica* 21 (1987) 271-297.

also suppress public associations (c. 320). The same is true of a private association "if its activity causes grave harm to ecclesiastical doctrine or discipline or is a scandal to the faithful" (c. 326, §1).

One might see these canons from the 1983 code on the suppression of associations as an outgrowth of a justification for the Holy See's treatment of the Society for the Propagation of the Faith just after wartime. Squabbling among French Catholics about support for German missionaries and vice-versa can hardly be said to manifest the unanimity which is supposed to characterize the Christian community.

At the same time, one cannot lose sight of the relative autonomy which private associations enjoy vis-à-vis ecclesiastical authority. This is the point underscored by the Congregation for the Council's decree, November 13, 1920 on the Society of Saint Vincent de Paul. A concise outline of such autonomy can been found in canons 321-326 of the revised code. For example, "the Christian faithful guide and direct private associations according to the prescripts of the statutes" (c. 321) and not according to the dictates or whims of ecclesiastical authority. "A private association of the Christian faithful freely designates its moderator and officials according to the norms the statutes" (c. 324, §1). Ecclesiastical authority does not appoint them although a spiritual advisor freely chosen by the association "from among the priests exercising ministry in the diocese ... needs the confirmation of the local ordinary" (c. 324, §2). Most importantly for the purposes of this handbook, "A private association of the Christian faithful freely administers those goods it possesses according to the prescriptions of its statutes .... " (c. 325, §1).

The autonomy described above is termed "relative" because it is not absolute. Each point is carefully circumscribed and limited by just enough power on the part of ecclesiastical authority to keep private associations smoothly operating with a view toward the general good of the whole church and especially that of the particular churches or dioceses within which they are functioning.

As noted above, canon 305, §1 expresses the general limitation:

> All associations of the Christian faithful are subject to the vigilance of competent ecclesiastical authority which is to take care that the integrity of faith and morals is preserved in them and is to watch so that abuse does not creep into ecclesiastical discipline. This authority therefore has the duty and right to inspect them according to the norm of law and the statutes. These associations are also subject to the governance of this same authority according to the prescripts of the canons which follow.

A particular example of exercising such vigilance and jurisdiction is the requirement just cited that associations have the spiritual directors they select confirmed by the local ordinary. Other examples include the duties of ecclesiastical authority "to be watchful and careful that dissipation of their energies is avoided and that their exercise of their apostolate is ordered to the common good" (c. 323, §2) and "to exercise vigilance so that the goods are used for the purposes of the association" (c. 325, §1). With regard to the administration and disposition of funds which have been donated or left to an association for pious causes, the local ordinary has special authority (c. 325, §2).

One might term these examples of "operational" vigilance and jurisdiction. They come into play only after a private association of the Christian faithful is functioning. Even more important is what might be called "constitutive" vigilance and jurisdiction, that which ecclesiastical authority exercises when an association is being formed. The most important of these are the review of statutes required for recognition (c. 299, §3), the approval of statutes required for the acquisition of juridic personality (c. 322, §2), which is roughly the canonical equivalent of incorporation of civil law, and the granting of juridic personality through a decree (c. 322, §1).

Constitutive vigilance and jurisdiction require much patience and discernment on the part of ecclesiastical authority. Often permission may be given for an organization to be formed with the understanding that the statutes will not be reviewed officially for a certain length of time, e.g., five years. In other words, the association remains "unrecognized" to give it a chance to prove to itself and to the church at large that the organization can actually function and to give ecclesiastical authority a perspective from which to decide whether granting recognition is actually worthwhile or even needed. During this time of discernment ecclesiastical authority may find itself lending all sorts of extra legal assistance to fledgling associations, e.g., advice on organization or property matters; suggestions on how to train members, how to lay ground work for future development of the association, etc. Examples of such development include how to prepare the association for approval of statutes and the reception of juridic personality.

At the same time, there are situations in which the Christian faithful may wish to organize themselves for pious and apostolic purposes with the intention of remaining unrecognized by ecclesiastical authority. This may be the future of the "going non-canonical" option discussed in recent years by religious congregations desiring greater independence.[5]

---

[5]The author does not mean to argue for such an option, which has many problems but simply to point out the possibility. One of the problems, of course, is that a religious congregation cannot simply declare itself an unrecognized association. There is also the problem of transferring property, which remains that of the congregation until it is legitimately alienated. In other words, even if a congregation managed to found an unrecognized association, it is unlikely that it would be able to sell or give its resources to the association.

Since juridic personality presupposes canonical recognition, the possibility of having unrecognized associations raises at least two important questions. Who owns or administers its property and to whom and when must reports be rendered?

Canon 310 clearly answers the question of canonical ownership:

> A private association which has not been established as a juridic person cannot, as such, be a subject of obligations and rights. Nevertheless, the members of the Christian faithful associated together in it can jointly contract obligations and can acquire rights and possess rights and goods as co-owners and co-possessors; they are able to exercise these rights and obligations through an agent or a proxy.

Civil law ownership may reside in a corporation even if the association is unrecognized canonically. The Canon Law Society of America, incorporated in the District of Columbia, is a good example. The Canon Law Society of America has no official canonical status. The corporation or its governing body, can easily act as the canonical agent and administer the association's property. For those associations which are not civilly incorporated, the situation is more complex. One would do well to contact a civil attorney on this issue.[6]

---

[6] Bryan G. Duhe, a partner in the firm of Duhe, Barnard Perfloff, P.C., was asked to read this text and responded to the issue as follows:

All states have different and somewhat varied laws that apply to organizations which are not recognized civilly.

Under the First Amendment of the U.S. Constitution, most states recognized as *de facto* all organizations. It is only those organizations that wish to limit the liability exposure of its individual member which require special recognition by most states. In order to benefit from a number of uniform laws designed to protect individuals from liability for corporate activity, the organization must file and request recognition as an incorporation. If granted by the local state authority the new incorporation becomes an "individual" of the state. All rights, remedies and liability exposure vest with the corporation and not its individual members (9 *Am. Jur.* BURGLARY 49).

Without the corporate identity conferred by state authority each individual member of the unincorporated group become personally liable in contract and under civil tort law for all activities conducted even for the group. Civil law allows and protects under the First Amendment to the US Constitution the right to organize but it is only the incorporation which allows organized individuals to speak and contract as a true corporate body within the civil law context (*Warrior River Terminal v. State*, 58 So. 2d 100).

As stated above, civil law ownership may reside in a corporation even if the association is unrecognized canonically. Conversely, an association may be accepted canonically and have absolutely no legal identity civilly unless an incorporation has been obtained.

Unrecognized associations are not the only ones without juridic personality, since the code provides that recognition – not incorporation or juridic personality – is all that is needed for an association to function with the most minimal relationship to ecclesiastical authority. In fact, as indicated above, granting recognition without juridic personality can constitute a second level at which an association may be allowed to operate while it and ecclesiastical authority discern the future.

The issues of ownership for merely recognized associations are the same as that of unrecognized associations. Canonically, "the Christian faithful associated together in it can jointly contract obligations and acquire rights and possess goods as co-owners and co-possessors. ... " At civil law they may or may not incorporate. If they do, the corporation or its governing body can act as the association's civil and canonical agent.

Private associations, whether recognized or unrecognized, are required to make few reports on their property to ecclesiastical authority. The statutes of individual associations may require this as a courtesy, but generally all reporting is internal. Local councils of the Knights of Columbus, for example, a well-known association of Catholic lay men with a large insurance fund, report only to the state, district, and supreme councils. Ecclesiastical authority might, for example, ask for a report – to which it would certainly be entitled – if there is a well-founded allegation that the funds are being misused.

The situation changes, however, if an association engages in fund raising activities or receives a gift or bequest for pious causes. Except for religious mendicants, "any private person, whether physical or juridic, is forbidden to beg for alms for any pious or ecclesiastical institute or purpose without the written permission of that person's own ordinary and of the local ordinary" (c. 1265, §1). Associations are also required to follow the fund-raising guidelines issued by the episcopal conference (c. 1301):

§1. The ordinary is the executor of all pious wills whether *mortis causa* or *inter vivos*.

§2. By this right, the ordinary can and must exercise vigilance, even through visitation, so that pious wills are fulfilled, and other executors are bound to render him an account after they have performed their function.

CONCLUSION

In great contrast to the silence of the 1917 code, the 1983 code clearly assert-ed the rights of lay Christian faithful to found and govern associations on their own initiative; it also provided sophisticated mechanisms for structuring and gov-erning them. At the same time church authority has been given enough remote control over financial and other internal matters of associations so that the diffi-culties encountered at the end of World War I can be avoided easily. What remains is for the whole Church – both authority and laity – to learn the mean-ing of exercising vigilance and jurisdiction between these two extreme examples. More associations need to submit their statutes for review by ecclesiastical authority. Perhaps the study of a sample would help, for example, the statutes of Magnificat, a private association of the Christian faithful, whose statutes were not only reviewed but approved by the Archbishop of New Orleans and which has now spread to more than twenty-six dioceses and several countries.[7]

This very example illustrates the kind of confusion which is easily understand-able in dealing with something new. By approving rather than merely reviewing the statutes, the Most Reverend Phillip M. Hannan, now retired, actually advanced Magnificat two steps instead of one. Though no harm and perhaps much good has been done in this case, part of the process of discernment needed by most associations is the experience of living in the lowest category of relation-ship to ecclesiastical authority until it grows capable of advancement, e.g., from unrecognized to recognized association, recommended association, association with juridic personality.

---

[7]The statutes are too long to include in this chapter. Copies can be obtained by writing Magnificat Central Service Team, 1201 Beverly Gardens Drive, Metairie, Louisiana 70002. A donation for postage and handling would be appreciated. One might also wish to consult the author's article, "Public Juridic Person Offers Flexibility," in *Health Progress* 17 (January-February 1996) 31-35. Many of the ideas are applicable to private associations.

FORMULARY 1:

From Bishop Deferring Review of Statutes to Leaders of an Association

---

The Chancery

Dear Leaders of the Association:

You are to be commended for sending me your statutes for review. That will be done once you have had the opportunity to function in an organized fashion for a suitable period of time. If you have not done so already, you might incorporate at civil law.

In the meantime, your association remains unrecognized by church authority, but I would appreciate your keeping in contact so that this period of discernment may be as fruitful as possible for all concerned.

Sincerely yours,

Diocesan Bishop

FORMULARY 2:

From Bishop Granting Recognition to Leaders of an Association

---

The Chancery

Dear Leaders of the Association:

Some time ago I received your statutes.

Having read them, I note that you are accomplishing the goals set by your organization and are operating according to your statutes. You are hereby recognized as a private association of the Christian faithful.

You are encouraged to remain in close contact with me so that I may follow your progress and make note of your achievements.

Sincerely yours,

Diocesan Bishop

FORMULARY 3:

From Bishop Granting Approval to Leaders of an Association

The Chancery

Dear Leaders of the Association:

I have carefully watched your association over the years and have noted not only that you are operating according to your statutes and accomplishing the goals of your organization but also the great good that you are accomplishing among the Christian faithful and others in our society.

For this, you are to be praised. I encourage the Christian faithful of this diocese to apply for membership and to regard your association as worthy of support.

I continue to encourage you to remain in close contact with me – especially if it seems opportune for your association to become a private juridic person.

Sincerely yours,

Diocesan Bishop

FORMULARY 4
From Bishop Granting Private Juridic Personality

DECREE

The association of the Christian faithful known as
_____,

having operated within the Diocese of _____
in accord with the norm of its statutes, which are hereby approved if
they have not been already, is hereby erected a private juridic person
in accord with the norm of canon 322 of the 1983 *Code of Canon Law*.

Anything to the contrary notwithstanding.

Given this _____ day of _____ in _____

Diocesan Bishop

Chancellor

[SEAL]

CHAPTER THREE

THE CODE OF CANONS OF THE EASTERN CHURCHES AND TEMPORAL GOODS

JOHN D. FARIS

The Catholic Church is a communion of twenty-two churches *sui iuris*, literally, churches "of their own law" (CCEO c. 27). This *sui iuris* status refers to the self-governing capacity of the hierarchies of these churches in all matters except those reserved to the Roman pontiff or ecumenical council. These twenty-two churches are generally categorized either as Western or Eastern, a reference to their historical origins in either the Western or Eastern Roman empires. One of the churches, the Latin Church, falls under the category of Western; the other twenty-one churches fall under the broad category of Eastern. The *Code of Canons of the Eastern Churches* (CCEO) orders the canonical life of twenty-one Eastern Catholic churches.[1]

It will be the task of this brief presentation to present an overview of the treatment of temporal goods in this code.[2] The limitation of space precludes a com-

---

[1] The *Codex Canonum Ecclesiarum Orientalium* (CCEO) was promulgated by Pope John Paul II with the apostolic constitution *Sacri canones* (*AAS* 82 [1990] 1033-1044) on October 18, 1990, (*AAS* 82 [1990] 1061-1353) and acquired the force of law on October 1, 1991. An English translation of the Eastern code was prepared by the Canon Law Society of America: *Code of Canons of the Eastern Churches Latin-English Edition* (Washington, DC: Canon Law Society of America, 1992).

A concordance of the CCEO and the CIC was prepared by C.G. Fürst, *Canones-Synopse zum Codex Iuris Canonici und Codex Canonum Ecclesiarum Orientalium* (Freiburg im Breisgau: Herder, 1992). See also the concordance in V. Pospishil, *Eastern Catholic Church Law*, revised and augmented edition (New York: Saint Maron Publications, 1996) 852-897.

An index was prepared by I. Zuzek, *Index Analyticus Codicis Canonum Ecclesiarum Orientalium*, Kanonika, vol. 2 (Rome: Pontificium Institutum Orientalium Studiorum, 1992). An addendum to the index was published in *Orientalia Christiana Periodica* 60 (1994) 635-639.

[2] For additional information on this subject, one can refer to Victor Pospishil, *Eastern Catholic Church Law*, revised and augmented edition (New York: Saint Maron Publications, 1996) 693-705; J. Abbass, "The Temporal Goods of the Church" in *Two Codes in Comparison*, Kanonika, vol. 7 (Rome: Pontificio Istituto Orientale, 1997) 177-205; Ioan Mitrofan, "Les biens de l'Église selon le *Codex Canonum Ecclesiarum Orientalium*" (Kaslik, Lebanon: USEK, 1996) 415-446.

prehensive treatment of the entire subject matter. Instead, we shall attempt only to address those salient points of the Eastern code that diverge from the *Code of Canon Law* (CIC). Consequently, certain points that are identical with the Latin code will be omitted, no matter their degree of canonical importance.

GOVERNANCE IN THE EASTERN CATHOLIC CHURCHES

Categorized according to the canonical status of their respective heads, the twenty-one Eastern Catholic Churches are gradated according to the degree of autonomy.

Patriarchal and Major Archiepiscopal Churches

The *patriarchal churches* (Armenian, Chaldean, Coptic, Greek-Melkite, Maronite, Syrian) enjoy the highest degree of autonomy, including the power to elect their own bishops (within the territory of their patriarchal churches) and their own patriarchs. The governance of these churches is articulated in canons 55-150 of the Eastern code.

The *major archiepiscopal* churches (Ukrainian and Syro-Malabar) are for the most part canonically equated with the patriarchal churches (CCEO cc. 151-154) with the exception that the election of the major archbishop must be confirmed by the Roman pontiff.

In the patriarchal and major archiepiscopal churches, the patriarch, major archbishop shares in the governance of the church with the *synod of bishops*, an assembly of all the bishops of the respective church. Generally speaking, the patriarch, major archbishop exercises executive authority while the synod exercises legislative, judicial and electoral authority in the church (see CCEO cc. 102-113, especially c. 110). The authority of the patriarch, major archbishop and synod is generally restricted to an "historical" territory of the patriarchal church; outside that territory, the Apostolic See fulfills the functions usually carried out by the patriarch, major archbishop and synod (CCEO cc. 146-150). Because the bishops of these churches can only be convened periodically, a *permanent synod*, comprised of four bishops and the patriarch, major archbishop serves on an on-going basis (CCEO cc. 115-121).

Metropolitan and Other Churches

The *metropolitan* churches (Ethiopian, Ruthenian [United States] and Syro-Malankara) are churches *sui iuris* with a lesser degree of autonomy in governance than the patriarchal or major archiepiscopal churches (CCEO cc. 155-173). In the metropolitan churches, a *council of hierarchs*, comprised of all the bishops of the respective church, is the superior legislative and electoral body. While comparable to the patriarchal synod of bishops, the power of the council of hierarchs is more limited: For example, legislation of the council of hierarchs cannot be promulgated without official reception on the part of the Apostolic See. Further, three candidates for the office of metropolitan are proposed by the council of hierarchs to the Roman pontiff, who makes the appointment.

The category of *Other Churches* (CCEO cc. 174-176) includes all those churches that, because of a variety of circumstances, have a limited degree of self-governing authority. These churches include the Albanian, Belorussian, Bulgarian, Greek, Hungarian, Italo-Albanian, Krizevci, Romanian, Russian, and Slovak churches. The church depends directly on the Apostolic See and the chief hierarch functions as a delegate of the Apostolic See (CCEO c. 175).

Terminology

The Eastern code employs a terminology appropriate to Eastern usage while the meaning of the terms is substantially identical to that the Latin code. An *eparchy* and *eparchial bishop* are the canonical equivalents of the *diocese* and *diocesan bishop* (CCEO c. 177 and CIC c. 369); hierarch is the counterpart of ordinary (CCEO c. 984 and CIC c. 134). Furthermore, *protosyncellus* is equivalent to the vicar general (CCEO c. 245 and CIC c. 475); *syncellus* (CCEO c. 246) is the counterpart of episcopal vicar (CIC c. 476). A *protopresbyter* (CCEO c. 276) is comparable to a vicar forane (CIC c. 553).

TEMPORAL GOODS IN THE EASTERN CODE

In consideration of the Lord's severe warning about the danger of money to his followers (Mt 6:24) and the possibility of abuses, the canons treating money and property are relatively few.

Title XXIII, "The Temporal Goods of the Church," *Code of Canons of the Eastern Churches* canons 1007-1054, is organized as follows: after three preliminary canons (cc. 1007-1009); four chapters treat respectively the acquisition of temporal goods (cc. 1010-1021); the administration of goods (cc. 1022-1033); contracts and alienation in particular (cc. 1034-1042); and pious wills and pious foundations (cc. 1043-1054).[3] However, matters relating to temporal goods are not restricted to Title XXIII, but are instead interwoven throughout the Eastern code.

Particular Law

The Eastern code is the common law for the twenty-one Eastern Catholic churches *sui iuris*.[4] Because the Eastern code must provide only the most general canonical norms, one finds numerous references are made throughout the code to the provisions of particular law (either at the level of the church *sui iuris* or at the level of the eparchy or religious institutes) throughout the code.[5] In Title XXIII, there are ten references to particular law.

Civil Law

The Eastern code provides for the protection of an author's intellectual rights, legal texts, official acts of ecclesiastical authorities and authentic collections of laws and acts (CCEO c. 666, §§1 and 2). Particular law of each church *sui iuris* can articulate more detailed norms about this matter in accordance with civil law (CCEO c. 666, §3).

The Eastern code requires that administrators of temporal goods be bonded in accordance with the requirements of civil law so that the Church might not suffer because of the death or departure from office of such administrators (CCEO c. 1027).

---

[3]The patterns follows that of the Latin code in Book V, "The Temporal Goods of the Church," cc. 1254-1310. See René Metz, "Le Canons communs à l'Église latine et aux Églises orientales à la fin du XXe Siècle," in Raffaele Coppola (ed.) *Incontro fra Canoni d'Oriente e d'Occidente* (Bari: Cacucci Editore, 1994) 73.

[4]CCEO c. 1493, §1. Beyond the laws and legitimate customs of the universal law, this code also includes by the designation "common law" the laws and legitimate customs common to all Eastern Churches.

[5]CCEO c. 1493, §2. Included in the designation "particular law" are all the laws, legitimate customs, statutes and other norms of law which are not common to the universal Church nor to all the Eastern Churches.

Juridic Persons and Ecclesiastical Goods

Similar to the legal fiction of a corporation in American civil law, canon law establishes *juridic persons* as aggregates of persons or things that are subjects of rights and obligations (CCEO c. 920). In its distinction between public and private juridic persons, the Latin code states that public juridic persons function in the name of the Church while private juridic persons do not (CIC c. 116, §1). No distinction between *public* and *private* juridic persons is made in the Eastern code; the juridic person of the Eastern code is to be equated with the *public juridic person* of the Latin code.

Only juridic persons are capable of acquiring, possessing, administering and alienating the temporal goods of the Church (CCEO c. 1009, §1).[6]

Certain entities are designated by the Eastern code as juridic persons: churches *sui iuris*, provinces, eparchies, exarchies (CCEO c. 921, §2), parishes (CCEO c. 280, §3), seminaries (CCEO c. 335, §1), monasteries, monastic confederations, orders, congregations and their provinces and houses (CCEO c. 423), societies of the common life along with their provinces and houses (CCEO c. 558, §1), secular institutes along with their provinces and houses (CCEO c. 567, §1), and public associations of the Christian faithful (CCEO c. 573, §1).[7]

Once temporal goods are acquired by a juridic person, they are designated as *ecclesiastical goods* (CCEO c. 1009, §2).[8]

Acquisition of Temporal Goods
1. Taxes and Offerings

The eparchial bishop can impose a tax on juridic persons only with the consent of the finance council (CCEO c. 1012, §1); in the Latin church, the diocesan bishop is required only to consult with the presbyteral council and the finance council before imposing such a tax (CIC c. 1263).

---

[6]The Latin code provides that *moral persons*, specifically referring to the *Catholic Church and the Apostolic See* (c. 113, §1), are also competent to acquire temporal goods (c. 1257, §1). The Eastern code is silent regarding moral persons. See *Nuntia* 18 (1984) 12.

[7]The Latin code foresees the constitution of private associations of the Christian faithful as private juridic persons, a status that does not include the competence to possess ecclesiastical goods (cc. 322 and 1257, §2).

[8]See also the title of chapter two, "The Administration of Ecclesiastical Goods."

The phrase "no tax can be imposed on the offerings received on the occasion of the celebration of the Divine Liturgy" (CCEO c. 1012, §1) is not found in the Latin code (CIC c. 1263 and 1917 CIC c. 1506); such an omission results in a difference between the power of the eparchial bishop and the diocesan bishop to impose taxes.[9]

With regard to the taxation of physical persons, the Eastern code stipulates that particular law of the church *sui iuris* can determine the level and the circumstances in which the tax can be levied (CCEO c. 1012, §2). The Latin code allows for the diocesan bishop to impose an extraordinary and moderate tax on physical and private juridical persons only in the case of grave necessity and in conformity with particular laws and customs (CIC c. 1263).[10]

The Eastern code states that within the limits, as determined by the particular law of the church *sui iuris*, the bishop can establish the amounts of these taxes and offerings (CCEO c. 1013) while taxes for acts of governance and offerings on the occasion of the administration of sacraments and sacramentals are set at the provincial level in the Latin Church (CIC c. 1264).

2. Collection of Alms

Differences between the two codes exist with regard to ecclesiastical fund raising. The Latin code prohibits physical and juridic private persons from raising funds (*persona quaevis privata, sive physica sive iuridica ... stipem cogere*) without the written permission of their own ordinary and that of the local ordinary (CIC c. 1265, §1). The Eastern code imposes a prohibition on physical and juridical persons from collecting alms (*Eleemosynas colligere personis physicis vel iuridicis*) without the permission of the authority to which they are subject and the written consent of the local hierarch (CCEO c. 1015).

One undisputed difference between the two codes is that the Eastern code imposes the need for permission on all physical and juridic persons; the Latin code is silent with regard to the requirement for public juridic persons to obtain such permission (in deference to the rights of mendicant orders).

The substitution of *eleemosynas colligere* for *stipem cogere* (found both in *Postquam Apostolicis* c. 240 and CIC c. 1265, §1) is held by one author to mean that the prohibition is now extended in the Eastern Catholic churches to collec-

---

[9]Abbass, 201.

[10]Anna Favergiotti, "Il Fondamento dell'Obbligazione Tributaria nello Stato Moderno e nel Diritto Canonico Latino ed Orientale. Note Comparative," in Raffaele Coppola (ed.) *Incontro fra Canoni d'Oriente e d'Occidente* (Bari: Cacucci Editore, 1994) 571-582.

tion by means of circular letters or the press.[11] However, to extend the need for permission based on the substitution of the two phrases does not seem to be justified since there is no canonical doctrine that gives such a broad definition to *eleemosynas colligere*. It should also be recalled that a strict interpretation is to be given when a canon restricts the free exercise of rights (CCEO c. 1500).

Administration of Ecclesiastical Goods

Extraordinary Administration

While the Latin code determines that it is the competence of the diocesan bishop to define extraordinary acts of administration (CIC c. 1281, §2), the Eastern code, in a more generic fashion, indicates that the authority to which the juridic person is subject is to define an act of extraordinary administration (CCEO c. 1024, §2).

Patriarchal and Major Archiepiscopal Churches

The governance of the patriarchal and major archiepiscopal churches is canonically equated in the common law except in those cases where it is expressly mentioned otherwise or it is evident from the nature of the matter (CCEO c. 152). Therefore, what follows regarding the patriarchal churches is also applicable to the major archiepiscopal churches.

1. Oversight of Ecclesiastical Property

The patriarch has the responsibility to oversee the ecclesiastical property of his church, with due regard for the primary obligation of the eparchial bishop to supervise the administration of temporal goods in his eparchy (CCEO c. 97; and c. 1022, §2).

2. Patriarchal Finance Officer

Distinct from the finance officer of the eparchy of the patriarch, there is to be a finance officer for the administration of the goods of the patriarchal church (CCEO c. 122). The patriarch appoints the patriarchal finance officer with the

---

[11]Abbass, 202-204.

consent of the permanent synod. The appointee must be a member of the Christian faithful, an expert in economic matters, and of outstanding honesty; anyone related to the patriarch up to and including the fourth degree of consanguinity or affinity is disqualified. The term of office is determined by the particular law of the patriarchal church; the finance officer cannot be removed without the consent of the synod of bishops or, in danger of a delay, the permanent synod. The patriarchal finance officer generally reports to the permanent synod regarding budgets and financial reports; however, the synod of bishops can also require the same administrative reports.

3. Reduction of Obligations of Pious Causes

In addition to the Apostolic See, the patriarch can be approached to reduce, moderate or commute obligations arising from pious causes. In order to act, the patriarch must have the consent of the permanent synod (CCEO c. 1054, §3).

Eparchies

1. Eparchial Bishop

In a manner similar to the Latin code (CIC c. 134, §3), the Eastern code stipulates that when a function of executive governance is explicitly attributed to the eparchial bishop, it can be exercised only by an eparchial bishop or exarch (CCEO c. 987), thereby excluding the protosyncellus or syncellus without a special mandate. As a result of the substitution of the term *eparchial bishop* for *hierarch* in the Eastern code in the canons relative to temporal goods, substantial differences arose between the two codes:

- ◆ Only the eparchial bishop can permit the taking up of special collections (CCEO c. 1014) while the Latin code allows for the local ordinary, e.g., vicar general and episcopal vicars, to grant such permissions (CIC c. 1266).

- ◆ Supervision of the administration of the ecclesiastical goods of the eparchy is the responsibility of the eparchial bishop (CCEO c. 1022, §1); the Latin code assigns this responsibility to the ordinary (CIC c. 1276, §1).

2. Finance Officer

The appointment of the eparchial finance officer by the eparchial bishop is made after consultation with the college of eparchial consultors and the finance council (CCEO c. 262, §1 and CIC c. 494, §1). While the Eastern code provides that the finance officer is *ipso iure* a member of the finance council (CCEO c. 263, §2), the Latin code is silent on the matter. Such a divergence results in some noteworthy differences:

- ♦ The Eastern code requires that an eparchial finance officer be a member of the Christian faithful (i.e., baptized, but not necessarily a Catholic [see CCEO c. 897]); the requirement is not *per se* made in the Latin code. If, however, the finance officer were to be appointed as a member of the finance council, he or she would need to be a member of the Christian faithful since the requirement is made of members of that council (CCEO c. 492, §1).

- ♦ A person related to the eparchial bishop up to and including the fourth degree of consanguinity or affinity is disqualified from membership on the finance council (CCEO c. 263, §3). Since the eparchial finance officer is to be a member of that council, the disqualification is applicable. In the Latin Church, however, the same disqualification is applied to members of the finance council (CIC c. 492, §3), but not *per se* to the finance officer. Therefore, if the finance officer were not appointed to the finance council, he or she could be related to the diocesan bishop.

- ♦ The term of office of the finance officer is determined by particular law, either at the level of the church *sui iuris* or the eparchy (CCEO c. 262, §2); in the Latin Church, the term is five years (CIC c. 494, §2).

In its delineation of the responsibilities of the finance officer, the Latin code states that he or she is to administer the goods of the diocese in accord with the approved budget to pay for authorized expenditures (CIC c. 494, §3). More expansive in its delineation of responsibilities (CCEO c. 262, §3), the Eastern code states that a finance officer is:

- ♦ To administer the temporal goods of the eparchy.

- ♦ To supervise the administration of all ecclesiastical goods in the eparchy and to provide for their preservation, safety and increase. The finance officer would assist the eparchial bishop in his administration of the temporal goods (CCEO c. 1022, §1).

- To supply for the negligence of local administrators.
- To administer those goods that lack an administrator designated by law.

Both codes exclude the possibility of a finance officer serving as administrator during a vacancy of the eparchy or diocese (CCEO c. 225, §2); the Eastern code additionally delineates the role of the finance officer during a vacancy (CCEO c. 232 and CIC c. 492, §1). If the eparchial bishop, after being warned, neglects to appoint a finance officer, the metropolitan or the patriarch can do so (CCEO cc. 80, 1°; 133, §1, 6°; 159, 7°).

3. Finance Council

No minimum number of members of the finance council is required in the Eastern code; the Latin code requires at least three members (CCEO c. 263, §1 and CIC c. 492, §1). The Eastern code assigns the presidency of the eparchial finance council exclusively to the eparchial bishop (CCEO c. 263, §1) while the Latin code affords the possibility of a delegate of the bishop presiding over the council (CIC c. 492, §1).

While the Latin code does not require any consultation before the diocesan bishop appoints a member of the finance council, the Eastern code requires consultation with the college of eparchial consultors or the observance of another process provided by the particular law of the church *sui iuris*. Further, the possibility of appointment by others, or election, to the council with subsequent confirmation by the eparchial bishop is also foreseen by the Eastern code (CCEO c. 263, §1).

According to the Eastern code, a person does not have to be a member of the Christian faithful to be appointed to the eparchial finance council (CCEO c. 263, §1 and CIC c. 492, §1). Hence, one does not need to exclude non-Christians in seeking experts as potential members of the finance council.

The Eastern code is silent regarding the duration of the term of office.

While the Latin code stipulates that the annual financial report is to be submitted to the finance council by the finance officer (CIC c. 494, §4), the Eastern code determines that the report is to be submitted first to the finance council and, through the council, to the eparchial bishop (CCEO c. 262, §4).

4. Support of Clerics

Both codes require the establishment of a special fund to be used for the support of clerics who serve the eparchy/diocese; the Eastern code calls for the "suitable and fundamentally equal" (*congruus necnon fundamentaliter aequali*) support of clerics while the Latin code, by its omission of that phrase would seem to allow for differences in the remuneration of clerics in the same diocese (CCEO c. 1021, §1 and CIC c. 1274, §1). Likewise, wherever health insurance and social security are not provided for the clergy, the particular law of each church *sui iuris* is to create institutes to safeguard these benefits (CCEO c. 1021, §2).

5. Support of Clerics' Families

Complementary to the right of clerics and their families to support (CCEO c. 390, §1), the Eastern code places an obligation on the eparchial bishop to see that clerics and their families are provided with adequate support, health insurance and social security (CCEO c. 192, §5).

6. Parochial Administration

While the Latin code makes specific reference to a parish finance council that is regulated by universal law and norms established by the diocesan bishop (CIC c. 537), the Eastern code makes a general reference to "appropriate parish councils" to deal with pastoral and financial matters that operate according to the norms of the particular law of the church *sui iuris* (CCEO c. 295).

7. Reduction or Modification of Obligations of Pious Foundations

With regard to the reduction of the obligations established by pious foundations to celebrate the Divine Liturgy, the Eastern code provides for the eparchial bishop to delegate certain powers to the coadjutor bishop, auxiliary bishop, *protosyncellus*, and *syncellus* (CCEO cc. 1052, §6 and 987). This expansion of possible competent authorities also extends those who are competent to transfer the obligations of celebrating the Divine Liturgy to other days or institutes (CCEO c. 1053).

8. Benefices

The Eastern code is silent regarding the reform of the benefice system referred to in the Latin code (CIC c. 1272).

ALIENATION OF ECCLESIASTICAL GOODS

Alienation is usually the transfer of any interest in the stable patrimony of a juridic person (see CCEO c. 1035, §1 and CIC c. 1291).

Requirements for Alienation

While the Latin code simply requires "the permission of the authority competent according to the norm of law" (CIC c. 1291) for the valid alienation of stable patrimony, the Eastern code is more detailed in its requirements (CCEO c. 1035):

♦ There must be an urgent necessity, evident advantage, piety, charity or a pastoral reason;

♦ There must be a written appraisal of the property by experts;

♦ The permission of the competent authority must be in writing; further, the competent authority can establish other safeguards to be observed lest the Church suffer loss.

Establishment of Limits

Inside the territory of a patriarchal church, the patriarchal synod of bishops can establish the minimum and maximum limits regarding the alienation of ecclesiastical goods.[12] Outside the territory of a patriarchal church and in metropolitan and other churches *sui iuris*, the Apostolic See establishes the minimum and maximum limits (CCEO c. 1036, §1).

Alienation within Established Limits

When the value of the ecclesiastical goods proposed to be alienated falls within the established limits, *consent* is required of:

♦ The finance council and the college of consultors for the goods of the eparchy;

♦ The eparchial bishop who obtains consent of the finance council and the college of consultors for the goods of a juridical person subject to that eparchial bishop;

---

[12] In addition to alienation, these prescriptions must be observed in any business transaction by reason of which the patrimonial condition of a juridic person can be worsened (see CCEO c. 1042).

- The authority as determined by the typicon or statutes of juridic persons not subject to the eparchial bishop (CCEO c. 1036, §1).

Alienation Exceeding, but not Double Limit

When the value of the proposed alienation exceeds, but does not double the established amount, consent is required of:

- The patriarch and permanent synod for an eparchy inside the patriarchal territory;

- The eparchial bishop, patriarch and permanent synod for goods of juridic persons subject to eparchial bishop inside the patriarchal territory;

- The patriarch and permanent synod for goods of a juridic person (even of pontifical right) inside the patriarchal territory (CCEO c. 1036, §2).

Alienation Double Limit

When the value of the proposed alienation is double the established amount, or there is a case of precious goods or goods donated to the Church by reason of a vow, the same procedure is to be followed except that the consent of the synod of bishops is required (CCEO c. 1036, §3).

In all other cases when the value of the proposed alienation exceeds the amount established or approved by the Apostolic See, or involves precious goods or goods donated to the Church by reason of a vow, the consent of the Apostolic See is required (CCEO c. 1036, §4).

Patriarchal Church and Patriarchal Eparchy

Specific provisions are also made regarding the alienation of ecclesiastical goods pertaining to a patriarchal church or the eparchy of the patriarch:

- If the value of the goods of the patriarchal church falls within the limits established by the synod of bishops, the counsel of the permanent synod is required; in the case of the goods of the patriarchal eparchy, the consent of the finance council and the college of consultors is required;

- If the value of the proposed alienation exceeds but does not double the established maximum amount, the consent of the permanent synod is required;

- If the value of the proposed alienation is more than double the established amount, involves precious goods or goods given to the Church by reason of a vow, the consent of the synod of bishops is required (CCEO c. 1037).

ECUMENISM AND TEMPORAL GOODS

Consequent to the collapse of communist regimes in Eastern Europe, the Eastern Catholic and Orthodox Churches are undergoing a restructuring of their ecclesial life. Disputes among the communities have arisen that quite often involve church property. Since the ecumenical dialogue of the past three decades has for the most part involved only the heads of the Orthodox Churches and the Vatican as participants, the Orthodox have called upon Rome to abandon claims to certain properties and effectively relinquish its rights in favor of the Orthodox. Such an appeal ignores the canonical role enjoyed by the Roman Pontiff regarding temporal goods.

Both codes state that the Roman Pontiff is the "supreme administrator and steward of all ecclesiastical goods" (CCEO c. 1008, §1 and CIC c. 1273); ownership of the property pertains to the various juridic persons of the Catholic Church (CCEO c. 1008, §2). Therefore, since the Roman Pontiff is not the canonical owner of the property, it would be improper for him to relinquish claims to church property; this can be done only by the claimants of ownership of the property.

The Eastern code includes provisions for the assistance of non-Catholic churches and ecclesial communions. Beyond the provisions of *communicatio in sacris*, the Eastern Catholic churches are also encouraged to cooperate with other Christians in works of charity and social justice (CCEO c. 908). If non-Catholic Christians lack appropriate facilities for divine worship, the eparchial bishop can grant them the use of a Catholic Church, building or cemetery according to the norm of particular law of his Church *sui iuris* (CCEO c. 670, §1).

CONCLUSION

This brief study has attempted to provide an overview of the general norms governing the stewardship of property in the Eastern Catholic churches. It must be kept in mind, however, that the general norms are only one facet of the law of the twenty-one Eastern Catholic churches, each of whom have various forms of particular law also regulating the subject.

CHAPTER FOUR

THE TEMPORAL GOODS OF RELIGIOUS INSTITUTES

JORDAN F. HITE, T.O.R.

This chapter will cover only those aspects of church law which apply specifically to religious institutes. The general principles for the administration and alienation of property can be found in chapters sixteen and twenty. The chapter will conclude with five case studies that illustrate the application and interpretation of the canons. The subjects of the five case studies are:

1. a religious institute closing its private high school;
2. a health care system sponsored by a religious institute borrowing four hundred million dollars;
3. refinancing a previously approved bond issue;
4. use of investments and borrowing from an institute retirement fund to make a purchase; and
5. a Catholic university sells its hospital.

The church law governing the temporal goods of religious institutes is a combination of the universal law applying specifically to religious institutes and the canons applying generally to the temporal goods of the church (c. 635, §1) as well as the proper law of the institutes. The laws governing temporal goods apply to religious institutes, secular institutes (cc. 710-730) and societies of apostolic life (cc. 731-746).

Religious institutes, their provinces and houses or equivalents are public juridic persons by law with the capacity to acquire, possess, administer and alienate temporal goods (c. 634, §1). This capacity may be excluded or restricted in the constitutions of institutes such as the Order of Friars Minor, Capuchin whose property is owned by the Holy See.

The canons pay special attention to the norm of poverty in institutes by providing that institutes have a special obligation to make appropriate norms for the administration of property that are consistent with the poverty appropriate to the institute (c. 635, §2). In addition, institutes are to avoid the appearance of luxury, immoderate wealth and amassing goods (c. 634, §2) as well as to do all in their power to use their resources to help the poor in order to give a collective witness to their charity and poverty (c. 640).

In religious institutes, the major superior, the financial officer (treasurer) and the council each have a role in the administration of property. The treasurer is to be someone other than the major superior and is responsible for the property of the institute, under the direction of the major superior (c. 636, §1) The treasurer and other administrators are to render an account of their administration to the competent authority (c. 636, §2).

For acts of administration, proper law, within the scope of universal law determines the nature of and the process for acts of administration (c. 638, §1). Thus, pontifical institutes have a broad grant of authority to set the limits and regulation for the administration of goods. This can be a very important area if an institute has large amounts of free capital (see case 7).

In regard to debts and contracts, it is the public juridic person that is responsible for debts and fulfilling the requirements of contracts (c. 639, §§1 and 2). Institutes should designate members authorized to make contracts or loans so that third parties are not harmed by members who apparently have the authority to act. Canon 639, §3 provides that a member who makes a contract without permission is personally responsible, but that may not be much help to a third party who made the contract in good faith, believing the institute was the contracting party. Finally superiors are not to permit debts to be contracted unless the institute is able to pay the debt.

In addition to the canonical structure of a religious institute, there is usually a civil law structure at the level of the institute, the province and sometimes a house. The most common civil law structure used by institutes to establish a civil law existence is the non profit corporation, which is also used by institutes to incorporate their apostolates (see chapter twenty-two).

Since civil law corporations represent the religious institute for civil law purposes (not all purposes), it is helpful if the governance structure of the corporation parallels the governance of the institute so that transactions that require both civil law and canon law approval can travel parallel but distinct paths without conflict between the two. For example, the alienation or sale of property which is stable patrimony in excess of the United States limit of $3,000,000 requires the consent of the council and the written permission of the superior (c. 638, §3). Most corporations established by religious institutes require a majority of the corporate members to approve such a transaction. A few religious institutes have divided the corporate members into two classes: Class A, the major superior and Class B, the members of the council and require the permission of both to reflect more clearly the canonical process in civil law. Some corporations sponsored by religious institutes have a policy that requires the canonical process to be complete before the transaction can be concluded. Most have no special provisions and to date the absence of major problems has been the result of the institute and their sponsored corporations being careful to determine that there is agreement on both the civil and canonical side before proceeding.

CASE 4

> A diocesan religious institute has closed its private high school and wants to sell the property to the diocese. It has been appraised at $5,000,000 dollars. What canonical process is required of the religious institute and the diocese?

First, the religious institute must complete the process designated by its proper law as well as the requirements of the canons. For the most part, religious institutes have repeated the canons in their proper law so that there is no difference. However, if an institute owned considerable properties or provided for the consultation of the local community prior to a sale such internal processes would need to be completed. Since the property is in excess of the $3,000,000 limit for the United States, the written permission of the competent superior and the consent of the council would be required (c. 638, §3). In addition, the valuation of experts (c. 1293, §1, 2°) should be included. The religious institute is a diocesan institute and therefore a diocesan juridic person and needs the permission of the bishop to alienate the property.

If the institute were a pontifical institute, the permission of the bishop would not be needed, but the Holy See would require the *nihil obstat* of the bishop where the property is located. The appropriate documentation should then be forwarded to the Holy See.

If the property was owned by a corporation, the appropriate corporate permissions would need to be secured.

CASE 5

A Pontifical religious institute which sponsors a hospital system of sixteen facilities estimates that over the next ten years it will need to borrow four hundred million dollars. It has a need for eighty million in the coming year, but it doesn't want to make repeated requests to borrow money every time there is a need. What process should the religious institute follow?

A long term borrowing of such a large amount is considered to be a transaction which may jeopardize the patrimonial condition of the institute because of the risk of default. Many large healthcare systems sponsored by religious institutes need to be able to borrow large sums of money, sometimes on short notice and often needing to move quickly to obtain the most advantageous interest rates. Just a small percentage point can mean hundreds of thousands of dollars during the course of a long term loan.

Religious institutes and the Congregation for Institutes of Consecrated Life and Societies of Apostolic Life (CICLSAL) have developed a practice over the years in which the CICLSAL gives a one time permission for the anticipated borrowing needs of the healthcare system sponsored by the religious institute.

The institute would follow its internal requirements, the requirements of the canons, submit the rationale and intended use of probable future borrowings and evidence it can pay back the borrowed amount. The recent practice of the Holy See for borrowings is not to require the *nihil obstat* of the local bishop or bishops for a petition to undertake debt by a pontifical institute. The sale or, transfer of property or other transactions still require the *nihil obstat.*

CASE 6

The Holy Faith Health System sponsored by the Sisters of the Holy Faith borrowed $100,000,000 to finance the construction of new buildings. In 1998, the System wants to refinance the debt at a lower rate of interest. Because of the lower rate of interest the System can add $20,000,000 to the principal without paying any more in principal and interest than it was obligated to pay under the original agreement. It plans to do this by retiring the old bonds issued for the debt and issuing new bonds at a lower rate of interest. The religious institute applied for and received a rescript for the original borrowing. Is this a transaction which needs the approval of the Holy See?

Two questions arise in such a transaction. The first is whether the additional $20,000,000 of principal debt since it is over the $3,000,000 limit requires a new petition? Since the overall debt burden of principal and interest is not increased, the risk to the borrower is not increased and therefore a new petition is not required for the refinancing. The second question is whether the issuance of new bonds in and of itself requires another petition. Since the new bonds are for the debt, which already received the approval of the Holy See, a new petition is not required.

CASE 7

> A pontifical religious institute wants to purchase a nursing home to use as a retirement home for its members. The purchase price is $10,000,000. The institute plans to use three million dollars from its investment portfolio and borrow seven million from the institute retirement fund. What approvals are needed?

Unlike the sale of property, the only requirements for the spending of funds, which have not been made a part of stable patrimony, are the requirements that are contained in the proper law of the institute. Normally, the investment portfolio of a religious institute is free capital. Most institutes have proper law that requires the permission of the major superior and council in order to spend an amount in excess of a certain limit. These may be relatively high or low depending on the financial circumstances of the institute. An amount this large would normally require permission of the major superior and council. It could also require the permission of the finance council.

The permission to borrow from the retirement fund would depend on the structure of the fund. Often these funds are governed by special internal regulations of the institute and perhaps are subject to civil law requirements if the fund is in a trust or a government approved retirement plan. The reason for such internal regulations and civil law safeguards is to ensure funds are available to care for the elderly and disabled.

If the retirement fund has not been the subject of a canonical act to make it stable patrimony, the fund is subject only to the internal regulations of the institute and the civil law provisions of the fund. It is possible to interpret canon 1295 as applying to retirement funds if the funds are recognized as stable patrimony (see chapter eighteen), thus making the retirement fund subject to the permissions required for stable patrimony. The difficulty with saying that a retirement fund is stable patrimony as a result of the interpretation of canon 1295 is that any number of accounting procedures that set aside funds for a particular use such as formation, missions or charitable works might also fall under the same interpretation. Institutes desiring flexibility in the use of funds might find it cumbersome to always seek the permission of higher authority (including the Holy See for amounts in excess of $3,000,000) to shift the use of funds. Thus, it seems clearer to recognize retirement funds as free capital until they have been established as stable patrimony by a canonical act.

CASE 8

A religious institute established a university in 1920. In 1925, the university established a Medical School and Teaching Hospital. Over the years the university along with the medical school and hospital grew receiving financial support from both the catholic and non catholic population of the area.

After the Vatican Council II the university reorganized to reflect the spirit of the Council to cooperate with the laity and to gain the expertise of laity in governing the university. Prior to the reorganization, the major superior and the council were the Board of Directors for the university. After the reorganization, the majority of the places on the Board of Directors were occupied by laity. Most of the laity were Catholic, but some were not. The change in structure from a corporation controlled by the leadership of the religious institute to one not controlled by the institute was not accompanied by a petition to the Holy See to alienate the property.

In 1998, the university decided to sell the hospital, but retain the medical school. The university received several offers, including an offer by a group of Catholic systems and an offer by a for profit health care group. The university decided to sell to the for profit hospital which offered the highest price and has agreed to operate the hospital as a Catholic facility.

The local bishop objects to the sale to the for profit corporation. The president of the university takes the position that the university was never a church entity since its original incorporation and it certainly passed from church control when it reorganized after Vatican II.

What is the canonical status of the university and the hospital? What, if any, canonical process should be undertaken regarding the sale?

The above case is similar to the recent sale of the St. Louis University Hospital to a for profit entity.[1] The university was founded by the Missouri Province of the Society of Jesus. According to a statement made by the Archbishop of St. Louis, the Archbishop met with the superior general of the Jesuits who took the position that the sale of the hospital could proceed only if the appropriate canonical procedure was followed. Also, it seems that no permission was obtained for the *de jure* alienation of the property of the university (presumably referring to the reorganization of the Board of Directors to a lay Board). The Jesuit superior general requested clarification of the canonical status of the university from the Congregation for Institutes of Consecrated Life and Societies of Apostolic Life and the Congregation for Catholic Education.

The response of the Congregations was:

1. The authorization of the Holy See is necessary for the sale of St. Louis University Hospital since the provisions of 1967 of appointing a self-perpetuating board of trustees, a majority of whom were not members of the Missouri Province of the Society of Jesus, did not constitute an alienation of ecclesiastical goods, whose owner, canonically considered, remains the Missouri Province of the Society of Jesus as public juridic person of the church, and therefore the properties pertaining to St. Louis University are still to be considered ecclesiastical goods. The goal of the action taken in 1967 was the incorporation of laypersons into the board of trustees in the spirit of the Second Vatican Council. It is in this light that the move was greeted in a positive way by the late Cardinal Ritter. The action was not a transfer of property, but a change in the structure of the governing body of the university.

2. It is the responsibility of the Society of Jesus to put into place a mechanism through which the society exercises control with respect to the president of the St. Louis University to ensure that the requirements of canon law as they pertain to St. Louis University are followed.

The letter from the Congregations also stated that the purchaser must observe Catholic principles and practices, including the *Ethical and Religious Directives for Catholic Health Care Services*, and maintain a program to meet the spiritual needs of the patients and their families; instruct students, interns, residents and fellows

---

[1] Archbishop Justin Rigali, "St. Louis University Hospital Sold to For-Profit Corporation," *Origins* 27:38 (March 12, 1998) 629-633.

51

in accord with the above, provide care for the needy consistent with past practice, and give assurances that existing education programs in pediatrics, obstetrics and gynecology at other Catholic hospitals will be continued.

A significant number of Catholic educational institutions and a few health care institutions restructured their board of trustees to a self-perpetuating Board of Trustees composed of a majority of laity following Vatican II. The canonical result of the restructuring had been a matter of debate. Some took the position of the congregation that an alienation never occurred, even though the civil law structure did not provide an avenue for control by the religious institute. Others were of the opinion that an alienation had occurred since the institute no longer had control over the property. Further, some understood such transaction as an "invalid alienation" since the permission of the competent authorities did not take place (cc. 1291and 1296).

If the facts of the case were presented to canonists, some would offer the opinion that the proper procedure at the time of the reorganization would have been to apply for permission to alienate and it is likely the permission would have been granted by the Holy See, provided the "just reason" of canon 1293, §1, 1° would have been supplied.[2]

It remains to be seen what mechanism will be acceptable for complying with the directive of the congregations to allow the Society of Jesus to exercise control with respect to the president and board of trustees. Since the facts of the above case and the St. Louis sale are replicated many times in the United States, the drafting of acceptable mechanisms will be of interest to the religious institutes which sponsor apostolates with similar civil law structures.

---

[2] See the discussion of Francis G. Morrisey on the Reorganization of Corporate Sponsoring Boards in "The Alienation of Temporal Goods in Contemporary Practice," *Studia Canonica* 29 (1995) 311-14.

CHAPTER FIVE

REMUNERATION FOR CHURCH EMPLOYEES

WILLIAM P. DALY

CASE 9

Father John Doe has been a priest for five years. He has just been assigned to his first pastorate at St. John's Parish. He is inheriting a staff of two full time and two part time employees, three student night receptionists, and one deacon who helps out several evenings and on Sunday. As he looks over the staff list, he wonders if the payroll figures he sees are internally equitable, consistent with church law on wages and benefits and sufficiently comparable with other employers in the area to maintain a reasonable amount of staff stability.

CASE 10

Sister Jennifer Jones has recently become chancellor of the Diocese. One of her roles includes overseeing the diocesan staff, comprised of two full time and three part time diocesan priests, three religious (one priest, one brother and herself), sixteen lay persons (both full and part time) and one full time deacon. She has been on the job for three weeks. Now Jim, a member of the staff, has asked for an appointment. As the grapevine has it, he will complain of being underpaid. What information will she need to determine if Jim and other staff are fairly compensated?

Canon law speaks in several places about proper remuneration of ministers and staff, about pensions, social security and insurance for priests, deacons and employees and about appropriate support for employees and their families. All of these items, covering issues of pay and benefits, can be subsumed under the title "compensation."

CANONICAL PRINCIPLES

Several canons guide remuneration in church settings and are related to these cases. Canon 1286 outlines the duties of administrators.
Administrators of goods:

1°   in the employment of workers are to observe meticulously also the civil laws concerning labor and social policy, according to the principles handed on by the Church;

2°   are to pay a just and decent wage to employees so that they are able to provide fittingly for their own needs and those of their dependents.

This canon requires administrators to follow applicable civil laws and pay a just and decent wage to staff. In the various situations described in our cases, staff includes clergy (priests and deacons), religious and lay persons. All should be compensated fairly according to their state in life and applicable work laws.

Canon 281 describes canonical expectations for remuneration of diocesan priests.

§1   Since clerics dedicate themselves to ecclesiastical ministry, they deserve remuneration which is consistent with their condition, taking into account the nature of their function and the conditions of places and times, and by which they can provide for the necessities of their life as well as for the equitable payment of those whose services they need.

§2   Provision must also be made so that they possess that social assistance which provides for their needs suitably if they suffer from illness, incapacity or old age.

This canon calls for sufficient salary and benefits (health and disability insurance and pension) to provide for the personal needs of priests and sufficient other income to provide equitable payment to those providing services.

Canon 281, §3 describes compensation expectations for *deacons*.

§3   Married deacons who devote themselves completely to ecclesiastical ministry deserve remuneration by which they are able to provide
for the support of themselves and their families. Those who receive
remuneration by reason of a civil profession which they exercise or
have exercised, however, are to take care of the needs of themselves
and their families from the income derived from it.

This canon distinguishes between deacons employed full time in ecclesiastical
ministry and those who work part time in a church setting while maintaining regular employment elsewhere.

The remuneration for deacons employed full time in church ministry (as in
case 10 above) is referenced by the code in similar terms to the full time lay
employees (see below). This compensation should be sufficient to provide for
their own support and that of their families.

Part time deacons with regular jobs elsewhere (as in case 9 above) are treated
as volunteers but should be reimbursed for expenses.

Canons 276, §2, 4° and 283, §2 describe canonical expectations for time-off
benefits for *diocesan priests and deacons fully employed by a church entity*.

276, §2, 4° They are equally bound to make time for spiritual
retreats according to the prescripts of particular law.

283, §2 They are entitled, however, to a fitting and sufficient time
of vacation each year as determined by universal or particular law.

These canons establish the expectation that priests and full-time deacons
should be provided time off for retreat and vacation. Canon 533, §2 states that a
pastor is entitled to a month's vacation. Canon 550, §3 notes that a parochial vicar
shall have the same vacation as the pastor.

Canon 681 covers members of religious institutes working in dioceses and
parishes. This canon addresses many instances in which religious work in church
settings. In other situations (e.g., religious working in hospitals, colleges, retreat
centers, institute or provincial offices, etc.), canon 681 and canon 231 (on lay
employment) can be referenced for guidance.

Canon 681, §2 In these cases, the diocesan bishop and competent
superior of the institute are to draw up a written agreement which,
among other things, is to define expressly and accurately those
things which pertain to the work to accomplished, the members to
be devoted to it, and economic matters.

Following canon 681, §2, administrators should ensure that an appropriate contract exists for religious workers. The contract will determine the amount of pay, appropriate benefits or certain payments in lieu of benefits, and allowances or support for housing and transportation where appropriate. It will also cover other related matters such as where payments should be directed.

Canon 663, §5 describes canonical expectations for time-off benefits for *members of religious institutes.*

They are to observe faithfully an annual period of sacred retreat.

This canon establishes the expectation that religious should be provided time off for retreat. Specific requirements are developed by the institute or individual religious but time-off must be requested of the employer and may need to be charged against accrued vacation, especially in situations where religious are compensated equivalently to lay employees.

Canon 231 describes compensation expectations for *lay persons.* Paragraph one describes the qualifications lay persons should bring to church service as well as the care they should take in performing their jobs. Paragraph two then describes what lay persons can expect for their efforts – decent remuneration to provide for their own needs and those of their families. Their compensation is to include key benefits: health insurance, social security and pension.

§1 Lay persons who permanently or temporarily devote themselves to some special service of the Church are obliged to acquire the appropriate formation required to fulfill their function properly and to carry out this function conscientiously, eagerly, and diligently.

§2 Without prejudice to the prescript of canon 230, §1 and with the prescripts of civil law having been observed, lay persons have the right to decent remuneration appropriate to their condition so that they are able to provide decently for their own needs and for those of their family. They also have a right for their social provision; social security, and health benefits to be duly provided.

Canon 231 speaks of decent compensation as a "right" based on proper fulfillment of job duties. Both pay and benefits (pension, health insurance) are spoken of as a right in return for effective work performance. (The reference to canon 230, §1 excludes compensation for lay persons installed as lector or acolyte.)

PAY ISSUES

Dioceses typically have well-developed systems of compensation for *diocesan priests*. These include cash salary, auto allowance or mileage reimbursement, mass stipends and stole fees or flat monthly amounts received in lieu of stipends and stole fees, a cash equivalent of the employee portion of the social security payments they must make as self employed persons, housing and food support and/or allowances. Sometimes these figures are all rolled into one salary. More often a schedule describes all the components separately.

Religious priests are often paid according to the schedule for diocesan priests.

Women and men religious are sometimes paid according to a stipend which applies to all religious in the diocese. This method often includes housing and automobile support. Another approach which is becoming more common in some dioceses is to pay religious lay equivalent salaries, i.e., pay rates similar to what lay persons are paid for comparable jobs. In this latter case, housing and auto allowances become part of the overall lay equivalent salary.

To meet the need to provide decent remuneration to lay employees, administrators need to be attentive to:

- Civil laws about pay;
- Standards of fair and just pay;
- Comparative pay data for key jobs.

Administrators need to adhere to two civil laws on pay. The *Equal Pay Act* requires that men and women doing the same job be paid comparably, i.e., in the same pay range. Men and women in the same job with comparable work performance records and seniority should be paid similarly.

The second noteworthy law is the *Fair Labor Standards Act (FLSA)*. It requires employers to pay covered workers an overtime wage rate of one and one-half times the regular pay rate for each hour worked in excess of 40 hours in a workweek and to maintain written records of hours worked by covered employees. This law extends to many workers and allows exemptions for certain positions. The FLSA categories are:

- **Exempt:** Positions which are responsible for developing, and administering general policies, and procedures or positions which require advanced specialized training or positions which perform original and creative work. Such workers are considered to be EXEMPT from the *FLSA* and overtime pay and record keeping requirements.

- ◆ **Non-exempt:** Positions which require the performance of routine, procedural, non-discretionary work. Such positions include those performing clerical, secretarial, drafting, computer operations, mechanical, food preparation, building and grounds maintenance, security, or custodial work. Such workers are considered to be NON-EXEMPT from *FLSA* criteria so that the employer must follow the law and pay for hours of work in excess of 40 per week at 1 1/2 times the regular pay rate. It will also be important to maintain time keeping records for these employees.

Since some states have stricter versions of the law on overtime, administrators should consult with local authorities.

Administrators should be aware of standards of fair and just pay and work to ensure that no adult worker on their staff falls below these standards. Many cities are passing "living wage" initiatives. These are good indicators of "decent remuneration" in that they attempt to ensure pay at or above the poverty line for a family. Trade union rates would be an appropriate level of reimbursement.

Finally, administrators should seek out information on comparable pay for jobs in their organizations. Sources of such information can be found in newspaper advertising, on the Internet, from diocesan agencies and from national organizations such as the National Association of Church Personnel Administrators.

BENEFITS ISSUES

Diocesan priests typically receive health and other insurance and are provided pensions. Administrators of these benefits need to exercise care in developing plan documents to address various issues including coverage for persons who enter the priesthood late in life, transfer to or from another diocese or leave active ministry before retirement.

Religious are typically covered for benefits by their institutes, which are compensated for benefits by their employers. Administrators should develop cost estimates of various benefits and provide equivalent amounts to religious institutes.

Deacons employed in full time church ministry positions should receive benefits comparable to lay persons (see below). Deacons with full time employment elsewhere are expected to receive benefits from their employers.

To best address the canon 1286 requirement to provide for the needs of lay employees and their families, administrators should strive to provide benefits that encourage substantial coverage for individuals and their families. This would mean:

- requiring at most, only a small employee contribution for both employee and dependent health insurance.

- providing health insurance continuation for up to eighteen months for a departing employee even though church organizations are technically exempt from this law.

- participating in government sponsored programs such as social security, workers' compensation, and disability insurance.

- providing unemployment insurance or severance pay in lieu of unemployment insurance in layoff situations.

- ensuring the viability of the employee retirement program through regular and sufficient employer contributions, a vesting schedule consistent with ERISA standards (even though church organizations are technically exempt from this law) and appropriate information and notification features.

- full application of the terms of the Family and Medical Leave Act (FMLA), even where a small entity may technically be exempt from the law. (The FMLA stipulates up to twelve weeks of unpaid leave with regular continuation of health insurance and guaranteed return to an equivalent job.)

Both Father John and Sister Jennifer found themselves in complex situations. The canons provide valuable guidance. But the deferral in canon 1286 to civil law on employment, pay and benefits, makes their situations even more complex. We have touched on a number of, but not all, of applicable laws at the federal level. States and localities also have laws pertaining to these issues. Both newly appointed administrators may have training in employment law, compensation administration and human resources management. If not, someone in Father John's shoes may be wise to seek out the human resource or finance director at the diocesan center or chancery for advice. Another avenue of information for Father John may be knowledgeable people on his parish pastoral council or finance council.

Sister Jennifer's responsibility for a large and diverse staff is even more complicated. Besides supervision of human resources issues in the central offices, she should exercise diocesan oversight of personnel practices in parishes. If she does not have sufficient background in employment law and compensation administration, someone on her staff may have human resources expertise and could be delegated this responsibility. She can also obtain assistance in developing policies, procedures and personnel systems from other church agencies, consultants or professional associations.

✠ ✠ ✠

ACQUIRING ECCLESIASTICAL GOODS

✠ ✠ ✠

CHAPTER SIX

SUPPORT FOR THE CHURCH

JOSEPH N. PERRY

Canon 1260: "The Church has an innate right to require from the Christian faithful those things which are necessary for the purposes proper to it."[1]

Providing for the church's material needs for ministry and education is a joint effort of clergy and faithful. This topic of church life, throughout history, has asked for constant reflection and renewal. In today's context, the following two scenarios exemplify the state of the question:

CASE 11

Mr. & Mrs. Average Member of Holy Apostles Parish, Anytown, USA, have three children currently attending the parish elementary school. Mr. Member is a traveling salesman. Mrs. Member is a housewife and works in the parish school's cafeteria for several hours four days a week. The annual family income, inclusive of a guesstimate of commissions Mr. Member receives from his job, is $52,000. Their parish has just launched its annual pledge drive for weekly support. Mr. & Mrs. Average Member are trying to determine what their support of their parish can be considering the family's expenses with school tuition costs, personal and household expenses, insurance, taxes and savings.

[1] *Code of Canon Law, Latin-English Edition*, (Washington, DC: Canon Law Society of America 1983) 451.

CASE 12

Their local pastor, Father James Smith, is also not without a challenge to motivate his congregation to respond generously to the parish's pledge drive. Holy Apostles is an urban parish of eight hundred households. Parish finances revolve around three areas: the annual operating budget, capital maintenance and improvements, and the diocesan assessment. Being a middle-income-working class parish, Father Smith knows that parish coffers will, probably, never overflow to abundance. But, he along with the parish council is desirous of maintaining a balanced budget while placing a percentage of income in savings and investments for the future. That future is as secure as the parishioners are willing to ensure it.

What kind of motivation is needed by the parish to meet its financial obligations? What is necessary to have administratively in place for the parish members to understand these material needs and fulfill goals in light of their abilities? What will move the parishioners beyond "obligation" to a genuine care for the church's mission? Answers to these questions have challenged the issue of church support for as long as the church has been around. Proper motivation and the setting of priorities connected with realistic needs is an arduous task.

Like other topics of church life and discipline, church support has run the gauntlet of social and religious change. A brief look at how the Church has handled church support might help to understand the present context.

If there is any consistent thread throughout this history, it is the fact that the issue of church support has always needed coaching by constant evangelical exhortation. This effect has met with varying degrees of reception by the faithful.

Several hundred years of persecution delayed formation of an administrative and procedural style within the early Church. No hard-and-fast rules are apparent with a method of church support prior to the first codification of laws (1917). Along the vast stretch of tradition, church support was understood in terms of the biblical concept of tithing. But tithing wore a different make-up and carried varying degrees of emphasis as the centuries marched on. Suffice it to say the Church has struggled with the exhortation and the corresponding cooperation of the faithful has always required a high degree of understanding of duty and spiritual fervor. Needless to say, an insured method of income to the Church for its ministries and administration has probably never been commensurate with the Church's realistic needs.

CHURCH SUPPORT IN SCRIPTURE

Scripture seems to address this subject beginning with the story of Cain and Abel and their disparate offerings in worship that ended in tragedy (Gen 4). Whereas tithes, tributes and taxes were practiced widely in the ancient world, the religious tithe mentioned in the Hebrew Scriptures was only hesitatingly reflected in the Church. The Hebrew practice of tithing was based on the notion that God is the sovereign Lord of all creation. The Lord says, " ... the land belongs to me and to me you are only strangers and guests" (Lev 25:23). This tribute was seen as an act of worship and, therefore, an obligatory act. The patriarch, Jacob, vowed to Yahweh: "I will surely pay you a tenth part of all you give me" (Gen 28:22). In time, the tithe took on institutional form in Israel and was scrupulously practiced as evidenced by the books of Leviticus and Deuteronomy but eventually, because of heavy prescription, could not be distinguished, in instances, from civil tributes paid to earthly lords.

In the Gospel, Jesus praised out loud a widow whom he observed placing *all she had to live on*, two copper coins, in the temple collection box. Jesus remarked that she gave more than all the rest who gave out of their surplus (Mark 12:41-44). Jesus lauded this woman's generosity because it far exceeded in spirit the legalistic notions of tithing that were propagated by the scribes and pharisees (Luke 11:42 and 18:12). Jesus replaced the meticulous formalism connected with religious tithes with the more unpretentious *almsgiving* which, along with prayer and fasting, became the new acts of religion for disciples (Matt 6:1-18). Yet, Jesus obliged himself to the temple tax (Matt 17:24).

THE EARLY CHURCH

The passage from Acts 2:44 sets forth an idyllic view that the earliest Christian communities were conspicuous in sharing their property and resources, even liquidating their assets for a broader distribution among themselves. Elsewhere in Acts 5:1-11 a couple's dishonesty indicates this ideal was not easily negotiated by even the earliest Christians. Generous support would remain a theme of preaching and exhortation up to the present day.

One sentiment of those early communities comes through strongly from the biblical text, namely, that the first Christians knew that there could be no rich and poor, no well fed and hungry in the kingdom of heaven. So, they sought to eliminate those differences in the kingdoms of earth. The early Church established the custom of collections for sister Churches for relief purposes in time of famine and poverty (Acts 11:28-30; Gal 2:10; Rom 15:26; 1 Cor 16:1). These efforts continued and are described in extra-biblical documents like the *Didache* (1st-2nd cent.); the *Didascalia* (1st half of 3rd cent.); and the *Constitutiones Apostolorum* (4th-5th cent.). The coaching at that time tapped the spirit of the Old Testament presentation of tithes and first fruits but without the former legal rigor of Jewish tithing.

THE PATRISTIC AGE

The era of the Fathers witnessed a different atmosphere for preaching tithes and offerings. The tone of exhortation found in some of the writings of the early Church Fathers, e.g., Origen (185-253/4) and Cyprian (200/210-258), would seem to indicate they met with the faithful's reluctance with the obligation to charity and support for the ministers that made the earliest communities so noticeable.[2] After the peace offered the Church by civil power (4th cent.), new organizational needs were evident with an increasingly expanding church territory-wise. The hierarchical system of the Church was developing to meet internal and territorial exigencies. The Church was taking pride of place alongside civil government. The Fathers appealed to the interior disposition of the faithful borrowing, again, from primary sources in the Hebrew scriptures for the purpose of more resolute giving patterns. The Fathers framed their exhortations in ascetical principles of charity following upon the great commandment of love to impress the faithful with the evangelical summons of sharing their goods and resources with the poor and to meet the sustenance needs of the clergy.

PRE-CODE LEGISLATION

In the period before the first code of 1917, both civil and church societies resorted to legislation to compel the faithful's compliance with taxation. The political and economic and moral upheaval of the European landscape cannot be underestimated. Church support lost its foundation in moral reasoning and now bore the clothing of juridics with the usual consequences enunciated for the violation of law. The Church was terribly preoccupied by the subject of church support as shown by a plethora of laws and exhortations to clarify who was due tithes,

---

[2]Citations from the Patristics taken from: *A Historical Essay on Tithes: A Collection of Sources and Texts*, (Rome: Terzo Natalini, 1973).

who collects tithes, what was tithable, to certain minute detail; who was exempt from paying tithes, specific monastic exemptions and their back-and-forth, and addressing abuses that naturally crept in. The topic of church support never lacked the interest of the official Church for no other reason than tithes and taxes always rubbed against the grain of human nature. The kind of giving that tithing represented fundamentally asked for altruistic and spiritual inclinations on part of the giver. The issue was buffeted by the changing European portrait relative to wars and the division of kingdoms, the flux of the economic situation, to say nothing of the burden of a variety of civil taxes upon the citizenry. In this mix, a variety of meanings was found attached to tithing – seen as an act of religion, whether as atonement for personal sin, adoration and thanksgiving, a form of petitionary prayer or a suppliant return to God. Needless to say, the faithful were not always moved to the highest spiritual considerations with what was preached as a fundamental Christian duty.

By the medieval period the system of tithing lost much of its original religious meaning and was smothered in a huge amount of legalism and surveillance. With the piety of this era, nonetheless, there was some return to biblical inspiration behind the subject matter and a theology of tithing was put forth that was given a scholastic tinge such as with Thomas Aquinas (1225-1274) or the spiritualist accents of Peter Lombard (1100-1160) and Bonaventure (1221-1274). The thought of the Church Fathers advancing tithing as a precept of the Church was not entirely lost on the medievalists.

The 16th century Reformers would attack the entire idea of money connected with ecclesiastical life. The Church was left demoralized by heavy critique of its institutional practices of taxes and tithes and tribute bound so closely to things holy. But the Counter-Reformation did not offer a thorough treatment of the questions posed about these and other practices of medieval Catholicism.

Old World and medieval methods were used to collect support for the Church until modern times. The *cathedraticum* (a tax from the throne laid against churches and confraternities subject to the diocesan bishop) of the 1917 code's legislation is the last vestige of an ancient way to collect revenues from the concept of tribute paid to a lord. Attempts were made all along to inspire motivation on part of the faithful about their giving. These took the form of obliging the faithful under precept or the threat of loss of the sacraments. But, by and large, the faithful were never terribly impressed by such firm exhortations. Civil power sometimes came to the rescue of church support with its own brand of civil consequences. The concept of ecclesiastical benefice eased much of the pressure for financial survival with use of land and buildings and other enterprises that were income generating. What was to be tithed and what wasn't tithed varied across the European landscape. Probably, the strongest voice of the Church on this issue was heard at the Council of Trent when it linked tithes directly with one's obligation to God (session 25.12). The refusal to meet one's tithes was punishable by excommunication. The penalty was lifted once restitution was made.

CODAL LEGISLATION

By the time of the first codification of laws (1917), the Roman Church still had no sure system of collecting revenues for its operations other than various *taxa* and the *cathedraticum*. No firm system had been in place with the arrival of the Catholic Church in the New World. In modern times, the bishops of the United States saw, clearly, that other methods, in exception to the code, were needed for the particular circumstances of the American church. The Second Plenary Council of Baltimore, no. 100 succeeded in gaining the Propaganda Fide's endorsement of parish assessment, which turned out to be a reorganized system of taxation of parishes and subordinate institutions, a method many bishops use to this day. The 1917 code asserted the right of the Church to own property (1917 CIC c. 1495) and to demand support from its faithful (1917 CIC c. 1496), reasoning that while the Church has from God all the supernatural means necessary for her sacred mission, e.g., jurisdiction, teaching power, sacraments, the purely material goods required for these same ends must come from the faithful themselves. In practice, the faithful supply these temporal goods voluntarily by the foundation of benefices, schools, hospitals and other charitable institutions. If these were forthcoming, then the 1917 code saw no reason for taxation of the faithful. Income following short-falls might be raised either by a general tax proportioned to the income of the individual, or by a special tax levied on the occasion of special services to the community as a whole such as collections taken up during divine services or on individuals on the occasion of some special spiritual ministration such as baptism, marriage and burial.

THE 1983 CODE

Does The Right/Duty To Support Depend On Good Will?

If by "good will" one means the initiative of the faithful essentially drives church support without any assertiveness on part of the Church to articulate the right to support or to remind the faithful of the church's needs, then, no, church support is not dependent upon the good will of the faithful. This "right" of the Church exists irrespective of the inclinations or the mood of the faithful to respond to the material needs of the Church. The Church as divinely instituted enjoys the right to require material support from its participating members and institutions for its ministries and services. The 1983 code describes the sources of this material support in the forms of free will offerings (c. 1261); taxation (c. 1263); fees (c. 1264); fund raising (c. 1265); special collections (c. 1266); prescription (c. 1268) and self-generating income (cc. 1271 and 1274). The modern means of requiring support would rule out force or imprisonment or any unusual penalties lacking the authorization of universal law and which would only bring harm to the Church. The Church is increasingly a voluntary society in this part of the hemisphere. This voluntarism is best complemented with exhortation to a reception of those obligations that follow upon voluntary association. It becomes a challenge reconciling the precept of church support (c. 222) with an appeal to the good will of the faithful for gratuitous support. Reconciling institutional needs with the faithful's economic ability is another challenge. Forming the faithful to a mind of stewardship is still another challenge.

But, if by "good will" one means the sympathetic support of the faithful is needed to respond to routine needs of the Church as well as its special missions and projects, then, yes, the good will of the faithful is heavily at root of the Church's current system of church support. We are recipients of the force of tradition, since the turn of this century if not before, with the bishops' endorsement of free will offerings as the manner in which church support, of whatever sort, is collected for the territory of the United States.

The Church is principally a spiritual force in the world. Existing in the world, the Church, of necessity, needs material resources to carry on its mission. Much of this comes from the faithful themselves in the form of voluntary offerings of money, in lesser instances, movable and immovable property (c. 1261, §1), foundations and trusts and other wealth generating interests. Certain Catholic institutions, usually, generate income, e.g., hospitals, health care facilities, schools, cemeteries and the like.

While the Church in the United States has, generally, refrained from enforcing a tithing system or imposing a coercive tax on its members, the new code envisions a moderate, ordinary tax levied on public juridic persons subject to the diocesan bishop (see chapter seven). The adjectives, *moderate* and *proportionate*, found in canon 1263, imply that bishops should avoid anything akin to heavy taxation or taxation that goes beyond what the faithful can reasonably respond to. The directive of a moderate tax would seem to imply that there should be other sources of income for a local church, such as other volunteer offerings from the faithful and lawful income generating enterprises, so that any tax, if decreed, will be moderate. The same canon envisions the possibility of an extraordinary tax for special needs; however the bishop may determine *special needs and grave necessity*, such as disaster or refugee relief, repair of diocesan buildings, building a school or seminary. In all this, much is left to the autonomous authority of the bishop in his own diocese with the legal obligation that he first consult his presbyteral council and finance council so that a collective pastoral wisdom can be applied to the onerous task of requiring the material support of the faithful. Canon 1263 represents a softened action by bishops in this regard from the sole directive action of the bishop enunciated in the former law (1917 CIC cc. 1502; 1504-1506). Although the National Conference of Catholic Bishops (NCCB) attempts to bring the bishops together with a collaborative style and consensus on many pastoral topics, still, the diocesan bishop is to use his own discretion with the administrative details of shepherding the diocese (c. 381).

The American bishops do a number of things requiring financial support of their parishes and institutions. Some enact a parish assessment in addition to a so-called *cathedraticum* tax. Others have traded the *cathedraticum* for a system of parish assessment. Fund-raisers and pledges on a large scale supplement the *cathedraticum* and/or parish assessment.

The assessment is best described as a kind of modern system of tax on the income of parishes and institutions subject to the bishop's jurisdiction since the canonical *cathedraticum* was legislated more as a coercive tribute to the person of the bishop from his benefices, and due to the fact that the *cathedraticum* never really covered modern diocesan revenue needs. American dioceses are often some of the largest in the world.

The traditional *cathedraticum* highlighted parishes and institutions as subjects of the bishop's authority. Parish assessment is often couched in terms of the faithful's participation in the life and ministry of the diocese and, therefore, carries more collegial implications. The custom of assessments appears to cover more adequately the work of the diocesan bishop, supporting those agencies and offices with which he carries out his episcopal ministry. Some bishops who retain it, apply the income from the assessment to support, for example; the strictly canonical offices of the chancery, tribunal, bishop's office, and direct the income from an extraordinary tax or free will collection or special fund drive for the diocesan seminary, high schools or other special projects.

The percentage of the assessment varies from diocese to diocese. Some dioceses do not have a collateral stewardship appeal with or without a mandatory goal or charities drive or Bishop's Fund Appeal, i.e., the free-will offering mechanisms to supplement the diocesan tax. So, the parish assessment can be formidable, up to 25% of parish income in some places. The average in the United States appears to be closer to 15% and as low as 3-4%. Necessarily, the faithful's personal support of their parish is taxed to support the ministerial and administrative functions of the diocese. The issue here is that no one system of generating income alone, namely, a so-called *cathedraticum* or an assessment taxing system, nor free will offerings alone adequately covers the needs of financial support for the average American diocese. Many dioceses appear to employ a combination of taxation and free will offerings to cover diocesan needs. This is not the situation in many third world countries that are restricted, in many instances, to a tax of their juridic persons and charitable free will offerings from the faithful beyond the local diocese or from other globally directed appeals. The 1983 code seems to recognize this situation and orders the bishops that should they need a tax, it should be moderate and not oppressive. Bishops often excuse or reduce the amount of the assessment for poorer parishes and other struggling juridic persons.

To complicate matters further, some dioceses still refer to assessment as parish tax, or use, incorrectly, the term *cathedraticum* for the sake of a practical label, or to distinguish, this collection from general diocesan fund or charities drives. Assessment is certainly a softer term and would attempt to embrace a broader reading of an institution's financial condition while educating the faithful towards better discipleship.

Bishops use varying methods for collecting the proceeds from other general diocesan fund drives or charitable appeals. Some collect what the faithful are willing to give after a campaign quota is announced. It is up to the local parish to collect from volunteer offerings of the faithful and, in some instances, make up any difference from parish coffers if a goal was levied on the parishes. Assessment is popularly based on a percentage of parish income, using a formula that considers such variables as membership numbers, parish debt, school expenses, or parish capital campaigns.

Baptism burdens the church member with the obligation, among others, to support the material needs of the Church (c. 221, §1). The Church refrains from determining what her members should hand over from their personal resources, leaving to them their private decision to donate to the Church. All the Church's collections (c. 1266) for ongoing and special projects and missions ask merely for voluntary contributions from the faithful. The Church, confidently, relies on her faithful to intuit the needs of the Church and to respond generously.

Unlike many of the Churches of the Reform, the principle under Mosaic Law of the tithe of one-tenth (Deut 14:22) or anything similar to first fruits (Num 18:19) has not enjoyed a consistent application in the Roman Church of the Western Hemisphere. Anything like this appears to be left to local custom in other places in the Catholic world. The Church in America began as mission territory and until shortly after the opening of this century was under the auspices of the Roman dicastery of the *Propaganda Fide* (now known as the Congregation for the Evangelization of Peoples). Implied in missionary service are found patterns of generous subsidy. Material exigencies of the frontier church and beyond were such that missionaries, religious and immigrant clergy, historically, gave much materially and spiritually to the poor masses they served. Generosity within pastoral service is still the style of many religious communities so much so that the idea that the Church provides or that the Church has wealth in abundance has not entirely disappeared from the consciousness of the faithful towards a more proactive stewardship on their part. Consequently, the right of the Church to material support is tempered, first of all, by the faithful's understanding of their duty to support and, secondly, their follow-through with actual support commensurate with the needs of the Church. The meaning behind alms or appeals as the Church so often employs these is that the Church begs and the faithful decide what they will give. Thus, the topic of church support merits a continual place among local evangelization initiatives of clergy, ministers and educators to aid the faithful in appreciating "the value of offering to God, as an act of worship, part of the gifts received from his bounty."[3]

What, Exactly, Is The Right/Duty To Support To Be Urged?

By right to support is meant the faithful have the right to support their church through their resources free of interference by civil power. Also, the Church has the right to receive support from its members free of interference by civil power.

By duty to support is meant the faithful's consciousness of their obligation to provide for the charitable works of the Church, the sustenance of the clergy and the support of local and parish ministries.

The Church in the United States has been fortunate to have been able to freely exercise its right to be supported by its faithful (c. 1261), and the faithful have enjoyed the right to freely donate to the Church. This situation differs, of course,

[3] Pope Paul VI, from the papal audience, October 3, 1973, International Stewardship Seminar, Rome.

in many parts of the world. The Church in Germany accepts the cooperation of the state in exercising its right to material support. In Canada, the situation in Quebec saw tithes enforced by civil law even after the British conquest.

Evangelical concepts are at the foundation of this right to require and duty to support the Church. Support can be encouraged by formation of a broader concept of stewardship, i.e., why it is necessary to give back to God through the Church. The term stewardship, as a substitute for church support, recalls the biblical notion of care for the possessions or gifts that God has given us and our corresponding duty to offer the best portion of these gifts back to God. In this sense, the concept, stewardship, appeals to an understanding of our participating role in God's creation.

The United States Bishops registered concern about this aspect of Catholic life with an appointment of a Stewardship Committee of the National Conference of Catholic Bishops (NCCB). This committee was initially appointed to examine ways in which diocesan and parish income could be increased. During the course of their research, it became clear that stewardship involves much more than the contribution of money, that church support is actually grounded in a theology of stewardship. The Bishops, then, produced a pastoral letter: *Stewardship: A Disciple's Response.*

> Only by living as generous stewards of these local Christian communities, their parishes, can the Catholics of the United States hope to make them the vital sources of faith-filled Christian dynamism they are meant to be. At the same time, stewardship in and for the parish should not be narrowly parochial. For the diocese is not merely an administrative structure but instead joins communities called parishes into a "local church" and unites its people in faith, worship and service. The same spirit of personal responsibility in which a Catholic approaches his or her parish should extend to the dioceses and be expressed in essentially the same ways: generous material support and self-giving. As in the case of the parish too, lay Catholics ought to have an active role in the oversight of the stewardship of pastoral leaders and administrators at the diocesan level. At the present time, it seems clear that many Catholics need to develop a better understanding of the financial needs of the Church at the diocesan level. Indeed, the spirit and practice of stewardship should extend to other local churches and to the Universal Church – to the Christian community and to one's sisters and brothers in Christ everywhere – and be expressed in deeds of service and mutual support.

For some, this will mean direct personal participation in evangelization and mission work, for others generous giving to the collections established for these purposes and other worthy programs.[4]

What Accountability Is There To Those Who Contribute?

In ways that exceed the previous code's legislation with temporalities, canon law now orders within finance structures consultation with certain individuals and groups like the diocesan finance council and the presbyteral council before certain acts are placed (cc. 1277 and 1280; see chapters twelve and sixteen). Closely allied with consultation is found a treatment of the issue of accountability that respects the variety of financial administration methods found around the Catholic world. Standard business practice in the United States sees as normative, annual audits, regular reporting and use of qualified accountants. Annual parish budgets publicized for parishioners have been common for years, although not mandated in some places. It follows that if we evangelize the faithful towards more responsible stewardship, the Church at the same time should follow up by regular and qualified reporting of the use of goods and monies contributed by the faithful. As parishes are asked to render annual financial reports to the diocese, the same should be done by the diocese to the faithful. The law now orders (cc. 1284, §2, 8° and §3; 1287) such reports on an annual basis to be presented to the local ordinary and the faithful but their form and shape are governed by particular law. It, therefore, falls to the local ordinaries to enforce local norms regarding accountability and to ensure that pastors and administrators honor these. The diocese and its parishes and institutions cannot go wrong with use of standard auditing and reporting procedures (c. 1284).

The experience of Church for most Catholics is their parish. Here, a portion of the faithful are united together to hear the Word, celebrate the sacraments and carry out other ministries in the name of education, service and social justice. Parishioner support for these endeavors enables the Church to continue to share Christ's message and make Christ's love a reality for everyone. Parish membership starts with baptism. With membership come certain rights, namely, the right to the Word, sacraments, education, and pastoral care (c. 213); and the obligation to support one's parish for education and programs for evangelization, worship and works of charity, the upkeep of parish buildings and grounds, just wages for parish employees and support of the clergy. Baptism positions each member within a community of fellow believers carrying on the legacy of Jesus Christ. As

---

[4]*Stewardship: A Disciple's Response*, (Washington, DC: NCCB-USCC [bilingual edition] 1992).

baptized members, God has made each one a steward (Matt 25:14-30) and has given each abilities and talents that are unique. Each should use his or her abilities and talents to serve God. The closest avenue for this stewardship is participation in one's parish. Parish participation is the most effective way to do one's part. "Like good stewards of the manifold grace of God, serve one another with whatever gifts each of you has received" (1 Peter 4:10).

What are the Obligations to Support the Local Church and the Universal Church?

Beyond one's private initiatives, for Catholics, the parish is the smallest unit of participation in building the kingdom. A collection of parishes, along with other non-parochial institutions, makes up the diocese governed by a bishop (c. 374). The diocese essentially shows forth the Church of Christ in its oneness, its catholicity and apostolic character (c. 369). All dioceses and similar configurations make up the universal church. The *Code of Canon Law* does not detail the financial obligations of the faithful towards their parish, the diocese or universal Church. Instead, the code both obliges and exhorts the faithful in general terms (cc. 222 and 1262) to be mindful of their duty to cooperate with building up the Body of Christ in accordance with their vocation and function within the Church (c. 208), namely, to maintain communion with the Church (c. 209, §1), to live a holy life and promote the growth of the Church and its continual salvation and to engage themselves actively in the Church's apostolate, (cc. 210 and 225, §1), and to assist the Church with their resources so that the Church has what is necessary for divine worship, the apostolate, works of charity and the sustenance of the ministers (c. 222).

At the level of the diocese, financial support will provide for the agencies and offices, which service the parishes and other institutions within the diocese, the retirement needs of clergy and religious, the seminary and the needs of the poor. A portion of the parish assessment may even be returned to the parishes for individual parish needs, education and specialized ministries. In addition, canon 1262 exhorts the faithful to cooperate with the various collections which the national episcopal conferences establishes for its broader apostolic concerns. At the level of the universal Church, there are the annual appeals that the pope regularly issues in the name of refugee relief, natural disaster relief, and any variety of needs of the poor from around the world as well as offerings for assistance towards expenses connected with universal governance of the Church by the offices and dicasteries of the Holy See. The diocesan bishops assist in this support of the financial affairs of the Holy See (c. 1271).

The Second Vatican Council propagated the idea of the common priesthood of the faithful in *Lumen gentium*, no. 10, the *Dogmatic Constitution on the Church*. With this teaching, associate concepts of community, collective responsibility and active participation are implied. The responsibility for church support appropriated by the faithful can find a valid emphasis in these concepts toward a renewed approach to this important facet of Catholic life. The purposes of church support have seen no change in direction over the vast stretch of church history, namely, to order divine worship; to provide decent support for the clergy and other ministers; to perform the works of the sacred apostolate and of charity, especially towards the needy (c. 1254, §2). The ideals of community and the sharing of resources that launched the first Christian communities provide us with a grounded tradition from which to understand the local church and its relation to the universal church. Joined in bonds of common worship and common mission, the Church witnesses to the world most authentically when each and every member shares in the life of the community and its burdens. Pastors will be the unifying forces in this expression of community charity, and the sense of community responsibility will thus be more keenly felt among the faithful in a renewed spirit of service and participation.

With these concepts, hopefully, Mr. & Mrs. Average Member and their pastor, Father James Smith, will appreciate an inspiration for action and commitment that will benefit their parish of Holy Apostles for the foreseeable future. As can be seen, the support the Church needs to carry out its mission in the third millennium is greatly enhanced if the faithful's consciousness can be enriched with a solicitude that nurtures an understanding that each parish is a member of the larger church on both diocesan and universal scales and that stewardship is kingdom behavior for the good of the Church now and in the future.

"It is indeed a duty and an honor for Christians to return to God a part of the goods they have received from him." [5]

---

[5] Vatican II, decree *Apostolicam actuositatum*, III, 10c, in *The Documents of Vatican II*, ed. Walter M. Abbott (New York: American Press, 1966) 502.

CHAPTER SEVEN

Taxation, Assessments and Extraordinary Collections

ROBERT L. KEALY

CASE 13

Bishop Ambrose has consulted with his diocesan finance council and presbyteral council about imposing a per capita tax on parishes. Is such a tax permissible according to canon law?

CASE 14

Bishop Brophy consulted with his diocesan finance council and presbyteral council about his intention to raise the diocesan assessment on parish income to thirty percent. Despite their opposition, he has signed a decree imposing the new assessment. A group of pastors want to know if they have any recourse.

CASE 15

The Diocese of San Pellegrino has a legitimately established assessment on parish income of seven percent. The assessment applies only to Sunday and Holy Day collections. Now Bishop Cosgrove has announced a new formula whereby the assessment is to apply also to parish fund-raising events, bequests, and school income. May he make this change without consulting the diocesan finance council and presbyteral council?

CASE 16

The Diocese of Chardonay has been hit with a $30 million dollar judgment in a sexual misconduct suit. It did not have insurance coverage for this type of case. Now, the bishop has consulted with the diocesan finance council and prebyteral council about imposing an extraordinary tax for the next five years of three percent of the income of every Catholic institution in the diocese, including parishes, schools, and hospitals. May he do so?

When the revised *Code of Canon Law* was promulgated in 1983, one of the controversial elements was the expanded taxation power of the diocesan bishop. Some canonists declaimed this as a departure from the canonical tradition; some bishops considered it merely a pragmatic necessity in view of modern day financial realities. However, the change in the law is actually a return to an older canonical tradition and it is based on a significant theological principle of the communitarian nature of ecclesiastical assets.

To understand the significant changes in the bishop's taxation powers, one has to understand that the Second Vatican Council's treatment of the temporal goods of the Church reflects a significant change in values from those underlying the 1917 code. In the old code, the treatment of church property was developed on the tradition of the benefice system. This system, which was a remnant of feudalism, looked on the income of a parish (or diocese) primarily as a means of support for the benefice-holder who held the office of pastor. This resulted in an exaggerated notion of autonomy for each parish. The assets of each parish were viewed as its and its alone. This disproportionate emphasis to the needs of the clergy diminished the Church's traditional teaching that one of the purposes of the temporal goods of the Church is to serve the needs of the poor.

The ecclesiology of the Second Vatican Council restored the notion that the diocese, rather than the parish, is the primary unit of the Church. In keeping with that ecclesiology, Vatican II recaptured the pre-feudal tradition of the Church regarding temporal goods, which saw the goods of the Church as a common patrimony meant to serve ecclesial communion as well as the particular ends of certain individuals or groups. The diocesan bishop, as the chief pastor of the local church, was to see to a more equitable distribution of the ecclesiastical goods within the diocese, keeping in mind also the needs of the Church outside his diocese.[1] The *Code of Canon Law* of 1983 incorporated that conciliar teaching into its treatment of temporal goods and the diocesan bishop's power of taxation.

METHODS OF RAISING FUNDS FOR THE DIOCESE

The 1983 *Code of Canon Law* contains a comprehensive restructuring of the means of diocesan financial support. The code provides a diocesan bishop with the following ways of raising funds for the diocese:

- a seminary tax on public and private juridic persons (c. 264);
- free will offerings (c. 1262);
- a tax on public juridic persons subject to him (c. 1263);
- an extraordinary tax on other juridic and physical persons (c. 1263);
- special collections (c. 1266);
- pious wills and bequests (c. 1299);
- administrative fees (c. 1264, §1);
- judicial fees (c. 1649).

TAXATION

Canon 1263 After the diocesan bishop has heard the finance council and the presbyteral council, he has the right to impose a moderate tax for the needs of the dioceses upon public juridic persons subject to his governance; this tax is to be proportionate to their income. He is permitted only to impose an extraordinary and moderate exaction upon other physical and juridic persons in case of grave necessity and under the same conditions, without prejudice to particular laws and customs which attribute greater rights to him.

---

[1]Cf., Robert L. Kealy, *Diocesan Financial Support: Its History and Canonical Status*, (Rome: Gregorian University, 1986) 228-281.

Canon 1263 is the most significant and most controversial canon in "Book V" on temporal goods. It is important, therefore, to analyze and interpret the various elements of the canon.

Consultation

While canon 1263 requires consultation with the finance council and presbyteral council (see chapter twelve) and not their consent, this consultation is no *pro forma* exercise. Canon 127, §1 states that these groups must be formally convoked to discuss the question and it requires for validity that the counsel of all those who are present be sought.[2] Likewise, canon 166 specifies the number of members who must be present.

More specifically, canon 127, §2 stipulates:

> 2° if counsel is required, the act of a superior who does hear those persons is invalid; although not obliged to accept their opinion even if unanimous, a superior is nonetheless not to act contrary to that opinion, especially if unanimous, without a reason which is overriding in the superior's judgment.

This consultation process obliges those who have been consulted to speak honestly and forthrightly: "All whose consent or counsel is required are obliged to offer their opinion sincerely and, if the gravity of the affair requires it, to observe secrecy diligently; moreover, the superior can insist upon this obligation" (c. 127, §3).

Since canon 1263 states that this moderate tax is for diocesan needs, those who are consulted should be provided with thorough information on the financial situation of the diocese in order for them to give informed counsel.

While the ultimate decision rests with the diocesan bishop, the advice of those consulted is essential to the decision-making process.

---

[2]C. 127, §1: "When it is established by law that in order to place acts a superior needs the consent or counsel of some college or group of persons, the college or group must be convoked according to the norm of can. 166 unless, when it concerns seeking counsel only, particular or proper law provides otherwise. For such acts to be valid, however, it is required that the consent of an absolute majority of those present is obtained or that the counsel of all is sought."

Public Juridic Persons

The term *public juridic person* was discussed in chapter one, but the question remains: Must the diocesan bishop impose such a tax on all public juridic persons equally, or may he distinguish a certain class or type of juridic person, e.g., parishes, to be subjected to the tax?

Since there is nothing in the canon which would prohibit the making of such a distinction, and cogent reasons could be adduced why parishes, for example, should be treated differently than other public juridic persons (since most voluntary offerings of the faithful are given to the parishes in collections at Mass), the diocesan bishop may impose this tax on a certain class of public juridic persons rather than all public juridic persons, natural equity being observed.

Subject To His Governance

This phrase is liable to cause some confusion. The Latin word used is *regimini*, which is more precisely translated as governance. All members of a diocese are subject to the governance or jurisdiction of the bishop except those who have been exempted. Those who are exempt from the governance of the diocesan bishop are still subject to his authority in other respects, because of his responsibility for the right ordering of the works of religion is his diocese.

By law, all institutes of consecrated life enjoy autonomy of governance as described in canon 586:

§1 A just autonomy of life, especially of governance, is acknowledged for individual institutes, by which they possess their own discipline in the Church and are able to preserve their own patrimony intact, as mentioned in can. 578.

§2 It is for local ordinaries to preserve and safeguard this autonomy.

Even those institutes which are of diocesan right, although they are under the particular care of the diocesan bishop, retain their autonomy of governance: "Without prejudice to can. 586, an institute of diocesan right remains under the special care of the diocesan bishop" (c. 594).

Members of institutes of consecrated life, while enjoying their autonomy of governance, are subject to the power of the bishop in regard to the public exercise of divine worship and in matters regarding the care of souls or other works of the apostolate (c. 678, §1). The bishop, then is responsible for the public order of public juridic persons of institutes of consecrated life, but this does not place them "under his governance" within the meaning of canon 1263. Thus, they are not subject to the taxation power of the diocesan bishop.[3]

It must be kept in mind, however, that often the apostolic care of diocesan parishes or institutions is entrusted to religious communities and so those parishes or institutions remain subject to taxation (c. 681, §1). In disputed cases, the contract between a diocese and the religious community must be examined (c. 681, §2).

Moderate

Does the canon mean moderate in absolute terms or in relative terms? Clearly it cannot mean moderate in absolute terms, or it would be impossible to raise the substantial sums of revenue required. Moderate means that it must be reasonable in relation to the economic situation of the parish or public juridic persons being taxed. The same understanding would hold for the second tax mentioned in canon 1263.

Proportionate to income

Does proportionate mean that a certain rate of tax must be used or can a graduated tax be used? Does this mean gross income, before expenses are deducted, or net income? Fairness would suggest that all of the factors affecting the financial situation of the juridic person be taken into account and that it not simply be a tax on gross income. Neither the wording of the canon nor equity would prevent the imposition of a graduated tax, with a higher tax for higher income scales. However, various factors should be taken into consideration. One parish could have a very high gross income because it is a large parish with a big school. Another parish could have a lower gross income, but be better off financially because it is a small parish with no parish school.

[3] See Lawrence G. Wrenn, *Authentic Interpretations on the 1983 Code* (Washington, DC: CLSA, 1993) 57-58. In 1989 the Pontifical Council for the Interpretation of Legislative Texts issued this authentic interpretation: *The Doubt: Whether external schools of religious institutes of pontifical right are included under the words of canon 1263, "public juridic persons subject to his authority." The Response: Negative. AAS* 81 (1989) 991. Wrenn points out that "to be subject to one's visitation and vigilance ... is not necessarily to be subject to one's governance."

For The Needs Of The Diocese

In determining the needs of the diocese, all of the obligations of the diocese, both legal and moral, should be taken into account. Canon 1271 states the obligation of the diocese to contribute to the support of the Apostolic See. Canon 1274, §3 articulates the obligation of richer dioceses to help poorer ones. Various texts from the Second Vatican Council present the obligation of each diocese to share its goods with other local churches.[4] Moreover, might not even secular needs, especially those of the poor, be considered as being among the "needs of the diocese?" Certainly care for the poor is one of the most important purposes of ecclesiastical goods and the tradition of Ambrose and Augustine who sold the communion plate to assist the poor[5] would serve as justification for this interpretation.

Ordinary and Extraordinary

The first tax in canon 1263 is termed neither ordinary nor extraordinary, but it is distinguished from extraordinary taxes which are treated in the second part of the canon. The term ordinary was not used because of a desire to adhere to the principle that every effort should be made to persuade the faithful to give voluntarily before resorting to taxation. This principle being granted, for all practical purposes, in situations in which the voluntary offerings fall short of the needed revenues, a tax of this sort can be imposed as an ordinary matter; whereas the second tax requires unusual circumstances and, it would seem, would usually be imposed on an *ad hoc* basis.

---

[4]E.g., *Lumen gentium*, The Pastoral Constitution on the Church in the Modern World, n. 23; *Christus Dominus*, Decree on the Bishops' Pastoral Office in the Church, n. 6. Cf., Walter Abbott, ed., *The Documents of Vatican II* (New York: Herder and Herder, 1966).

[5]Ambrose, *De offic.*, II, 28, 137-38 (*MPL*, XVI, 140); Possidius, *Vita August.*, XXIV (*MPL*, XXXII, 54).

Physical persons

During the evolution of this canon there were several comments that a tax on physical persons would be unrealistic.[6] However, there is a history of such taxes being imposed on cardinals, prelates, and clergy since the time of the Crusades.[7] This provision also relates to *Christus Dominus*, number twenty-eight, which said that priests are to contribute from their clerical income for the needs of the diocese "according to the bishop's determination."[8]

Other Juridic Persons

Does this mean that public juridic persons, who are subject to the first tax, are not also subject to the second tax? Common sense says, "no." Other juridic persons is meant to include private juridic persons, not to exclude public juridic persons.

Grave Necessity

The second tax mentioned in canon 1263 can be imposed in case of grave necessity. Of course, this is a matter of judgment to a certain extent, but the notion conveys the idea that a need is particularly urgent and important. It is not for ordinary recurring needs.

Under The Same Conditions

The same conditions which apply to the ordinary tax also apply to the extraordinary tax, especially the need for consultation with the diocesan finance council and presbyteral council. Could this tax be imposed on juridic persons who are not subject to the governance of the diocesan bishop? Some have concluded that this is possible[9] because the second part of canon 1263 does not repeat the phrase, subject to his governance. A more reliable opinion seems to be that subject to his governance is one of the elements of "under the same conditions."[10]

---

[6] Pontificia Commisssio Codici Iuris Canonici Recognescendo, *Relatio: complectens synthesim animadversionum ab Em.mis atque Exc.mis patribus commissionis ad novissimum schema Codicis Iuris Canonici exhibitarum, cum responsionibus a secretaria et consultoribus datis.* (Vatican City: Typ. Polyglottis Vaticanis, 1981) 281-82.

[7] Lateran Council IV, unnumbered appendix (Mansi, J.D., ed., *Sacrorum conciliorum nova et amplissima collectio*, XXII, 1062-63); cf., Kealy, 135.

[8] *Christus Dominus*, n. 28.

[9] John J. Meyers, "Collection and Taxation," in *The Code of Canon Law: A Text and Commentary*, ed. James A. Coriden et al. (New York/Mahwah: Paulist Press, 1985) 865.

[10] See *Code of Canon Law Annotated*, ed. Ernesto Caparros et al. (Montreal: Wilson & Lafleur, 1993) 751.

Particular Laws and Customs

This considerable exception to the restrictions of canon 1263 was inserted after the plenary meeting of the Commission.[11] This canon does not allow the introduction of new particular legislation granting broader powers to bishops, for to do so would make the restrictions of the canon meaningless.[12] It seems that this exception was introduced particularly with Germany and Austria in mind because, at least in some regions where there is a church tax collected by the state, the state is acting as the agent for the Church and not in its own name and the particular dioceses have to empower the civil finance ministry to collect the tax. Thus, without this clause in canon 1263, they would be unable to do so.[13]

Tax on Mass Offerings

Although throughout the evolution of canon 1263 there was a clause prohibiting a tax on Mass offerings, such a prohibition does not appear in the final text. Does this mean that Mass offerings can be taxed?

We find the prohibition of a tax on Mass offerings in the 1917 code in canon 1506. Throughout the revision process there was always agreement that such a tax should be prohibited. Reference to this prohibition was omitted from the final text of canon 1263 apparently because the *coetus* had recommended that this prohibition be moved to a more appropriate place in the code.[14] Through an apparent oversight, the Secretariat failed to do this, however. Thus no explicit prohibition of Mass offerings appears in the code. However, there is such a prohibition in canon 1012 of the Eastern code: " .... no tax can be imposed on the offerings received on the occasion of the celebration of the Divine Liturgy." Thus, there was no intention of introducing a tax on Mass offerings in the revised *Code of Canon Law* and such a tax would be inappropriate, despite the fact that it has been introduced in some dioceses.[15]

---

[11]After the plenary session of the Commission for the Revision of the *Code of Canon Law* was concluded, the pope created a commission of cardinals to which he reserved the consideration of six canons, including this one. The final form of canon 1263 in the new code buttressed the bishop's broad powers even further by adding at the end of the canon the phrase "without prejudice to particular laws and customs attributing greater powers to him." Kealy, 330.

[12]See Velasio De Paolis, "Questiones miscellaneae," *Periodica* 73 (1984) 462.

[13]Alexander Hollerbach, "Kirchensteuer und Kirchenbeitrag," *Handbuch des katholischen Kirchenrechts*, Joseph Listl, et al., eds., (Regensburg: F. Pustet, 1983) 897.

[14]Pontificia Commissio, "De Iure Patrimoniali," *Communicationes*, V (1973) 95; cf., Kealy, 312, f. 62.

[15]See Francis G. Morrisey, "Acquiring Temporal Goods for the Church's Mission," *The Jurist* 56 (1996) 594-96.

Voluntary Offerings

Taxes on juridic persons, for the most part, depend indirectly on voluntary offerings of the faithful, for that is the main source of revenue for most public juridic persons, especially parishes.

Canon 1262 deals with such voluntary offerings given to support the works of the Church. It states: "The faithful are to the support to the Church by responding to appeals and according to the norms issued by the conference of bishops."

Free-will offerings of the faithful are the most basic form of church support. Implicit in these canons is the significant power of making direct appeals to individuals or foundations for various financial needs of the diocese. It should be noted that the canon gives conferences of bishops the authority to issue norms regarding appeals and contributions.[16]

Special Collections

A companion canon to 1263 is canon 1266, which gives the local ordinary the right to take up special collections. This canon, which emerged virtually unchanged from the 1977 Schema, reads as follows:

> In all churches and oratories which are, in fact, habitually open to the Christian faithful, including those which belong to religious institutes, the local ordinary can order the taking up of a special collection for specific parochial, diocesan, national, or universal projects; this collection must be diligently sent afterwards to the diocesan curia.

This canon is intimately linked to canon 1263 because it is a means of raising substantial revenues and revenue-raising must be viewed as a whole. In general, persuasion is preferred to taxation. Too great a burden must not be placed on parishes and pastors. At the same time, too many appeals to the faithful can become an obstacle to the primacy of spiritual concerns. What is called for, then, is a comprehensive plan, formed in consultation and established with prudence.

It should be noted, too, that a common form of special collection is an annual collection for the central operating expenses of the diocese. While this collection takes the form of a direct appeal to the people, often some quota is assigned to each parish. Insofar as parishes have to make up for deficiencies in their quotas from parish funds, this really constitutes a tax and falls under the provisions of canon 1263.

---

[16] See chapter eight on "Solicitation of Funds."

SEMINARY TAX

Canon 264 concerns the seminary tax and reads:

§1 In addition to the offering mentioned in can. 1266, a bishop can impose a tax in the diocese to provide for the needs of the seminary.

§2 All ecclesiastical juridic persons, even private ones, which have a seat in the diocese are subject to the tax for the seminary unless they are sustained by alms alone or in fact have a college of students or teachers to promote the common good of the Church. A tax of this type must be general, in proportion to the revenues of those who are subject to it, and determined according to the needs of the seminary.

This canon begins by taking cognizance of the local ordinary's power to take up a special collection for the seminary and notes that the right of the bishop to impose a seminary tax is an additional means of obtaining the necessary funding for the seminary. The exemptions to the seminary tax remain the same as the old code, and those bound by the tax are essentially the same as in the old law, but translated into the new terminology of juridic persons.[17]

As in the old law, the seminary tax must be general, proportionate to income and in correspondence with the true needs of the seminary. The old restriction of a five per cent ceiling on taxable income is not mentioned in the new code. In fact, the notion of taxable income is abandoned in the new code and is replaced by the more general term of revenues.

PIOUS WILLS AND BEQUESTS

Another significant source of revenue for the diocese is that of wills and bequests. Canon 1299 is exactly the same as the parallel canon in the 1917 code, canon 1513, except for a stylistic change for greater clarity.[18] It asserts the right of an individual to bequeath goods for religious or charitable purposes. This canon is directed against civil law limitations on such bequests.

---

[17] 1917 CIC c. 1356; cf., Kealy, 184-85.
[18] In 1917 CIC c. 1513, *mortis causa* was used in §1 and *in ultimis voluntatibus* was used in §2 to make it clear that the same thing was meant in both places; the 1983 code uses *mortis causa* in both paragraphs. See Kealy, 194.

ADMINISTRATIVE FEES

Fees for certain administrative acts are not so much a source of revenue as they are a reimbursement for administrative expenses incurred. Canon 1264 assigns to a meeting of the province of bishops the responsibility for setting the amount of such fees for acts of discretionary executive power or for the execution of rescripts of the Holy See. Such fees attached to the execution of rescripts of the Holy See must be approved by the Holy See. Except for stylistic changes these provisions are the substantially the same as the provisions set forth in the 1917 code in canon 1507, §1.

JUDICIAL FEES

Because the expenses for maintaining an ecclesiastical tribunal can be significant, canon law allows for fees to be assessed to the parties using the court. In the 1917 code, these fees were to be set by a meeting of the province of bishops.[19] The 1983 code gives this authority to the bishop whose responsibility it is to supervise the tribunal (c. 1649, §1).

REVENUE SOURCES OMITTED FROM THE 1983 CODE

Tithes and First-Fruits

Under canon 1502 of the 1917 code, particular law or customs regarding tithes and first-fruits were to be observed. Where such particular laws or customs still existed at the time of the promulgation of the revised code, they would continue to be in force by virtue of the final clause in canon 1263, "without prejudice to particular laws or customs which give him greater rights."

---

[19] 1917 CIC cc. 1057, §2 and 1909, §1; see Kealy, 191-92.

Cathedraticum and Foundation Tax

In the 1917 code, the *cathedraticum* was provided for in canon 1504[20] and the foundation tax was provided for in canon 1506.[21] Neither tax is mentioned in the revised *Code of Canon Law*. What is their status?

Both taxes have been eliminated by virtue of the fact that they are not provided for in the new code. Canon 6, §1, 1° states that the 1917 code was abrogated when the new code went into effect. Under the 1917 code, the *cathedraticum* and the foundation tax were universal law, not custom or particular law. Since they have been omitted in the 1983 code, they have been abrogated. The argument that they have continued existence under the rubric of custom or particular law (by virtue of the final clause of canon 1263) is wrong.[22] They were not custom or particular law; they were universal law and so were abrogated.

CONCLUSION

It is very important for the good of the Church that the diocesan bishop's power of taxation be carefully understood. Because the Second Vatican Council called for a more communitarian understanding of the Church's goods and the provisions of the new code are based on this conciliar vision, the old ways of thinking of this power are no longer adequate. This is one area of the new code in which a new *habitus mentis* is especially called for.

---

[20]1917 CIC c. 1504: "All churches and benefices subject to the jurisdiction of the bishop, and also all confraternities of lay persons, must pay to the bishop annually, as a sign of subjection, the *cathedraticum* or a moderate tax to be determined according to can. 1507, §1, unless it has already been fixed by ancient custom." In common parlance, *cathedraticum* has been misused to refer to diocesan assessments on parishes. Properly used, the canonical term is more precise and more limited.

[21]1917 CIC c. 1506: "The Ordinary can impose another tax for the good of the diocese or in favor of a patron on churches, benefices, and other ecclesiastical institutions, even though they are subject to him, only on the occasion of its foundation or consecration ... "

[22]See CLSA *Commentary*, 866.

Responses to the Cases:

CASE 13: A *per capita* tax is not permitted. A tax must be "proportionate to income."

CASE 14: A thirty percent tax on parish income would not be moderate. Recourse to Rome could be taken against a tax of this amount.

In regard to the issue of consultation, while the consent of the diocesan finance council and presbyteral council is not required, the validity of the consultation process requires that certain steps must have been taken: the finance council and presbyteral council must have been formally convoked to discuss the question; the counsel of all present must have been sought; those offering their counsel must have had the information necessary to make an informed judgment; and the bishop must have listened to the advice. Also, the bishop should not act contrary to the advice given unless he has an overriding reason.

CASE 15: A change in the elements on which a tax is imposed is a change in the tax and requires a new consultation process.

CASE 16: After the appropriate consultation, the bishop may impose a moderate, extraordinary tax, but on whom? Does it apply to "public juridic persons subject to the bishop's authority," who are mentioned in canon 1263 in connection with the "ordinary" tax but not in connection with the extraordinary tax? Yes, in this case it amounts to a temporary increase in their diocesan tax. To whom else does it apply? It applies only to those subject to the bishop's governance. Thus religious institutes of pontifical right and their schools, or hospitals, are exempt. It could apply to private juridic persons and individuals (e.g., priests) subject to the bishop.

CHAPTER EIGHT

SOLICITATION OF FUNDS

WILLIAM A. VAVARO

CASE 17

About 20 years ago, Pastor Jones helped to establish a Knights of Columbus Council in St. Mary's Parish. The members of the Council were stalwart members of the parish and supported many parish activities. In recognition of this assistance, the pastor permitted the Knights to sell chance books for the benefit of the Council at the doors of the church on the first two weekends of October. This situation went along fine until a new pastor arrived and refused permission for this fund raising activity, claiming that the law of the Church forbade it. The Knights were totally flabbergasted at this turn of events and indicated that they would no longer support parish activities if the parish were not going to support the Council in meeting its own expenses.

Canon 1265, §1 reads: "Without prejudice to the right of religious mendicants, any private person, whether physical or juridic, is forbidden to beg for alms for any pious or ecclesiastical institute or purpose without the written permission of that person's own ordinary and of the local ordinary."

The origins and sources tell us much about particular abuses which existed in our Church especially in recent times.

The sources (*fontes*) for this canon are found in those of canon 1503 of the 1917 code as well as subsequent responses which deal in large part with priests coming from territories under the Oriental Congregation. One of these decrees is dated October 16, 1919. Another decree of the Sacred Oriental Congregation dated January 7, 1930 dealt with Oriental clerics going to America or Australia for any purpose other than the spiritual care of the faithful of their own rite. A concern was raised about Oriental clerics who are found "sometimes collecting Mass stipends and alms without permission."[1] A third and similar decree is dated July 20, 1937.

The significance of canon 1265 is that it restricts the fund raising activities of private persons in the Church. Such persons can be physical, that is, individual persons or several individuals together. Thus an individual is restricted from seeking funds by making an appeal in a church. Obviously an appeal made from the pulpit would be the clearest example. For instance, if an individual sought financial assistance for a sick child needing an operation or a family whose home burned down by making such an appeal from the pulpit.

Likewise, there are private juridic persons in the Church. These can be members of some association with a good purpose in mind, such as a fraternal organization for priests made up of priest members and guided by some rules or by-laws or constitution approved by the membership. While such groups can certainly seek monies from their members, they cannot approach the Christian faithful in general.

This legislation does not restrict public persons, parishes or dioceses, for example, they do not require permission to take up a collection within the area of their own competence. Thus a parish could seek funds for the rebuilding of the organ, or to establish an outreach pastoral program for the elderly.

There may arise conflicts of interests involving individuals who are members of mendicant orders since the rights of mendicant religious are protected in this legislation.

The only mention of "mendicants" in the 1983 *Code of Canon Law* is found in canon 1265.[2]

Canon 621, §5 of the 1917 code provided for mendicant orders, by institution or by fact, to have the legal right to "quest" (i.e., to gather alms) in any diocese where they possess a house which was subject only to their religious superior. The orders founded by Francis of Assisi and Dominic Guzman are the classic and probably best known of the mendicant orders. They were approved in 1215, and later they were followed by the Carmelites (approved in 1245) and the

---

[1]Decree of the Sacred Oriental Congregation, 7 January 1930: *CLD* 1: 24-26.
[2]Xaverius Ochoa, *Index Verborum ac Locutionum Codicis iuris Canonici*, (Citta del Vaticano: Libreria Editrice Lateranense, 1984) 274, under *Mendicans, antis*.

Augustinians (approved in 1256).[3] The Servites were added to the list about 150 years later. In 1578, Pope Gregory XIII added the Minims, Jesuati, Trinitarians and Mercederians to the list also.

The rights of mendicant orders to gather alms was modified by Pope Paul VI's motu proprio, *Ecclesiae Sanctae*: "Religious should not proceed to collect funds by way of public subscription without the consent of the Ordinaries of the places where such collections are being made."[4]

The actual seeking of alms by the mendicant orders should be stated in their constitutions and statutes. Bishops inviting these mendicant orders to serve in their dioceses should be aware of this basic right. It would be wise for them to stipulate the manner in which mendicants can exercise their rights in the diocese.

The commentators seem to affirm that these restrictions apply to verbal solicitation strictly. A person must be at the doors of the church, or on the sidewalk outside, and verbally solicit funds for a cause or a group in the strict interpretation of this canon.

Commentators on the 1917 code did not apply restrictions to mail solicitation or advertisements. Yet, it seems that most of current day solicitations are frequently made by mail. Requests have become more frequent for elderly religious needs, missionary works, and appeals for food and medicine. We can only wonder what new electronic media such as the Internet will bring in making it possible to solicit funds. It would appear that the inclusion of a pamphlet, or religious article, whose monetary value could be minimal, would not exclude these restrictions. An offering given for a medal or a prayer card does not seem to be a reasonable *quid pro quo* since the value of the medal or card does not approach the contribution sought.

In the code of canons of the Eastern Churches, there is no mention of the rights of mendicants since apparently this is not part of their tradition. Their legislation appears more, simple but more encompassing as it affects all persons, physical and juridic. Canon 1015 of CCEO reads: "Physical and juridic persons cannot collect alms without the permission of the authority they are subject to and without the written consent of the hierarch of the place where the alms are collected."

---

[3] Historically it can be shown that the Franciscans were actually approved prior to Lateran Council IV and therefore were able to have their own particular rule approved, whereas later approvals required that a Rule approved before 1215 be chosen. These were the four mendicant orders approved by the Second Council of Lyons in 1274. See *New Catholic Encyclopedia*, 9: 648-649 s.v. "Mendicant Order."
[4] Pope Paul VI, *Ecclesiae Sanctae* I, 27, §2, *AAS* 58 (1966) 770; *CLD* 6: 279.

Norms Established by the Conference

Canon 1265, §2 reads: "The conference of bishops can establish norms for begging for alms which all must observe, including those who by their foundation are called and are mendicants."

There is clearly a need for norms to be established on a national level to provide greater uniformity within the same ecclesiastical territory. If national norms do not exist, it could be left to each diocese to establish particular law or synodal legislation to regulate this area of fund raising activity by individuals.

Permissions

The permissions needed must be given in writing. This written permission can be given only by a "proper ordinary" of the person doing the solicitation. In practice, it is often lay people, sometimes consecrated persons also, who are seeking funds for some "good" or "charitable" purpose. This written permission must be sought from the proper ordinary of the person soliciting. It would seem that since this matter belongs to the good order of the diocese that the written permission should be given by the diocesan bishop.

Administration of Funds

The administration of funds collected is the ultimate responsibility of the collectors who have received the permission to solicit the funds. They should do so for the purposes stated so that the donors give without any deception or misleading statements. The benefactors of the appeal must also remain true to the intentions that were stated for the solicitation. They should use the funds for the purposes that were stated and should follow the will of the donors if any are stipulated.

FINANCIAL REPORTING

There must always be accurate and clear financial reporting of any funds sought from the Christian faithful. This is part of good stewardship.

Some occasional reporting, even in a general way, must be available when seeking funds. For example, "we have used our funds to begin the establishment of an outreach program and now we come to you again to be able to staff our program with a professional counselor." Some summary on an annual basis of income and expenses should be available for review by any person being solicited for funds.

A recapitulative report may be more difficult to provide. Possibly a listing of accomplishments over a period of time (five years for example) would provide a good basis for letting others know how the funds have been used and if they have been used in accord with the goals of the person or persons seeking the funds.

In case 17, it appears that the new pastor is within his rights to forbid this type of solicitation at the doors of the church since there has been no formal, written permission given for such activity.

CHAPTER NINE

Mass Offerings and Stole Fees

EUGENE J. FITZSIMMONS

CASE 18

The pastor informed his newly assigned parochial vicar that "in our parish we do not accept Mass offerings and do not write Mass cards. People who want a Mass card can get that at the Franciscan shrine two blocks away." The pastor adds: "In this parish each priest gets an extra $300 in monthly salary to compensate for what he might receive from Mass offerings."

CASE 19

The provincial assembly of bishops recently determined $125.00 as the amount of the offering to be made by the faithful throughout the province on the occasion of marriage. Within that province diocesan bishop "A," with the advice of his presbyteral council, has directed that in his diocese the priest officiating at each marriage be paid $35.00 by the parish of the celebration for his ministry. Fr. John, a pastor in the diocese of bishop "A," refuses to make such payment contending that neither the bishop nor the presbyteral council is the administrator of his parish's funds and they have exceeded their authority.

THE NATURE OF A MASS OFFERING

The Mass offering is a contribution which has become almost exclusively monetary. Canon 950 speaks of a sum of money offered for the application of Masses.[1] The faithful offer that contribution to some priest requesting that he apply the Mass according to the intention of the donor. The faithful thus share the Church's concern for its ministers and its activities.

The Specific Purpose of a Mass Offering

The faithful make a Mass offering in order that the Mass will be applied for their intention (cc. 945, §1 and 946). Such intention does not exclude the other intentions for which the Mass is offered as specified in the Liturgy itself, e.g., "Lord, may this sacrificea … advance the peace and salvation of all the world,"[2] "Lord, remember those for whom we offer this sacrifice, especially N. our pope and N. our bishop."[3]

---

[1]Research sources for the Church's canons on Mass offerings include: (1) *Code of Canon Law, Latin-English Edition* (CIC), 1983; (2) *Code of Canons of the Eastern Churches, Latin-English Edition* (CCEO), 1991; (3) Congregation for the Clergy Decree, *Mos iugiter*, February 22, 1991, *AAS* 83 (1991) 443-446; and (4) Archbishop Gilberto Agustoni, "Commentary on Collective Mass Intentions Decree, *Origins* 20:43 (April 4, 1991) 705-706. Note that the Decree *Mos iugiter* meets the requirements of the Apostolic Constitution *Pastor Bonus* to derogate from the prescriptions of current, universal law. See John Paul II, 28 June 1988, *AAS* 80 (1988) 841-924, 1867, art. 18. The closing paragraph of the decree reads: "On January 22, 1991, the Supreme Pontiff approved the norms of the present decree in their specific form and ordered that they be immediately promulgated and take effect."

In addition to the commentaries on CIC and CCEO, noteworthy are the advisory opinions of Richard Hill, SJ, the advisory opinion of Louis Naughton. *CLSA Advisory Opinions, 1984-1993* (Washington, DC: CLSA, 1995) 292-296. For commentaries on *Mos iugiter*: Gilberto Augustoni, Commentary on the Collective Mass Intentions Decree published together with the Decree in *L'Osservatore Romano*, March 23, 1991, and *Origins* 20:43 (April 4, 1991) 705-707; Julio Manzanares, "De stipendio pro Missis ad intentionem 'collectivam' celebratis iuxta Decretum *Mos iugiter*," *Periodica* 80 (1991) 579-608; and Tomas Rincon-Perez "El Decreto de la Congregacion para el Clero sobre accumulación de estipendios (22-II-91)," *Ius Canonicum* 31 (1991) 627-656.

One should note that CCEO does not use the terms *stips* or *stipendium* or *eleemosyna* in the context of Mass offerings but prefers *oblationes*. Victor Pospishil in his commentary on CCEO has observed that *Mos iugiter* about the so-called "collective" Mass intentions "does not affect the Eastern Catholic Churches but the principles have been accepted by most Eastern Catholic Churches. CCEO c. 715, §1 leaves the regulation of this question to the particular law of theses Churches." See Victor J. Pospishil, *Eastern Catholic Church Law*, 2d ed., (Staten Island, NY: Saint Maron Publications, 1996) 405-406.

[2]Eucharistic Prayer III.

[3]Eucharistic Prayer IV.

Accepting a Mass Offering

Any priest or bishop of the Latin Church (c. 945, §1) or an Eastern Church (CCEO, c. 715, §1) who will celebrate or concelebrate a Mass has the right to accept a Mass offering. Notice it is a right, not an obligation to accept a Mass offering.[4] This is worth noting in discussing case 18

Obligation Arising from Accepting a Mass Offering

The priest who accepts the offering for a Mass for a particular intention is bound *ex iustitia* to satisfy personally the obligation assumed or to commit its fulfillment to another priest.[5] "The priest may refuse to accept an offering, but once he has accepted it, the relationship of justice is not based on the offering but on the *acceptance*."[6]

The Number of Masses to Be Offered

The principle of one Mass per offering (*Tot Missae quot stipendia*) remains firmly in place both in canon 948 and in *Mos iugiter*, art. 1, §1. Separate Masses are to be applied for the intentions for which an individual offering, even if small, has been made and accepted. Pospishil states: "The various Eastern Catholic Churches have copied the norms which regulated in the Latin Church the acceptance of so-called *Mass stipends*. This means that for each liturgy only one stipend may be accepted."[7]

Unlawful "Collective Intention"

Priests who indiscriminately collect offerings for the celebration of Masses for particular intentions, and combine them into a single offering, and without the knowledge of those who have made the offering, satisfy them with a single Mass celebrated according to an intention which they call "collective" act in violation of canon 948 and violate justice.[8]

---

[4]"While an individual priest or group of priests may voluntarily agree to forego the exercise of this canonical right, an individual can change his mind and withdraw from the plan and a newcomer could not be compelled to surrender the exercise of his right." Richard A. Hill, "Mass Stipends and Offerings for Special Intentions," in *CLSA Advisory Opinions, 1984-1993* ed. Patrick J. Cogan, SA (Washington, DC: CLSA, 1995) 293.

[5]*Mos iugiter*, art. 1, §1.

[6]Angel Marzoa, in *Code of Canon Law Annotated*, Capparos, Theriault, Thorn, eds., (Montréal: Wilson & Lafleur Limitée, 1993) 603-604.

[7]Pospishil, 405-406.

[8]*Mos iugiter*, art 1, §2.

Lawful "Collective Intention"

By exception to the rule of canon 948 it is lawful under certain conditions to satisfy several intentions with a single Mass applied according to a "collective intention."[9]

Two requisite conditions are that the persons making the Mass offering have been "previously" and "explicitly" informed that those offerings are being accepted for fulfillment as part of a "collective intention."

A third and necessary condition is that the donors have "freely consented" to having their Mass offerings combined with those of other donors for the celebration of one single Mass at which the intentions of all the donors are fulfilled.

A fourth condition imposed by the legislator is that public notice needs to be given identifying the place, the date and the hour when a "collective intention" Mass is to be celebrated. A restriction has been imposed by the legislator, namely in a given place of worship the "collective intention" Mass may not be offered more than twice weekly. The restriction aims to ensure that the "collective intention" Mass remains the exception to the norm which is a single Mass for a single intention. Note that the "only twice weekly" restriction does not prevent the two celebrations from being on the same day.

Mos iugiter makes the observation that the "collective intention" is an exception to the norm of law. As an exception to the law it is to receive the strict interpretation required by canon 18.

Determination of the Amount of the Mass Offering

The sum of money to be offered for the application of a Mass is to be determined by the bishops of an ecclesiastical province, either at a provincial council or a provincial bishops' meeting (c. 952, §1). The provincial bishops are free to determine the amount of stipend for Mass to be celebrated at a particular day and hour (sometimes called "announced Mass") and a different stipend amount for the application of a Mass at the convenience of the celebrant.

In the absence of such determined amount for an ecclesiastical province, lawful diocesan custom is operative (§2).

Diocesan priests, as well as, members of religious institutes of all kinds are required to abide by the decree of the provincial bishops or by the lawful diocesan custom (§3). No one in that territory may demand more than the prescribed stipend amount. If a larger amount is freely offered a priest may accept it, just as he may also accept a smaller amount than that prescribed (§1).

[9] *Mos iugiter*, art. 2

Priest May Fulfill Several Mass Intentions within One Day

A priest celebrating more than once daily is permitted to apply each Mass for the intention for which an offering was made (c. 951, §1). By exception, should one of the Masses on a given day be "concelebrated" no Mass offering can be accepted for one of those Masses unless the priest was principal celebrant at the concelebration (c. 951, §2). Daily celebration or concelebration is encouraged (c. 904); once daily is the norm (c. 905, §1). Bination and trination are permissible exceptions, which are governed by the local ordinary (c. 905, §2).

Priest May Retain For Himself Only One Mass Stipend Daily

Such is the norm apart from Christmas day when the priest may trinate and retain all three stipends. All other stipends fulfilled on a given day must be sent to or used for the purposes described by the ordinary, though some compensation can be made for the priest's extra efforts in bination or trination. The "ordinary" is the ordinary of the place where the Mass was celebrated when the celebrant is the pastor or parochial vicar; otherwise it is the ordinary of the priest celebrant.[10]

The commentators on the 1983 code are agreed that the pastor or diocesan bishop may satisfy the Mass *pro populo* and on the same day retain a Mass offering for a binated Mass.

Celebrant of Lawful "Collective Intention" Mass Retains Only One Mass Offering Daily

Mos iugiter allows the celebrant of such a Mass to retain for himself only that stipend which is lawful in the diocese where the Mass is celebrated. He is required to transmit the remaining stipends to the ordinary who will apply them to uses he has designated. "Ordinary" here is understood in the sense determined by the Pontifical Commission.[11]

Determining the Use for Mass Offerings That Can't Be Retained

Ordinaries, both diocesan bishops and religious major superiors, are required to determine some purpose in keeping with canon 946 to which will be applied the binated or trinated Mass offerings and the amount of offering beyond the

---

[10]Pontifical Commission for the Authentic Interpretation of the Code of Canon Law, August 6, 1987, *AAS* 79 (1987) 1132.

[11]Ibid.

diocesan norm in the event of "collective intention" Masses which the priest celebrants are required to transmit to the ordinaries. The activities of the Church and the support of its ministers are generic statements, which the ordinaries are to concretize.

Determining the Number of Masses to Be Applied

A practical rule for determining the number of Masses to be applied in fulfillment of Mass offerings given without specification of the number of Masses is set forth in canon 950. Unless the donor's intention must lawfully be presumed to have been otherwise, let the offering for each single Mass be that sum of money which was the lawful Mass offering in the diocese of the donor's residence at the time the donation was made. It is not uncommon that such a determination needs to be made in the case of a bequest arising from a Last Will and Testament.[12] The expression *nisi aliam fuisse eius intentionem legitime presumi debeat* emphasizes the strong respect canon law has for the intention of the donor (cf., c. 1300).

The Number of Mass Offerings A Priest Can Accept

Every priest is restricted by canon 955, §4 to accepting no greater number of Mass offerings to be fulfilled by himself than he can discharge within one year. In the present day, this restriction is practically meaningless. While the canon repeats in substance the provision of the 1917 code (c. 835), it has to be understood in a different way since a priest may now lawfully fulfill, but not retain for himself, more than one Mass intention on a given day. He may compute into the number of Mass offerings he will accept those Mass intentions which he foresees he will fulfill by legitimate bination and trination, warranted by the pastoral needs of a parish with diminishing numbers of priests, sending the binated/trinated Mass offerings to the ordinary (c. 951, §1).

Mos iugiter reflects a preference for transfer of Mass obligations to another priest when one priest has numerous Mass offerings to fulfill rather than use the "collective intention" (art. 5, §1), though it does not exclude the use of a "collective intention" provided all the conditions required for "collective intention" Masses have been fulfilled (art. 5, §2).

---

[12]In 1993, the Congregation for the Clergy obtained from the Holy Father for a USA diocese the reduction of the obligation of Masses to accord with the more recently increased approved diocesan Mass offering. Cf., "Canon 950: Mass Offerings" in *Roman Replies and CLSA Advisory Opinions, 1996*, eds. Kevin W. Vann and James I. Donlon (Washington, DC: CLSA, 1996) 11-15.

Recall that recent commentators are agreed that the pastor or diocesan bishop can fulfill the *pro populo* Mass and on the same day retain a Mass offering for a binated Mass.

Each priest is required to keep an accurate personal Mass register (c. 955, §4) which is subject to examination by his ordinary (c. 957).

The Number of Mass Offerings That Can Be Retained In A Particular Church

It is a common occurrence in places of pilgrimage and even in parish churches that the faithful wish the Mass for their intention to be celebrated in that place, even if it will be considerable time, even more than a year, before that Mass offering can be fulfilled there. This is noticeable in parish churches when Masses are requested by parishioners for a deceased parishioner or family member. Again, respect for the intention of the donor prevails (c. 1300). The Mass offering may be retained there to be fulfilled there. *Mos iugiter* encourages that the norms of the universal law be observed as regards transfer to another place for celebration (art. 4), though it also allows the "collective intention" norms to be implemented (art. 4). Pastors and rectors of churches and shrines are required to keep an accurate Mass register, subject to an annual inspection by the ordinary (c. 958).

Transferring Mass Offerings

Provision is made in canon 955 to transfer Mass offerings to another priest who will fulfill them. The sender is required:

- not to delay in transmitting the requests;

- to select a priest whom he knows will be responsible in fulfilling the Mass offerings;

- to send the Mass offering in its entirety for each intention, subtracting nothing for himself, unless it can be demonstrated with certainty that the excess above the diocesan approved amount was intended for him personally by the donor. The sender is not released from his responsibility in justice to fulfill those Mass offerings until he is certain that the recipient has accepted the obligation to fulfill those Mass offerings and the sum of money he sent has been received. Practically, this means that the recipient is to acknowledge the receipt of the Mass offerings and his intent to fulfill them.

The priest recipient, in accepting the obligation to fulfill the Mass offerings, accepts as well that requirement of the law that he will have satisfied those obligations within one year from the time of his acceptance (c. 955, §2) unless clearly present is some other lawful stipulation such as anniversary Masses, feast day Masses. Further, the priest recipient is required to keep an accurate Mass register of the Mass offerings he has accepted (c. 955, §4).

The sender is required to keep an accurate record in a Mass register indicating the specifics of the transfer (c. 955, §3). It is subject to examination by his ordinary (c. 957).

If the offerings transmitted were lost in transit, even through no fault of the sender, he remains personally responsible for the fulfillment of those Mass intentions (c. 949).

Vigilance over Mass Obligations

The law assigns to the local ordinary, or the religious or similar superior the serious responsibility of exercising vigilance that Mass obligations are fulfilled (c. 957). Administrators of pious causes must ensure that Mass obligations not fulfilled within the year are brought to the notice of the proper ordinary who will see to their fulfillment (c. 956) or reduction (c. 1308) either personally or through the Congregation for the Clergy.[13] Reduction, however, is allowed only when both just and necessary. Private persons do not have the authority to arrange decreases in the obligations or changes in their fulfillment.[14]

Founded Masses

At times, a donation or bequest is made to an existing juridic person such as a diocese or a parish with the understanding that the recipient assumes the long term obligation of applying from the annual income the celebration of Mass or Masses as specified by the donor. In the matter of bequests careful attention must be paid to the intention of the donor as expressed in a Last Will and Testament.[15] The applicable canon law is that governing non-autonomous pious foundations (c. 1303ff.). The valid acceptance of such a foundation requires the written per-

---

[13] *Pastor Bonus*, art. 97, 2§.

[14] M. Lopez Alarcon, in *Code of Canon Law Annotated*, Capparos, Theriault and Thorn, eds., (Montréal: Wilson & Lafleur Limitée, 1993) 813-815

[15] Cf., Barbara A. Cusack, "Pious Foundations and Mass Intentions," in *Roman Replies and CLSA Advisory Opinions, 1994*, eds. Kevin W. Vann and James I. Donlon (Washington, DC: CLSA, 1994) 141-142.

mission of the ordinary. He is not to give such permission until he is satisfied that the new obligation to be undertaken can be fulfilled together with any earlier obligations, and that the income from the foundation would be appropriate for the obligation to be assumed. The duration of the "long term" is to be defined by particular law. Abandoned is the concept of "perpetual" foundation as found in the 1917 code. When the "long term" has expired the assets of the foundation become the property of the diocesan fund for the support of the clergy, if the juridic person accepting the foundation was subject to the diocesan bishop, unless some other intention was expressed by the donor. Otherwise the goods belong to the juridic person itself, such as a clerical religious institute or a monastery. The pastor or rector of the obligated parish or other juridic person is required to maintain a current written record of the foundation Mass obligations, their fulfillment, and the offering. Such record is to be separate from the required record of manual masses (c. 1307, §2).

Mass Offerings Are Not Subject To Prescription

Repeating the canon law previously in force are canons 199, §5 of the Latin Church and 1542, 5° of the Eastern churches. Thus the mere passage of time will not free one from the obligation to satisfy an unfulfilled Mass offering once the obligation has been accepted.

Profiteering From Mass Offerings

The Church has long been preoccupied with simony, the deliberate intention of purchasing or selling the sacred for a price. Thus, canon 947 enacts that "any appearance of trafficking or trading is to be excluded entirely from offering for Masses" which is the same as the 1917 code (c. 827). Thus, many of the canons in Book IV, "The Blessed Eucharist," Chapter III, "Mass Offerings" are designed to prevent abuses in the matter of Mass offerings. Many commentaries on these canons recall a history of abuse that has given rise to the numerous regulations on Mass offerings. Early in *Mos iugiter* one reads: "Because the matter directly affects the most blessed sacrament, even the slightest appearance of profit or simony would cause scandal. Therefore the Holy See has always followed the evolution of this pious tradition with attention, with opportune interventions ... in order to prevent or correct any eventual abuses wherever they might occur" (see cc. 947 and 1385).

Penal Canon

Canon 1385 states: "A Person who illegitimately makes a profit from a Mass offering is to be punished with a censure or another just penalty." The canon prescribes a mandatory penalty once the competent authority is satisfied that a grave external violation of the law has occurred which is gravely imputable. While mandatory, the penalty is indeterminate. It may be a censure or some other expiatory penalty. The commentators are forceful in describing what constitutes this canonical crime. For example:

> The offense is committed when someone benefits unlawfully from the money or goods received for the celebration of the Mass, e.g., (1) a priest who accumulates offerings against the prescriptions of canon 948 and the decree *Mos iugiter*; (2) a priest who takes more than one offering each day against the prescription of canon 951; (3) a priest who requires an offering higher than that established in accordance with canon 952; (4) a priest who retains part or all of the offering when transferring the obligation of celebrating Mass in accordance with canons 951, §1 and 956. (5) The offense may also be committed by those who have the responsibility of receiving offerings for Mass at churches, shrines, and places of pilgrimage.[16]

Stole Fees[17]

The Nature of Stole Fees

"Stole Fees," as they are called, are the offerings received on the occasion of some parochial liturgical ministry such as the celebration of baptism, marriage, funeral, or the blessing of homes. In canon 1707, §1 of the 1917 code such fees were called *taxa solvenda*, whereas in the current code the more benign *oblationes* is found (cc. 531; 848; and 1264, 2°). The term "stole fee" is the conventional translation of the canonist's term *iura stolae*, which identified the offerings

---

[16]Gerard Sheehy, et al. eds., *The Canon Law, Letter and Spirit* (Collegeville, MN: The Liturgical Press, 1995) n. 2778.

[17]The Canon Law in force: (1) *Code of Canon Law, Latin-English Edition* (CIC), 1983; (2) *Code of Canons of The Eastern Churches Latin-English Edition* (CCEO), 1991. In addition to the Commentaries on CIC and CCEO, helpful is Francesco Cocopalmerio, *De Paroecia* (Rome: Pontifical Gregorian University, 1991) 201-203 and the advisory opinions of James H. Provost in *CLSA Advisory Opinions 1984-1993*, (Washington, DC: CLSA, 1995) 139-143.

received on the occasion of ministering some sacrament or sacramental, a ministry performed with the use of a white stole or a black stole. The canon law of the Church does not mandate that a parochial function must have an offering or stole fee attached, although the provincial bishops are directed to determine for the province what offering will be made on the occasion of sacraments and sacramentals (c. 1264, 2°). Such offering is presupposed on the occasion of funerals (c. 1181). "Stole fees" have their origin in custom. Stole fees differ from stipends or offerings given for the celebration or application of Mass. They differ also from "voluntary offerings" intended for the person of the minister of the sacrament or blessing or officiant at marriage.

The Specific Purpose of a Stole Fee

In the 1917 code the parish was considered a benefice and the pastor was entitled to the revenue from the benefice for his support. Baptisms, marriages and funerals and the blessing of homes were listed among the "reserved parochial functions," i.e., ministries reserved to the pastor. Thus offerings received from such ministry were, according to the 1917 code, to support the pastor (cc. 462 and 463). Vatican Council II ordered abandoning or at least reforming the "benefice system."[18] The 1983 code describes those same functions as "especially entrusted to the pastor" (c. 530), assigns stole fees as belonging to the parish treasury, and authorizes the diocesan bishop to determine the purpose for which they will be used (c. 531).[19]

The Amount of a Stole Fee

A provincial meeting of the bishops is to determine for the province what are the amounts of the offerings that can be asked on the occasion of ministering sacraments or sacramentals (c. 1264, 2°) and on the occasion of funerals (c. 1181). If the provincial bishops have not made such determination, analogy with canon 952, §2 would require that the custom existing in the diocese be observed.

For the Eastern Catholic churches the amounts of those offerings are determined by the eparch for his territory, but they are to be the same in places where more than one patriarch or eparch of the different churches *sui iuris* exercise jurisdiction. Thus the need for prior consultation among such hierarchs (CCEO, c. 1013).

---

[18] *Presbyterorum Ordinis*, Decree on the Ministry and life of Priests, in *The Documents of Vatican II*, ed. Walter Abbott, (New York: Herder and Herder, 1966) 572-573.
[19] James H. Provost, "Disposition of Stole Fees," in *CLSA Advisory Opinions 1984-1993*, (Washington, DC: CLSA, 1995) 142-143

The Obligation to Pay a Stole Fee

Clearly the faithful have the obligation to provide for the needs of the Church and the support of its ministers (c. 222, §1), and the diocesan bishop has the obligation to call that to the attention of the faithful (c. 1261, §2). The 1917 code made the statement that the pastor had the right to receive the lawfully established stole fees but could not demand a greater amount (1917 CIC c. 463, §1). Thus the correlative obligation on the part of the faithful to provide the approved amount. In the 1983 code the minister of the sacraments is not to ask for anything more than the offering approved by competent authority (c. 848).

The earlier code enacted the principle that the pastor was not to refuse his ministry gratis to the poor (1917 CIC c. 463, §4) and repeated that instruction in the matter of providing a becoming funeral liturgy and burial for the poor (1917 CIC c. 1235, §2). The current code states the principle that the minister must be careful not to deprive the needy of the help of the sacraments because of their poverty (c. 848) and that the poor are not deprived of suitable funeral rites (c. 1181).

The Ownership of Stole Fees

Profoundly changing canon law is the statement of canon 531, assigning ownership of the stole fee to the parish rather than to the person of the pastor. The juridic person of the parish is entitled to the stole fee. The Church's minister who receives that offering on the occasion of performing some parochial function, even if he be a cleric not attached to that parish, is directed to give it to that parish's treasury. If the minister of that parochial function is the pastor himself, he is the administrator of the public juridic person, which is the parish (c. 532) and the offering or stole fee belongs to that parish's treasury in virtue of canon 1267, §1.

Determining the Use of Stole Fees

The diocesan bishop is to decide how stole fees will be used. He is also to determine how those ministers, including the pastor, who carried out the parochial function are to be remunerated. He is to issue regulations in these matters after consultation with the presbyteral council (c. 531). Herein is the solution to case 19 above. Richard Hill, S.J. offers the opinion that the bishop could decide that the stole fee is to be given to the priest or deacon who performed the liturgical function.[20]

---

[20]Hill, *CLSA Advisory Opinions 1984-1993*, 142.

Voluntary Offerings Intended for the Minister

When the donor clearly intends the offering for the person of the minister, that portion in excess of the "approved amount" belongs to the person of the minister; if the donor's intention is doubtful, that portion given in excess of the "approved amount" belongs to the parish treasury.[21] Such is in keeping with the fundamental principles of canon law that offerings made are presumed to belong to the juridic person (c. 1267, §1) and that the intention of the donor must be carefully respected (c. 1267, §3). Canon 531 authorizes the diocesan bishop to determine the purpose of the "approved offering," not of the excess amount when it is clear that the donor intended the excess for the minister.[22]

---

[21]Canon 531 reads " .... *nisi de contraria voluntatis offerentis constet.*"
[22]Cocopalmerio, 203.

$\oplus$ $\oplus$ $\oplus$

ADMINISTERING
TEMPORAL GOODS

$\oplus$ $\oplus$ $\oplus$

CHAPTER TEN

ECCLESIASTICAL FINANCIAL ADMINISTRATORS

MATTHEW P. HUBER

Aside from the diocesan financial administrator, there are other financial administrators, individuals appropriately appointed, to oversee directly the administration of a public juridic person, namely a parish.[1] Since parishes are vital to the life of the church, it is easy to understand why the church would place such emphasis on how a parish is to be financially administered and who properly exercises this office.

CASE 20

> It has been several months now that Holy Savior Parish and its two missions situated in a fast developing area in the Rocky Mountains have been without a pastor. Fr. Algreed had been a dynamic and well-liked pastor for several years. He enjoyed the parishioners and knew their potential. The three church communities were comprised of modest facilities, which they were fast outgrowing.
>
> So concerned for the future and working with the communities, Fr. Algreed began a process of merging the parish with the two missions. Ultimately they would build a single parish facility to meet their needs adequately now and to provide for the future growth of the area. But after three years of promoting the capital campaign, Fr. Algreed suffered a debilitating stroke. Bishop Brondel must decide what should be done with the parish in assigning pastoral leadership. He has great hope for Holy Savior and its missions in coming together to build a

---

[1]Canon 1279, §1 insures that every public juridic person is to have an administrator, whose responsibility is the direct administration of its ecclesiastical goods.

strong and vibrant parish community in the near future. Yet at the same time, the bishop knows he has an increasingly limited number of priests to minister as pastors in his diocese. He knows Holy Savior and its missions need someone in place who can hold their confidence, lead them pastorally and properly administer the goods of the communities.

Bishop Brondel is keenly aware that he needs the right person for this situation. The future of this parish is vital to the area. He knows he cannot assign a team of priests to work together *in solidum* with a moderator. He is faced with the options of assigning another priest as pastor; a priest as administrator; a deacon with a lay person or community of persons to serve as the pastoral administrator with parish leaders. He wonders what impact this assignment will have on the life of these communities, how they are financially administered given all they have experienced and the promising future he hopes will unfold for them.

Among the many concerns of any bishop today the care of parishes is paramount, both pastorally and in the good administration of parish resources. Three types of financial administrators may exercise the duties of financial administration in a parish. They are the parish priest; the parochial administrator; and in the case of a parish without a resident pastor, the pastoral collaborator (a deacon, lay person or community of persons) appointed by the diocesan bishop according to universal and particular law.

Canon 515 defines a parish as a definite community of the Christian faithful established on a stable basis within a particular church (a diocese), with the pastoral care of the parish entrusted to a pastor under the authority of the diocesan bishop. In the absence of a pastor, the diocesan bishop may appoint a priest as parochial administrator of a parish (c. 539),[2] or he may appoint a deacon or lay person as a pastoral administrator of a parish (c. 517, §2). All these persons would have direct supervisory authority over the parish in their responsibilities as financial administrators.

Each of these three positions would generally oversee the financial obligations of a parish for which they are given charge. Canon 515, §3 states that a parish legitimately erected has public juridic personality by the law itself, is therefore a

---

[2]Canon 517, §1 speaks of a team of priests assigned jointly to a parish or parishes *in solidum* with one assigned as moderator. The moderator in this case, like a pastor, is responsible to the bishop and represents the parish(es) in all juridic affairs according to canon 532.

public juridic person and as such is to have an administrator. This then becomes the scope of accountability of these financial administrators to oversee and administrate all the goods of the parish.

The Pastor of a Parish

Canon 515, §1 states that the parish priest is the proper shepherd of a parish entrusted to him under the authority of the diocesan bishop. As such he exercises pastoral care of the parish in cooperation with diocesan bishop sharing in the ministry of Christ. The pastor shares in the threefold *munera* of teaching, sanctifying and governing as noted in canon 519: The pastor (*parochus*) is the proper pastor (*pastor*) of the parish entrusted to him, exercising the pastoral care of the community committed to him under the authority of the diocesan bishop in whose ministry of Christ he has been called to share, so that for that same community he carries out the functions of teaching, sanctifying, and governing, also with the cooperation of other presbyters or deacons and with the assistance of lay members of the Christian faithful, according to the norm of law.

The governing duties of the pastor include those of a financial administrator. Canon 1279, §1 gives this responsibility of administration to the parish priest as the one who immediately governs the juridic person, in this case the parish.

Therefore, the pastor acts in the name of the parish in all juridic affairs, and must faithfully observe the canons regarding the administration of parish property (see c. 532). These duties are wide and varied including all the patrimony and goods of a parish. Basically, the responsibilities of a pastor as financial administrator entail the good stewardship and administration of all parish property and assets.

To assume the duties of a pastor the church would expect the priest to possess all the necessary qualification of a good shepherd. In outlining these norms, canons 519-524 give the requirements for the appointment of a parish priest.[3] As the pastor, he has primary responsibility of the parish and represents it in all juridic affairs (c. 532). One requirement of the code before he takes office is to take an oath before the ordinary or his delegate that he will be an efficient and faithful administrator (c. 1283, §1). Canon 1279, §1 admonishes that once he take office he is bound to fulfill the responsibilities of an administrator.

---

[3]Canons 519-524 list several items. The parish is entrusted to the parish priest under the authority of the diocesan bishop. The diocesan bishop can entrust a parish to a clerical religious institute or to a clerical society of apostolic life with one of their number being the parish priest. To be appointed parish pastor one must be in the presbyteral order, and possess those qualities that make for a good shepherd. The parish pastor is to enjoy a stability of office and is to be freely appointed by the diocesan bishop, after hearing from the area vicar or dean and others if appropriate.

Authority of the Parish Pastor

Since the pastor is the one who immediately governs the parish, it is his duty and responsibility to administer faithfully the goods of the parish entrusted to him, (c. 1279). He is limited in his authority as administrator to acts of ordinary administration, unless he first obtains written authority from the ordinary (c. 1281). These acts of extraordinary administration are to be defined in the statutes of the parish, or in the absence thereof, defined by the diocesan bishop (c. 1281, §2). For a further discussion of acts of extraordinary administration, see chapter sixteen.

In carrying out this ministry as pastor, the priest should be aware that it is ultimately for the good of the Church that he exercises prudence in all his decision-making pertaining to administration. Canon 1282 reminds him he is bound to fulfill these duties in the name of the Church and in accord with the norm of law.

Duties of the Parish Pastor as Administrator

The duty of a pastor as financial administrator of a parish is a position of trust. All those obligations and responsibilities that one would expect of person placed in management of a business should be also be expected of a pastor as financial administrator. The pastor is the one who directly oversees the whole financial operation of the parish. It is he who exercises decision-making power that will affect the future well being and development of the parish. The following are canonical expectations of the parish priest as administrator of a parish.

- ♦ Canon 1283, 1° – The administrator must take an oath before the ordinary or his delegate that he will be an efficient and faithful administrator.

- ♦ Canon 1283, 2° – The administrator is to prepare and sign and regularly update a detailed inventory of all parish property and assets. This list should be detailed and reflect the true standing of the parish. It should include a detailed description of all goods movable and immovable, either precious or of cultural value, along with all the material holdings of the parish. Insurance records along with current valuations of holdings should be utilized to determine actual worth.

- ♦ Canon 1283, 3° – Copies of this inventory are then to be kept on file with the parish archives and the chancery archives and regularly updated as needed.

- ♦ Canon 1284, §1 – The administrator is bound to fulfill his duties with the diligence of a good householder.

116

- Canon 1280 – The pastor is to preside over the finance council (c. 537) and through the assistance and expertise of its members as advisors in financial matters, is to supervise carefully the administration of all parish goods.[4] (See chapter twelve for a discussion of finance councils.)

- Canon 1279, §1 – The pastor acts, assisted by the finance council, according to the norms of the statutes of the public juridic person (the parish). Since many, if not most parishes, do not have statutes of their own, diocesan statutes and/or policies, validly enacted, would constitute statutes for the parish. These policies should include various details which pertain to good financial administration, such as: establishing an annual budget (c. 1284, §3), providing for annual upkeep and maintenance of the facilities, providing for salary and benefits for all employees, providing for the diocesan assessment (c. 1263), adequate insurance, investment strategies or diocesan procedures for investments, debt payment policies, etc. These policies assist the pastor and ensure the financial health and stability of the parish.

- Canon 1284, §2 – outlines several duties of the administrator in carrying out his responsibilities of sound fiscal management of the parish. Administrators must:

  1° – take care of the goods entrusted to their care and make sure that nothing is in any way lost or damaged and see that proper insurance policies are in place to meet the needs of the parish;

  2° – take care that the ownership of ecclesiastical goods is safeguarded through civilly valid methods;

  3° – observe the prescriptions of both canon and civil law, and particular law of the diocese, and especially be careful so that the Church is not harmed through non-observance of civil laws;

  4° – accurately collect the revenues and income of goods when they are legally due, safeguard them once collected and apply them according to the intention of the founder or according to legitimate norms;

  5° – pay the interest on a loan or mortgage when it is due and take care that the capital debt itself is repaid in due time;

---

[4] See canon 532 and also reference canon 1276 on ordinaries entrusted with overseeing administration.

6° – with the consent of the ordinary invest the money which is left over after expenses and which can be profitably allocated for the goals of the parish;

7° – keep well-ordered books of receipts and expenditures;

8° – draw up a report on their administration at the end of each year;

9° – duly arrange and keep in a suitable and safe archive the documents and deeds upon which are based the rights of the Church or the institution to its goods; deposit authentic copies of them in the archive of the curia when it can be done conveniently.

- ♦ Canon 1285 – The Church encourages financial administrators of parishes to be charitable in contributing to the needs of the poor and other apostolic works for the good of the Church. Within the limits of ordinary administration, the pastor can make appropriate donations from the assets of the parish. He is to determine within the limits of ordinary administration what amount can be given and is encouraged to share these assets especially with the needy (c. 1254, §2). Parishes are encouraged to contribute to the broader needs of the community and to share in the needs of the poor, and others involved in apostolic activity.

- ♦ Canon 1286 – Administrators are also to observe meticulously all the civil laws pertaining to employment and social order (c. 1286, 1°). This is especially true in attending to those areas which surround an individual's employment and the requirements of the state in providing for various kinds of insurance, worker's compensation, social security and other benefits or taxes.

Additionally they are to pay employees a just and decent wage so that they may provide appropriately for their needs and those of their family (c. 1286, 2°). From this social justice canon, administrators are to provide an honest wage for the labor they receive from their employees. No employee should be paid less than minimum wage for any work in the parish, and administrators are to provide a decent salary for all employees.

- ♦ Canon 1287, §1 – Administrators must present to the local ordinary an annual financial report of their administration.

- ♦ Canon 1287, §2 – According to particular law administrators are to give an accounting to the faithful of the finances.

- Canon 1288 – And finally, administrators are neither to initiate nor contest a lawsuit on behalf of the parish in civil court unless they obtain the written permission of their own ordinary.

THE PAROCHIAL ADMINISTRATOR

The distinction of parochial administrator from that of pastor is quite clear. The parochial administrator is a priest assigned to a parish who acts in place of or substitutes for the pastor. He is not the pastor of the parish. The bishop may need to appoint a parochial administrator if the pastor is impeded and for some reason incapable of exercising his duties or if the parish has become vacant due to his transfer, removal, resignation, retirement or death (c. 539).

The appointment of a parochial administrator is understood as an interim position to protect and safeguard the parish. His primary duty is to ensure the ongoing pastoral activity and administrative responsibilities in a parish. He carries out this duty until either the pastor is capable of returning or, in the case of a vacant parish, another pastor is appointed. The parochial administrator's primary role is one of guardianship.

Appointment of the Parochial Administrator

When a parish becomes impeded or vacant it is the diocesan bishop's responsibility to appoint as soon as possible a parochial administrator (c. 539). This is to ensure that the immediate interim governance of the parish may continue, either, in the case of an impeded parish until the pastor is able to resume his duties or, in the case of a vacant parish, a new pastor is assigned.

Authority of the Parochial Administrator

Once appointed, the parochial administrator is the one who immediately governs the parish, just as a pastor. He is to be faithful in fulfilling this duty according to law (cc. 540; 1279, §1; and 1282). Like the pastor he is limited to acts of ordinary administration. He must follow approved procedures to obtain written permission of acts beyond the limits of ordinary administration (c. 1281).

As a temporary guardian, the parochial administrator is not to do anything in the parish that could prejudice the rights of a returning or a newly appointed pastor or in any way harm the patrimony of the parish (c. 540, §2).

Duties of the Parochial Administrator

The duties and rights of the parochial administrator are the same as for the pastor unless the diocesan bishop has informed him otherwise.[5] Though generally understood that there would be no major changes or innovations during this time,[6] the parochial administrator nonetheless would have all the administrative powers of a pastor to govern effectively the parish during this interim (c. 1279, §1). Just as for the pastor, the canons on administrators and their duties (cc. 1279-1288) equally apply to the parochial administrator, unless the diocesan bishop determines otherwise (c. 540, §1). He is likewise bound to be faithful in fulfilling his duties in the name of the Church and in accord with the norm of law (c. 1282).

The final duty of the parochial administrator is to render an account of his guardianship to the pastor reassuming his duties or the newly appointed pastor (c. 540, §3). This provision is to provide for pastoral accountability of his stewardship of the parish in the pastor's absence. The administrator's report will also facilitate the pastor's involvement in the parish as he resumes or newly undertakes his administrative duties to the parish.

THE PASTORAL COLLABORATOR OF A PARISH

The parish pastoral collaborator found in canon 517, §2 is a relatively new position in the church. The canon reads: "If, because of a lack of priest, the diocesan bishop has decided that participation in the exercise of the pastoral care of a parish is to be entrusted to a deacon, to another person who is not a priest, or to a community of persons, he is to appoint some priest who, provided with the powers and faculties of a pastor, is to direct the pastoral care." The concept of a pastoral collaborator envisioned in this canon is a new inno-

---

[5] Canon 540, §1: A parochial administrator is bound by the same duties and possesses the same rights as a pastor unless the diocesan bishop determines otherwise.

[6] This follows from the same idea regarding a vacant see canon 428.

vation to the 1983 *Code of Canon Law*. By this provision the church seeks to provide for the realities of supplying for parochial ministry in the face of diminishing numbers of priests.[7]

Distinct from the *parochial administrator*, it is the position envisioned when, due to a dearth of priests, the diocesan bishop would entrust a share in the exercise of the pastoral care of a parish to other "non-presbyteral" pastoral leadership. A deacon, male or female religious, lay person or a community of persons may provide for this pastoral leadership.[8] In any case, the diocesan bishop is to appoint a priest with the powers and faculties of a pastor to supervise the pastoral care.[9]

When a diocesan bishop is faced with this situation, he must decide how this position of pastoral collaborator is to be conferred. Since it is the pastoral collaborator who will directly share in a participation of the exercise of the pastoral care of a parish, it is appropriate that the scope of this authority be mandated. Much will depend upon the how the pastoral collaborator is appointed by the diocesan bishop and what authority this person is given.[10]

---

[7]Because the code does not give this position a title, arriving at a common title in praxis has been problematic. Various titles have been offered: "Lay Pastor," "Parochial Minister," "Lay Administrator," "Parish Leader," "Parish Life Coordinator," "Pastoral Administrator," etc. To one extent or another, there are difficulties with each. "Pastoral Collaborator" is the title used in this text. This title also conveys the reality of the full scope of the pastoral and administrative responsibilities generally expected of this position. The August 15, 1997 Interdicasterial Instruction approved *in forma specifica*, "Some Questions Regarding Collaboration of Non ordained Faithful in Priests' Sacred Ministry" states: "It is unlawful for the non-ordained faithful to assume titles such as pastor, chaplain, coordinator, moderator or other such similar titles which can confuse their role and that of the pastor who is always a bishop or priest." Congregation for the Clergy, et al., *AAS* 89 (1997) 852-877 at art. 1, no. 3.

[8]The case of assigning a "community of persons" though not frequent could parallel canon 517, §1 in assigning team ministry with one moderator exercising pastoral care.

[9]This provision in canon 517, §2 does not imply that this priest is the proper pastor of the parish, rather that he would moderate the pastoral care. Canon 515, §1 reminds us: "A parish is a certain community of the Christian faithful stably constituted in a particular church, whose pastoral care is entrusted to a pastor (*parochus*) as its pastor (*pastor*) under the authority of the diocesan bishop." In this case, the particular parish does not have a pastor as its own shepherd, and so another priest endowed with the powers and faculties of a pastor (c. 517, §2) is to supervise the pastoral care. Canon 526, §1 reaffirms this when it states: "A pastor is to have the parochial care of only one parish; nevertheless, because of a lack of priests or other circumstances, the care of several neighboring parishes can be entrusted to the same pastor."

[10]For a more complete and detailed exploration of the canonical implications and description of this position see: Barbara Anne Cusack and Therese Guerin Sullivan, S.P., *Pastoral Care in Parishes without a Pastor: Applications of Canon 517, §2* (Washington, DC: CLSA, 1995).

Appointment of the Pastoral Collaborator

The position of pastoral collaborator is seen as an extraordinary situation in the code and its primary concern in its implementation is to provide for the pastoral and administrative care of a parish in the absence of a resident pastor. The determination for the appointment is to come as a decision of the diocesan bishop after he decides he is truly lacking priests to assume this ministry.[11] Given the scope of pastoral and administrative responsibilities generally assumed with this position, it is appropriate that the diocesan bishop would create a stable office of pastoral collaborator by particular law. In doing so, he should enumerate the necessary qualifications for the position,[12] list the responsibilities to be lawfully assumed[13] and define the term of office.[14]

Authority of the Pastoral Collaborator

Regarding the exercise of authority relating to the temporal goods of a parish, the pastoral collaborator by virtue of lawfully assisting in the exercise of the power of governance may be granted all those powers that do not directly require the exercise of sacred orders. This question is addressed in canon 129:

§1 Those who have received sacred orders are qualified, according to the norm of the prescriptions of the law, for the power of governance, which exists in the Church by divine institution and is also called the power of jurisdiction.

[11]Canon 517, §2 reminds the bishop that this determination can only be made when there is a "dearth of priest" to serve in parochial ministry in his diocese.

[12]Canon 149, §1 states: "To be promoted to an ecclesiastical office, a person must be in the communion of the Church as well as suitable, that is, endowed with those qualities which are required for that office by universal or particular law .... " These qualifications could be modeled after the qualifications for parish priests found in canon 521, §§ 2 and 3, and in canons 528-535 to the extent that they could apply to a non-presbyter.

[13]See canon 145 on the creation of ecclesiastical offices.

[14]Canon 145, §1 states that an ecclesiastical office is constituted in a stable manner. Canon 1279, §2 states that when a public juridic person (a parish) does not have its own administrator (parish pastor) the ordinary to whom the public juridic person is subject is to appoint a suitable person (pastoral administrator) as administrator for a three year term; and the law allows them to be reappointed by the ordinary. This would argue for exercising certain stability by defining a specified term of office for the pastoral administrator.

§2 Lay members of the Christian faithful can cooperate in the exercise of this same power in according to the norm of law.

Canon 1279, §1 reaffirms that this person may lawfully assist in all aspects of the administration of parish goods. The authority of the pastoral collaborator once defined in particular law creating the office is to be given to the person appointed to the office by a written decree of the diocesan bishop (c. 156).

Duties of the Pastoral Collaborator

Like the pastor and the parochial administrator, the pastoral collaborator immediately governs the parish and is bound to the canons on administrators of juridic persons (cc. 1281-1288). The pastoral collaborator must also be mindful of these responsibilities in assisting the priest-moderator. These responsibilities are enumerated under, "Duties of the Parish Pastor as Administrator," presented earlier. In relationship to the finance council of the parish, to whom are the members accountable in offering their aid in the administration of the parish goods? The priest supervisor mentioned in canon 517, §2 is not the proper pastor of the parish, nevertheless, he is juridically responsible. In such a case, the pastoral collaborator should work with the finance council to assist the priest-moderator.

CONCLUSION

Having explored these other ecclesiastical financial administrators in light of the issues that face Bishop Brondel, we can see he is left with some weighty decisions to make. The bishop knows Fr. Algreed can no longer function as pastor of these communities. He is concerned for the welfare and stability of the parish. The bishop believes that it is essential to assign a pastor with just the right skills and temperament to deal effectively with this delicate situation and still be able to lead the community. Knowing how pressed he is for priests in his diocese, finding the right priest to appoint as pastor will take time.

A parochial administrator would provide for the spiritual and administrative needs of the community while they come to terms with what happened. He could provide for some continuity until a pastor could be assigned. Yet, he may not be able to really be effective in planning for and addressing the long-range goals they have set.

Given his shortage of priests, a pastoral collaborator may be an option. This person could help the ongoing plans for development. It would be essential for this person to work well with a priest moderator assigned from the area. The pastoral and administrative needs of the parish would be met, and the parish itself would have the time it needs to truly plan in even greater ways for the future. This option would give Bishop Brondel the advantage of time in finding the right priest for the post when one becomes available while still providing for the essential leadership the parish needs.

No matter whom Bishop Brondel decides to place, it will be important that his designee make an accounting of the assets and needs of the three communities. Once completed a new report can be compared against the one on record with the diocese and may help to establish if anything is missing from the patrimony of the parish. The administrator's report may further assist the bishop in his determination of what is the best future direction for the parish and its missions.

Bishop Brondel is left with several decisions. As he ponders what actions to take he is guided by his understanding of the canons and the authority and duties of each of the possible financial administrators.

CHAPTER ELEVEN

THE DIOCESAN FINANCE OFFICER

FREDERICK C. EASTON

CASE 21

Joe has just gotten off the telephone. His wife, Angela, notes that he has become quite pensive. She has known for some time her husband has been sought after by the local bishop for some high position with the diocese handling its finances. Joe has been doing work as a controller for a big communications firm in town. But now there is this offer. What happened on the phone? As she wonders what he will say, she remembers their previous discussions of the matter. She recalls what he told her he had learned about the proposed position and what it would mean to the family from a financial standpoint. They had been over all of that together and she remembers how she told him that she was all right with whatever he would decide.

"Well, Angie," he says sheepishly, "I guess we're into a whole new way of life. I just said 'yes' to the bishop. I'm going to be what he calls 'my chief finance officer'. From what I have learned in the job interviews, I have some idea of what this job entails because I could just intuit I would feel comfortable doing what he described. However, now as I think about it, we've probably just moved into a whole new world!" He moves over to the kitchen table and sits down, thoughtfully: "I guess I should know what a 'chief financial officer' does; I have been working for one for the past six years. But, being a CFO for a diocese? There is so much more I would like to know. I guess I'll be finding out. Like ... where does this position fit in? I do not remember my priest-uncle who had been Vicar General ever speaking of this position and I am sure he would have mentioned such a position when he would go over the old years working closely with the old bishop. Yet, there's been the Vatican Council since his time. The bishop men-

> tioned a couple of groups that I shall work with: one seemed to make sense to me, the 'finance council' and I remember my uncle speaking of the 'consultors'."
>
> Joe got up now and moved to the kitchen window and looked out then turned around: "The bishop spoke often when I had my interview with him and his advisors about canon law. I did not get the idea I had to know all of church law to be good candidate for this job, but he did say I would quickly have to get acquainted with some of it. I guess I'll have to get a good idea just how the church and the diocese work in order to do well as the chief financial officer."

Joe's thoughtful concern on the threshold of becoming a diocesan finance officer is well taken and appropriately leads to this chapter on this position in diocesan governance.

The selection of the seven "deacons" by the Apostles (see Acts 6:1-4) shows how the early church sought to have certain tasks delegated to skilled administrators so that the Twelve would be free for a more direct pastoral ministry. During the first five centuries of the church, some ecclesiastic was always required to administer the properties throughout a diocese. However, during the period between the fifth and thirteenth centuries there was a gradual lessening of the requirement for a diocesan administrator of ecclesiastical goods distinct from the bishop. In fact, there is no specific mention made in the 1917 *Code of Canon Law* of any finance officer. Nevertheless, the Church's history supports the wisdom of the 1983 code which now requires that "[i]n every diocese, ... the bishop is to appoint a finance officer ... " (c. 494, §1).

THE APPOINTMENT OF THE
DIOCESAN FINANCE OFFICER

Process of Selection

The diocesan bishop must personally appoint the diocesan finance officer. The vicar general or an episcopal vicar does not have this authority according to canon 494. However, there are two consultative bodies which must be involved in the assessment of qualifications for candidates for this office: the college of consultors[1] and the diocesan finance council.[2] At minimum, the bishop must hear the college of consultors and the finance council about the candidate to be selected (c. 494, §1).

Church law allows for any method to be used to involve these two bodies in the process for selection of the diocesan finance officer. However, the code intends that the bishop must listen to each body separately in order to receive the individual wisdom of each body.[3] Any method that leaves the bishop free to make his choice after hearing their advice is acceptable. There are two general ways in which this consultation can happen:

1. For example, the college of consultors and the diocesan finance council would be free to propose two or more candidates for the bishop's selection. In such an arrangement, the specific recommendations in favor or against each candidate should be candidly presented.

2. Alternatively, the bishop might propose a candidate to each of these bodies and hearing their opinions. Nevertheless, each body must have sufficient information about the candidate's qualifications in order to make an intelligent recommendation to the bishop.

---

[1] The college of consultors is a body required by canon 502, §1 and consists of "not less than six nor more than twelve" priests chosen from the membership of the council of priests. This group "is established for a five year term." It is frequently involved as a consultative and even deliberative body in certain financial matters. Further details about this body's responsibility will be addressed in chapter sixteen.

[2] Canon 492 requires the bishop to establish a finance council for his diocese. The details of this body will be treated more extensively in chapter twelve.

[3] Canon 127, §1 gives directions for consultation of such bodies. It is clear the group must be convened according to the norm of canon 166 which requires that each member be personally invited to a meeting of the group.

Qualifications for Diocesan Finance Officer

The *Code of Canon Law* specifies only two general qualifications for the finance officer. Canon 494, §1 simply states that the finance officer is to be a person who is "truly expert in financial affairs and absolutely distinguished for honesty." This may be a simple phrase but its meaning is manifold and must be considered very carefully.

1. Financial Skills

The finance officer must have true skills in financial matters. As will be mentioned below, often the diocesan structure allows for various persons with different roles to handle the various aspects of managing the temporal goods of the diocese, both liquid assets and real estate. Thus, the chief diocesan finance officer is the one who not only must have the ability to comprehend the breadth of a given diocese's temporal holdings, but he/she is also able to supervise others for the purpose of accomplishing the common goal.

2. Canonical Awareness

Candidates for this office do not have to be clergy.[4] Often, the chief financial officers come from the corporate world. They will likely not be skilled at the time of their selection and appointment about matters concerning ecclesiastical law and temporal goods. Nonetheless, they are assuming a position of responsibility for the finances of an ecclesiastical institution. Thus, they must be able and willing to make the necessary mental adjustments to accommodate themselves and their understanding of financial matters to the ecclesiastical world as determined by the *Code of Canon Law*.

If the person assuming the role of chief finance officer is not a cleric, it is especially necessary that he or she become well acquainted with the canonical understanding of pastors and parishes. Although the diocese or bishop may own all the property in a diocese according to civil law, canon law determines that the bishop and those who assist him must also respect the rights of parishes within the Church. For example, pastors and their equivalent in canon law are the official administrators of dependent juridic (corporate) persons that also have rights. Further, parishes are capable of owning temporal goods according to church law. It is true that the bishop has the right of oversight over the financial administra-

---

[4]There is no mention of either clergy or laity in canon 494, which establishes the requirements for office.

tion of parishes. The chief financial officer usually acts in the name of the bishop in the exercise of this right. Similarly, the bishop has the right to issue special instructions governing the administration of temporal goods in the parishes. Undoubtedly, the finance officer will have a pivotal role in the drafting of such instructions. For that reason, the diocesan finance officer should be acutely conscious of the canonical relationship of the diocese to the parish and the bishop to the pastor.

3. Honesty

The code says that the finance officer must be "absolutely distinguished for honesty" (c. 494, §1). This preeminent honesty must be evident in everything that he/she does. Of course, the finance officer is accountable to the bishop. However, the officer is required to make certain reports to the finance council and is therefore accountable to that body (c. 494, §§3-4). Among the duties mentioned below, it is the annual report of receipts and expenditures that the finance officer must give to the finance council (c. 494, §4). The bishop and his other advisors must have a true and accurate picture of the financial situation of the diocese in order to make pastoral planning decisions.

Persons skilled in financial matters naturally have a considerable power by reason of their expertise. Bishops rely on these experts particularly when financial matters are complex and highly technical. Thus, the honesty and integrity of the finance officer is so important so that the bishop and the finance council can safely trust the decisions and recommendations of the officer. Further, the finance officer should always give as candid as possible a report of the financial conditions of the diocese in a manner which he knows will be understood by the bishop and the finance council.

Special Situations during Vacancy of a Diocese

In some dioceses, the financial officer may also be a priest. If the finance officer who is a priest is elected the diocesan administrator by the college of consultors after a vacancy of the office of bishop, he can no longer serve as the finance officer for the diocese. In such a case, the diocesan finance council must select a temporary diocesan finance officer (c. 423, §2). Likewise, if the diocesan finance officer should resign during a vacancy, it would be the task of the diocesan finance council to elect a temporary officer.

Term of Office

The *Code of Canon Law* determines that the term of office for the finance officer is five years. Nonetheless, after the completion of a term, the officer may be appointed for other five-year terms. There is no limit on the number of terms for which the officer may be re-appointed (c. 494, §2).

DUTIES OF THE DIOCESAN FINANCE OFFICER

There are four canonically mandated duties of the officer (see c. 494, §§3-4):

1. to administer the goods of the diocese;
2. to follow a budget determined by the finance council;
3. to meet the expenditures authorized by the bishop or other legitimate authorities; and
4. to submit to the finance council at the end of the fiscal year a report of receipts and expenditures.

The canon is quite succinct but it is obvious the duties mentioned are complex and detailed in nature. Therefore, it is clear to accomplish these many duties in dioceses of any size the assistance of others will be needed. Thus, the finance officer will need to supervise the staff since he is accountable in virtue of his office for the accomplishment of these duties. Moreover, he must ensure that these duties are accomplished wholly in accord with the requirements of church law. Other chapters will take up in greater detail these requirements of church law regarding such matters as alienation of property (chapter twenty) and general management of diocesan finances (chapters fifteen and sixteen).

Other Duties for the Local Diocese

Besides the direct responsibilities for the ecclesiastical goods properly belonging to the diocese as a public juridic person, the bishop ordinarily assigns the diocesan finance officer to fulfill the episcopal duty of supervising the administration of the temporal goods belonging to the parishes or other public juridic persons subject to the bishop (c. 1276, §1). Here as well, the finance officer will undoubtedly employ the assistance of other staff whom he must supervise.

Other Financial Duties

In some dioceses, there may be foundations (aggregates of temporal goods) or other kinds of public juridic persons, which have been established without having any financial administrator. In such case, the *Code of Canon Law* states: "In the administration of the good of a public juridic person which does not have its own administrators by law, the charter of the foundation, or its own statutes, the ordinary to whom it is subject is to appoint suitable persons for three year; the same persons can be reappointed by the ordinary" (c. 1279, §2).[5] For example, there may be a foundation established within a diocese without a determination of who would be the administrator. Until articles of the foundation or its constitution could be properly changed, the bishop might well appoint the diocesan finance officer to administer the foundation. Certainly, if the lack of an administrator were more protracted, the ordinary could appoint the diocesan finance officer or another suitably qualified person for the task.

REMOVAL FROM OFFICE

The bishop is perfectly free not to renew the canonical appointment of the diocesan finance officer at the expiration of a five-year term. However, he may not remove the finance officer during a term of office without grave, that is, very serious reason.

Further, there is a process required for such a removal. The college of consultors as well as the diocesan finance council must be thoroughly informed of the situation so that they can give their considered opinion to the bishop. The bishop must then assess the reasons for removal from office after taking into account the opinions of both the college of consultors and the diocesan finance council. The bishop is then free either to remove the person from office or to leave him or her in the position (c. 494, §2).

[5] According to canon 134 the term, "ordinary" can apply equally to the bishop of the diocese, his vicar general or episcopal vicar or, the major superior of clerical religious institutes of pontifical right and of clerical societies of apostolic life of pontifical right as long as they possess ordinary executive power.

CONCLUSION

Although a new canonical position, the finance officer of a diocese is another example of the church's desire to have a system of checks and balances in its administration. Such a system is particularly important for responsible caring for the patrimony of the church. The confidence of the people of God in the bishop is inevitably undermined by any serious failures by the finance officer.

As mentioned above, it is most important that anyone who has this position make it his/her priority to be thoroughly familiar with the manner in which the church administers its temporal goods. Therefore, more than a nodding acquaintance with the canons on temporal goods is mandatory. Not only is the knowledge mandatory, but a skilled implementation of canons in keeping with the spirit of the law should also be a priority of the finance officer. This handbook was inspired by a desire to be of some service to finance officers and those who work in the financial arena for the church.

All who minister in the financial area of the diocese should have a proper appreciation of the ecclesial nature of their work so that people of God and all others whom they encounter may have reason to see them as ecclesial servants and stewards and trust their ministry. The finance officer should take the lead in inspiring such a consciousness among those who safeguard and directly administer those temporal goods, which serve the otherworldly mission of the Church.

A Sample Position Description for a Diocesan Financial Officer

---

DIOCESE OF ELICROCA

Position Description

I. Identifying Information

Position Title:	*Chief Financial Officer/Secretary for Finance and Administrative Services*
Status:	*Full-time, Exempt*
Secretariat:	*Finance and Administrative Services*
Reports to:	*Bishop, Moderator of the Curia, Diocesan Finance Council*
Supervises:	*Director, Accounting Services*
	Director, Internal Auditing
	Director, Information Systems
	Director, Management Services
	Director, Human Resources
	Director, Catholic Cemeteries
	Secretary, Chief Finance Office

II. Primary Functions

The Chief Financial Officer is responsible for the overall financial management of the Diocese of Elicroca and the stewardship of fiscal resources in order to support the Mission and Goals of the diocese. Additional responsibilities include the leadership and general supervision of offices that provide administrative services to the parishes, schools, and agencies of the diocese to ensure high levels of quality and professionalism.

FORMULARY 5:
continued

III. *Position Content*
Major Responsibilities and Regular Activities

1. Provide pro-active leadership for the offices in the Finance Secretariat to ensure overall effectiveness and continuous improvement of services

2. Promote greater cooperation and teamwork within the Finance Secretariat and between Secretariats

3. Develop strategic plans for this secretariat which forecast needs and allocate resources in a pro-active fashion

4. Supervise and empower staff members in order to foster the development of their gifts and abilities

5. Keep the bishop informed of all issues of importance for the patrimony and general fiscal health of the diocese

6. Consult with the Finance Council on all major strategic and operational issues and keep members properly informed of ongoing financial matters

7. Properly administer all employer benefit programs and ensure that the diocese is adequately safeguarded through proper liability coverage

8. Develop long-range financial plans that support the mission and goals of the diocese

9. Prepare the annual diocesan budget, which forecasts sources of revenue and anticipated expenditures, both operational and capital

10. Assist parish leadership with parish financial planning and management

11. Develop and implement fiscal policies to ensure efficiency, accountability, and sound financial management

12. Supervise and approve the development of all diocesan financial reports

13. Review parish annual reports and identify situations where assistance and pro-active intervention is appropriate

14. Cooperate fully with the independent accounting firm, which is contracted to perform the annual audit and supervise the implementation of management letter recommendations

15. Ensure that all dealings in the financial area comply with legal and canonical requirements and meet the highest ethical standards

16. Perform other duties as assigned by the bishop or moderator of the curia or the diocesan finance council

CHAPTER TWELVE

THE DIOCESAN AND PASTORAL FINANCE COUNCIL

KEVIN M. McDONOUGH

Mundane and unglamorous though their functions may be, effective finance councils represent important advances in church life and a practical application of Vatican II reforms. Since the 1983 *Code of Canon Law* focuses most of its legislation on the diocesan finance council, much of this chapter will consider the diocesan specification of the more general reality of finance councils. Toward the end of the chapter, nevertheless, we will examine some particular aspects of parish finance councils and those of other church institutions.

Historical Notes about the Finance Council

The finance council has taken on particular prominence as a result of discussions preparatory to and during the Second Vatican Council. A variety of structures have been used throughout most of church history to encourage financial discipline and prevent or correct abuses. Monasteries and religious orders developed detailed structures for handling monies and approving financial transactions. These structures – including the separation of financial offices from other governance positions, a regular role in financial decision-making for the provincial or abbey council, and the requirement of full membership approval for certain major transactions – all served to prevent the concentration of financial authority in the hands of one individual. In regard to dioceses, provincial councils have long had the authority to regulate matters such as the amount to be collected from Mass offerings, the charge for certain services, and concerns about clerical lifestyle. Within dioceses, the cathedral chapter in theory constituted a kind of check for financial accountability by a bishop or his administrative staff.

Key American bishops in the late nineteenth and early twentieth centuries came to believe that the cathedral chapter, as they knew it from European experience, was a form, which had lost all practical function. The bishops united in their resistance to urgings of the Vatican's Congregation for the Propagation of the Faith to establish chapters in American dioceses. In place of chapters, they established boards of consultors, small groups of senior priests appointed for a limited term who were granted some role in the supervision of diocesan financial matters. This provided the bishop with some flexibility, potentially open to abuse: an advisor with a limited term of office is theoretically less likely to challenge misconduct than will someone with protected tenure in a benefice. On the other hand, it allowed the bishops to appoint as consultors those priests who had a genuine expertise in financial matters.

The search for expertise was a significant motivator for greater involvement of individual lay people as advisors as well. American bishops took a lead in involving prominent lay financial leaders as informal advisors in the early and middle part of the twentieth century. Based on this experience, several key American bishops went to the preparatory sessions for the Second Vatican Council intending to urge greater formalization for the role of lay experts in diocesan financial matters. Among these bishops was Francis Cardinal Spellman of New York, who intervened repeatedly in favor of expanded lay involvement during the meetings of the preparatory commission on the sacred hierarchy.

It was this appeal for the involvement of experts, so typical of the council in many matters, which won the day. When the council fathers approved the establishment of diocesan finance councils in their Decree on the Bishops' Pastoral Office in the Church (*Christus Dominus*) they did so for this particular reason. The 1983 *Code of Canon Law* enshrines expertise as the fundamental contribution which a finance council brings to a church institution.

Post conciliar developments have led to a second functional emphasis. This is particularly so in the American scene. That emphasis is on openness of information. Neither the council discussions nor the subsequent authentic documents place great emphasis on the finance council as a means of open communication with donors and other "constituents" of the diocese or other institution. Nevertheless, American pastoral practice in the 1960s to the 1980s placed greater and greater weight on this contribution. In fact, structured disclosure of financial information appears to have been a key element in the unprecedented success of US diocesan fund appeals during this period. Thus, when key American church administrators and financial experts were called on by the Holy See to address its financial difficulties in the 1980s, they brought this experience with them to Rome. The publication of an annual financial report from the Holy See in recent years has been the result.

It may be said, on the basis of this history, that the primary role of the finance council is to provide a forum for the application of genuine expertise to church institutional financial matters. A secondary, but increasingly important role is to provide a forum for the disclosure of information aimed at creating a climate of public trustworthiness.

Expertise and Openness: Two Potentially Competitive Functions

An American reader of the *Code of Canon Law's* requirement for a diocesan finance council will probably be surprised by the small minimum size established there: at least three members (c. 492, §1). Administrators steeped in the ecclesiastical politics of late twentieth century America can anticipate the objections to a three – or four – member finance council: "too closely held," "the bishop's cronies," "representatives of the in-group." The code provides for a structure, which is charged minimally with providing technical, expert advice on the prudent handling of fiscal matters. One might envision a banker, an accountant, and a tax attorney all of whom are well respected in their professions and loyal to the Church, constituting such a council.

Diocesan practice in the United States has leaned toward structuring for community credibility, and therefore has tended to opt for much larger finance councils. These include members who are chosen because they represent constituencies within the diocese rather than because they have a particular financial expertise. Members may be chosen from other consultative bodies, such as the diocesan pastoral council or the presbyteral council. They may represent the elements of church leadership: women and men religious, permanent deacons, parish business administrators. They may be chosen on a geographical basis. Most American dioceses with ethnic and linguistic diversity attempt to represent the "faces of the diocese" on the council as well.

In structuring a finance council, the bishop or other institutional leadership should seek to balance these two values, expertise and openness. Too exclusive an emphasis on expertise tends to create too small a finance council whose membership is chosen from among a particular economic class with fairly similar social outlooks. Too great an emphasis on openness of communication, however, can result in a body whose membership represents interest groups rather than expert knowledge and which is too large to be effective in its discussions. A diocesan finance council with fewer than ten members might be charged with exclusivity and excessive staff control. One of more than twenty members could be unwieldy and unable to discuss technical issues with any depth of understanding.

What a Finance Council Does

There are two main groups of tasks over which a finance council exercises some supervision. The canonical tradition styles them as ordinary administration and extraordinary administration (see chapter sixteen). In American practice, ordinary administration means the development of the annual budget and regular review of compliance with it. Extraordinary administration includes major one-time financial transactions, such as construction projects and purchases and sales of property, and significant structural changes to diocesan financial administration.

The structures of the finance council should be set up and its membership chosen with a view to discharging both of these functions, which may require their own particular procedures and expertise. For example, preparing a budget requires some clarity about diocesan or institutional plans. Keeping track of compliance with the budget requires regular financial reports and the ability to read and understand those reports. As a result, at least some finance council members should have some knowledge about programmatic planning, while others should be familiar with key principles of accounting and the roles that outside auditors can play for an institution.

Assistance with extraordinary administration calls on another sets of skills, which, although not incompatible, are different from those for ordinary administration. Expertise in the funding of indebtedness, the management of investments, and the construction of a balance sheet will all be needed on a finance council. Certain collateral skills may also be useful. These would include some knowledge of insurance and risk management, for example. Some dioceses have found it useful to include civil attorneys on their finance councils, both for their particular expertise in the law and also their experience with complex business transactions. In fact, the code itself suggests that knowledge of civil law is a good criterion for finance council membership (c. 492, §2). A finance council may also profit from having one or more members particularly attentive to the impact of good financial management on fund raising and development.

Relationship Between a Finance Council and Diocesan Staff

The code envisions a close and positive relationship between the diocesan finance officer and the finance council. The finance officer reports regularly to the finance council (c. 494, §4). The finance officer's nomination must be reviewed by the finance council, although not approved thereby, before the bishop may make the appointment (c. 494, §1). Even so, there are tensions inherent in such a relationship. After a generation of experimentation, diocesan staff members have come to realize just how time consuming is the "care and feeding" of volunteers, including finance council members. New members must be carefully selected and thoroughly oriented to their work. They must be kept informed in a timely manner. Provision must be made for the smooth functioning of their meetings, with materials prepared and mailed ahead of time and minutes provided for. Members must be rotated off the council, thanked as they leave, and replaced with competent successors. Some diocesan fiscal managers can come to wonder whether the volunteers are not more work than they are worth.

From the side of the council, there is a tendency to depend excessively on financial staff and then to worry about that dependency. Can we trust the reports we are receiving? Are we getting the whole picture? Are we being brought into the process too late and merely asked to rubber-stamp a decision, which has already been made?

Difficulties such as these can be minimized if careful use is made of committees within the finance council structure. If, as suggested above, the diocesan finance council consists of between ten and twenty members, then staff will become overburdened in attempting to keep every member fully informed of all relevant business. Inevitably, then, the council membership will fear that it is being left in the dark on critical questions. When smaller groups of council members work with a portion of the council's responsibility on a stable basis, however, they acquire a level of familiarity that serves two purposes. First, it helps reduce redundancy of communication since committee members develop their own understanding of ongoing questions and pass that understanding on to new members. Second, it increases the confidence level of the advisors since they recognize that they have a relatively sophisticated knowledge of the matters which they are expected to address.

Advice or Consent: What Does a Finance Council Provide?

We have spoken about the sort of matters which are addressed in a finance council, but not about what the council actually does in regard to those matters. Once again, clarity about the specific roles to be discharged by the finance council will assist in establishing proper procedures.

The particular statutes of a religious institute will delineate when the community leadership must seek the advice of the finance council and when they must seek its consent. Parishes too are required to have finance councils, but the code is silent about the specifics of its work. Particular legislation in a diocese may establish some required consultations or even consents on the part of the parish finance council. The code provides more detail, however, when it comes to diocesan finance councils. There are two levels of required involvement by the finance council in fiscal decision-making of the diocese.

The more frequent requirement is that the bishop hears the finance council on a matter before the he can commit himself to a particular decision. The bishop must seek the council's advice, but is not required to follow it. Nevertheless, if he acts before having sought the advice, the action is invalid. A list of the matters on which he must consult the finance council is provided below.

The bishop must consult with the diocesan finance council before completing the following decisions:

1. Approve the annual budget (c. 493);

2. Accept the end-of-the-year financial report (c. 493);

3. Appoint the diocesan finance officer (c. 494, §1);

4. Remove the diocesan finance officer (c. 494, §2);

5. Impose a new diocesan tax (c. 1263);

6. Place "more important acts" of ordinary administration (c. 1277);

7. Accept the financial reports of subordinate administrators (c. 1287, §1);

8. Approve the means for investing endowments (c. 1305);

9. Diminish the obligations associated with endowments (c. 1310, §2).

In a small number of cases, the bishop cannot act without the consent of the finance council. The code is reluctant to bind the decision-making authority of the bishop, and therefore makes the consent of the finance council a prerequisite for particularly grave matters only. In fact, the specification of which acts are to require consent is left to the national conference of bishops (see cc. 1277 and 1292).

In its normal functioning, the finance council is an advisory body. Its function should not be thought of as merely advisory, however, because the strength of the finance council is derived not from its control but from its expertise. Because it is primarily advisory, the finance council is not bound to give political necessity the weight, which the final decision-maker must. Rather, the finance council is free to consider many alternatives, to weigh them without concern for their short-term cost, looking rather to the long-term advantages which more expedient decision-making might otherwise ignore. Genuinely expert advice offers as wide a variety of alternative approaches to a problem as possible, laying out the positive and negative consequences of each. It provides a broader perspective than bishop or staff, caught in the day-by-day challenges of diocesan administration, are likely to have the time to develop.

Establishing the Diocesan Finance Council

Having looked at what the council provides for the diocese, and having examined the scope and formality of what it provides, we can now look directly to the establishment of the council.

The diocesan finance council should be established by a decree of the bishop. It should be published according to the formalities of other diocesan decrees, being signed and dated by the bishop and notarized properly.

The decree should outline or make reference to the canons, which specify the role, scope, and authority of the finance council. A particular bishop may not narrow any of these elements for his own diocesan finance council: they are obligatory by the universal law. He could, however, expand one or another element of the finance council's role. This should be avoided, however, since it may place the bishop's successor in the difficult position of having to take away, for legitimate reasons, what was granted by a previous bishop for equally legitimate reasons.

The decree should provide for some regular schedule of meetings, for the selection of officers, and for any permanent committees. It ought to make specific provision for appointment, term of office, and removal of members.

This decree should be given to all new members at the time that they are considering an invitation to serve on the finance council. While the decree itself is too technical for more generalized communication, it would be useful for the diocese to acknowledge the existence of a finance council more or less regularly. At the time that new members are appointed, for example, it may be helpful to let the people of the diocese know that church leaders are seeking advice regularly from people like themselves.

The Parish Finance Council

Each parish in the Latin rite is required by universal law to have a finance council (c. 537). The single canon, which addresses this particular structure, has two emphases. First, although making reference to universal law, the canon invites the establishment of more particular norms at the diocesan level: "(it) is regulated … by norms issues by the diocesan bishop." In particular, such diocesan norms should establish the procedure for choosing council members. Second, the canon makes it clear that the council does not substitute for the pastor as the chief administrator and legal representative of the parish's goods. In fact, this canon makes specific reference to canon 532, which charges the pastor to care for the parish's goods and to represent the parish in all juridic affairs.

In the years immediately after the Second Vatican Council, many parishes also established parish pastoral councils. These pastoral councils were given a wide variety of responsibilities in different parishes. They worked according to widely differing sets of procedures and understandings of their authority. The 1983 code acknowledges the existence of such councils, but does not make their implementation a requirement of universal law (c. 536). Specific regulations, including whether or not to have such councils at all, are left to the diocesan bishop. Many dioceses and parishes have wrestled with how best to coordinate parish pastoral councils and finance councils.

Three arrangements are theoretically possible. First, the two bodies may be seen as entirely separate from each other, each communicating directly and independently with the pastor. Second, the finance council may function as a committee of the pastoral council, often alongside other parish committees. Third, this relationship may be reversed: the pastoral council may be a committee of the finance council, providing the pastoral input, which flavors and reshapes the economic advice of the finance experts. Of these three arrangements, the second appears to be the most common in current US practice.

Not only are all three theoretically possible, but all three can be in conformance with the *Code of Canon Law*. The determinative factor will be whatever regulations the diocesan bishop chooses to give.

FINANCE COUNCILS OF INSTITUTES OF CONSECRATED LIFE

While specifically naming only dioceses and parishes, the code establishes a further general requirement for all "official" church organizations. Canon 1280 requires that "each juridic person is to have its own finance council or at least two advisors." This requirement is extended, by canon 635, to institutes of consecrated life. It even extends to any of their subordinate structures (provinces and some houses, c. 634 and even to local houses, c. 636, §1) which are capable of owning or administering temporal goods.

Beyond this general requirement, however, the code is silent on the specifics of the constitution of the finance council in an institute or subordinate structure. Is the finance council necessarily identical with that council which provides members a share in the leadership of their community? Just as with parishes, one can imagine a variety of relationships between the community council/councilors, on the one hand, and the finance council/advisors, on the other. Defining this relationship is a matter for the particular constitution and statutes of the institute.

FINANCE COUNCILS IN ASSOCIATIONS OF THE CHRISTIAN FAITHFUL

Associations of the Christian faithful may also be required to have a finance council or at least two financial advisors. All public associations, which by the law itself have juridic personality in the Church once they have been properly erected (c. 313), must make some provision in their statutes to conform to canon 1280. Diocesan officials who review such statutes in preparation for the bishop's approval should ascertain that the association has set up an appropriate vehicle for bringing financial expertise to bear in decision-making processes. Private associations may or may not have juridic personality in the Church (c. 322), and consequently may or may not be bound by canon 1280. Even so, it would not be unreasonable for a bishop to withhold his approval of the statutes even of a private association until they include some means of internal fiscal accountability.

CONCLUSION

Finance councils at all levels of church organizational life fulfill a two-fold purpose. Their primary aim is to serve as a vehicle by which church leaders obtain expert help in caring for the temporal goods of their diocese, parish, community, or association. Secondarily, they foster a climate of trust and participation by opening up the flow of information about matters economic. A carefully structured and well-employed finance council may be more noteworthy for the fiscal crises and managerial scandals it helps prevent than for creative programming or captivating statements. In just such a manner, however, the council helps the church community to remain intent on its real business, which is the salvation of souls.

STATUTES FOR THE FINANCE COUNCIL OF THE ARCHDIOCESE

ARTICLE I The name of this body shall be the Archdiocesan Finance Council referred to sometimes as "AFC"

ARTICLE II Purpose
The Archdiocesan Finance Council is one of the three major councils of the Archdiocese of N. It is established by the Archbishop for the purpose of advising and assisting him in financial matters.

ARTICLE III Membership
AFC shall be composed of not fewer than 19 persons, including the Archbishop of N., or the person who, in his stead, exercises ordinary jurisdiction over the spiritual and temporal affairs of the Archdiocese of N. in accordance with legislation of the Roman Catholic Church and the Vicar General of the Archdiocese.

1) Two members of this Council shall be elected by the Archdiocesan Pastoral Council.

2) Two members of this Council shall be priests serving the Archdiocese of N., elected by the Presbyteral Council of the Archdiocese.

3) One member of this Council shall be a religious sister serving the Archdiocese of N., elected by the Sisters Council of the Archdiocese.

4) One member of this Council shall be a permanent deacon, serving the Archdiocese of N., elected by the Deacon Council of the Archdiocese.

5) At least eight members of this Council shall be appointed to at-large positions by the Archbishop.

6) Three members of this Council shall be appointed by the Archbishop as:

a) Chair of the Archdiocesan Financial Council

   b)   Chair of the Revenue Committee

   c)   Chair of the Allocations Committee

The Vicar of Finance shall also be an ex-officio, non-voting member of this Council.

It shall be the responsibility of each of the six elected members of the AFC to communicate the activities and recommendations of the AFC to the body which elected each such member and to encourage that body to exercise care in the election of its members to ensure its representatives have the interest and time to serve, and to communicate to the AFC its observations or recommendations in regards to matters being considered by the AFC.

ARTICLE IV Term of Office

   1)   The regular term of office of the elected or appointed at-large members of the AFC shall be five years, with approximately one-third of those members' terms expiring each year.

   2)   No elected or appointed at-large members shall serve more than two consecutive five-year terms.

   3)   The Chair of the Revenue Committee and the Chair of the Allocations Committee shall be appointed to a two-year term. These Chairs may not serve a more than three consecutive two-year terms. The Chair of this Council shall be appointed for a one-year term.

ARTICLE V Vacancies

Vacancies on the AFC by reason of resignation, death, disability, termination of office, or otherwise, shall be filled by the same constituency or person which originally selected the member whose position has become vacant.

ARTICLE VI Officers and Duties

The officers of the AFC shall be a Chair and a Vice-Chair.

   1)   The Chair of this Council shall conduct all meetings of the AFC and its Executive Committee.

   2)   The Vice-Chair of the Council shall act in the place of the

FORMULARY 6:
continued

Chair when the Chair is absent or unable to attend a meeting of the AFC or the Executive Committee and shall assist the Chair in the performance of the Chair's duties. The Vice-Chair shall be appointed by the Archbishop from among the membership of the Council for a one-year term.

ARTICLE VII Meetings

Meetings of the AFC shall be held at the call of either the Archbishop, the Chair, or by a majority of the full membership of the AFC. All meetings of AFC will be staffed by the Vicar of Finance.

ARTICLE VIII Committees

There shall be an Executive Committee and two standing committees of the AFC. The standing committees shall be the Revenue Committee and the Allocations Committee. The Vicar of Finance shall staff all committees of the AFC.

1) Executive Committee: There shall be an Executive Committee composed of the Archbishop, or his delegate, the Chair of the AFC, who shall be the Chair of the Executive Committee, the Vice-Chair of the AFC, the Chair of the Revenue Committee, the Chair of the Allocations Committee, and two members of the AFC elected to one-year terms by the AFC.

    The Executive Committee shall be responsible for the affairs of the Council between meetings, adoption of a yearly schedule of AFC meetings, for preparing agendas for the AFC meetings, for assigning AFC members to the standing committees, for approving the annual plans and schedules of standing committees, for recommending policies and procedures guiding the budget process and the operations of the AFC, and for determining the purpose, membership and term of each ad hoc committee. It shall report all of its activities and actions to the AFC at the next meeting of the AFC for ratification.

    All AFC members shall serve on at least one of the three committees. Members may indicate their committee preference prior to appointment.

2) Revenue Committee: The Revenue Committee shall consist of a Chair appointed by the Archbishop, at least five members of the AFC appointed by the Executive Committee and up to five or six others recommended by the AFC Revenue Committee members and approved by the Archbishop for three-year terms.

The Revenue Committee shall review and coordinate revenue projections of all sources of operating and capital funds, and assist and advise on the annual and multi-year fundraising strategies and efforts of the Archdiocesan Central Corporation prior to any major fundraising campaigns.

The Revenue Committee acts as a central area for communications on all major fundraising by agencies, departments, and institutions both inside and outside the Archdiocesan Corporation to help monitor and coordinate these efforts.

3) Allocations Committee: The Allocations Committee shall consist of a Chair appointed by the Archbishop, at least five members of the AFC appointed by the Executive Committee and the Chairs of the Allocation Panels. Allocation Panel Chairs shall be suggested by the Allocations Committee Chair, recommended by the AFC and approved by the Archbishop for a one-year term.

The Allocations Committee and its panels, each consisting of up to six persons appointed to staggered three-year terms by the Allocations Committee Chair, shall review the three-year and annual proposals for new and expanded programs, the three-year goals and annual objectives and the three-year and annual budgets of each department and agency requesting funds from the Central Corporation and it shall prepare recommendations for the AFC on them. The panels shall further establish contact with their respective agencies/departments, conduct budget hearings, and prepare and present to the Allocations Committee recommendations from their respective Panels.

The Allocations Committee shall annually prepare a recommended total budget including funds and comments on existing, expanded and new programs, from the panel recommendations and submit it to the Archbishop's Cabinet and the AFC.

The Allocations Committee and its panels shall review needs on a year-round basis and recommend to the AFC such changes in allocations as it deems necessary.

The Revenue and Allocations Committees shall work closely with the division directors and other staff as appropriate, to become informed about proposals, plans and studies that can impact on revenue or spending, the goals or objectives of departments and agencies, and strategies and funding to achieve them.

ARTICLE IX Quorum and Voting

A majority of the full membership shall be necessary and sufficient to constitute a quorum for the transaction of business at all meetings of AFC and its committees so long as all the members of the council or its committees were properly notified of meeting in accordance with canon 127. The act of a majority of the members present at any meeting at which there is a quorum shall be the act of the AFC or its committees.

ARTICLE X Amendments

Amendments to these statutes shall be proposed at any meeting of the AFC, following a two-week notice, upon a two-thirds vote of the full membership of the AFC. They would be effective upon the approval by the Archbishop.

Amendment Proposed: _____ 200_.
Amendment Approved: _____ 200_.

Most Reverend N.
Archbishop of N.

CHAPTER THIRTEEN

THE INVENTORY OF PROPERTY

LAWRENCE A. DiNARDO

CASE 22

The Reverend Peter Paul has recently been appointed Pastor of Mary, Mother of the Hills Parish. He was very pleased with his appointment since he knew the previous pastor, who had recently died. Father Paul had been assigned to the neighboring parish as a resident and had visited the rectory and church several times during his priestly ministry. In his visits to the parish, to assist the previous pastor over the last several months, he was impressed with the care of the facilities and the many beautiful amenities that decorated the church and rectory.

The rectory contained antique furniture, oriental carpets, two beautiful grandfather clocks and a great deal of crystal glassware. In addition, there were several murals and paintings that had been imported from Italy. The rectory contained a large Madonna collection that had been procured from various parts of the world. Father Paul remembers the pastor giving the history of the rectory, its contents and in particular the Marian collection.

The church was also well appointed. Candlesticks that had been imported from Czechoslovakia flanked the altar and the vestments were imported from Belgium. The church had several chalices and a monstrance imported from Spain. Father Paul remembers the Bishop speaking, at the funeral of the pastor, of the Church's beauty and the work of the pastor in enhancing both the church and rectory.

Upon his arrival at the parish, Father Paul discovered that the both the rectory and church had been stripped of the beautiful artifacts. The furniture, oriental carpets, grandfather clocks, crystal glassware and other goods had been removed. In fact, the rectory contained only one bedroom suite and a few chairs. Most of

CASE 22: *continued*

the other furniture had been removed. The situation in the church was similar. The candlesticks, vestments, chalices, monstrance and an assortment of albs and other altar linens had also been removed.

When Father Paul made inquiry with the parish staff about the goods, he was told that the family of the former pastor had removed them, contending that these were the personal property of the pastor and thus part of his estate.

Father Paul asked whether or not the parish archives contained an inventory of the parish property. He was informed that no such inventory existed. He then contacted the dean and chancery office and made an inquiry as to whether or not an inventory of the parish property had been filed in the curial archives. He was told that no inventory existed and that the diocese had not requested any inventory of parish property for many years.

Canons 1282-1284 of the *Code of Canon Law*[1] outlines the duties and obligations of an administrator of ecclesiastical goods. Canon 1282 states: "All clerics or lay persons who take part in the administration of ecclesiastical goods by a legitimate title are bound to fulfill their functions in the name of the Church according to the norm of law."

This canon establishes the foundational principle that administrators have an obligation to care for the goods of the Church. The goods delineated in this canon refer to those possessed by public juridic persons.[2] The duties of the administrator, whether clerical or lay, are to be carried out in the name of the Church and for the welfare of the Church.[3] The canon presumes that the persons

[1] Cf., the *Code of Canons of the Eastern Churches*, canons 1025-1028, contains similar provisions for the obligations and responsibilities of the administrator of ecclesiastical goods.
[2] Cf., canons 1258 and 116. Canon 116, §1 states: "Public juridic persons are aggregates of persons (*universitates personarum*) or of things (*universitates rerum*) which are constituted by competent ecclesiastical authority so that, within the purposes set out for them, they fulfill in the name of the Church, according to the norm of prescripts of the law, the proper function entrusted to them in view of the public good; other juridic persons are private."
[3] Francis G. Morrisey, "The Administration of Goods," in *The Canon Law Letter and Spirit*, ed. Gerard Sheehy, et al: (Collegeville, MN: Liturgical Press, 1995) 727.

who are entrusted with the administration of ecclesiastical goods desire to pursue the objectives of the Church, which are outlined in various conciliar texts and canon 1254, §2.[4]

Canon 1283 establishes the practical steps that are to be taken by administrators of ecclesiastical goods before they undertake their responsibilities. The canon states:

Before administrators begin their function:

1°   they must take an oath before the ordinary or his delegate that they will administer well and faithfully;

2°   they are to prepare and sign an accurate and clear inventory of immovable property, movable objects, whether precious or of some cultural value, or other goods, with their description and appraisal; any inventory already done is to be reviewed;

3°   one copy of this inventory is to be preserved in the archive of the administration and another in the archive of the curia; any change which the patrimony happens to undergo is to be noted in each copy.

This canon outlines the practical steps that are to be taken by administrators prior to taking office. The taking of an oath underlines the importance which the law attaches to the administration of ecclesiastical goods (see c. 1199). The oath should be drawn up by the ordinary and should specify the importance of caring for ecclesiastical goods as well as indicating the necessity of undertaking and submitting an inventory of the goods as prescribed in the canon. In addition, the oath should also bind the administrator to abide by all particular regulations concerning the administration of the temporal goods of a public juridic person that may have been established by the ordinary.

The canon further outlines what goods are to be inventoried by the administrator. The canon establishes three categories of goods that are to be part of the inventory. The first is immovable goods. Immovable goods are "corporeal property that cannot be removed."[5] These would include buildings and contents that are fixed, such as altars, pews, chandeliers, etc. The second category is moveable goods which

---

[4]Cf., *Presbyterorum ordinis* 17; *Apostolicam actuositatem* 10; *Ad gentes divinitus* 41. Both the conciliar texts and canon 1254, §1 point out that the ends which are especially proper to the Church are: to order divine liturgy; to provide for the decent support of the clergy and other ministers; to perform the works of the sacred apostolate and of charity, especially toward the needy.

[5]Adam J. Maida and Nicholas P. Cafardi, *Church Property, Church Finances, and Church-Related Corporations: A Canon Law Handbook* (Saint Louis: The Catholic Health Association of the United States, 1984) 315.

are precious or in any way of cultural value (see cc. 638, §3; 1189 and 1292, §2). The canon notes that goods that are precious are to be carefully inventoried. Goods such as chalices, monstrances, candlesticks, tabernacles, certain vestments, oriental carpets, antique furniture, crystal, etc., would easily be precious goods that hold special value for the Church. In addition, moveable goods that have a cultural value such as paintings, murals or notable artistic designs are to be clearly indicated in the inventory. In the third category are any other goods that are part of the public juridic person. The intention of this last category is so that all the property owned by the public juridic person is accounted for in the inventory. To give a complete assessment of the goods, which have been inventoried, the canon also requires that a description and estimate of their value be part of the inventory. It is clear that this provision applies to all categories of goods to be inventoried by the administrator.[6]

Finally, the canon requires that a copy of the inventory be kept in the administrative office of the public juridic person and one copy sent to the curial archives. This provision is important so that a copy of the inventory is always available to the ordinary as well as to the succeeding administrator of the public juridic person. Significant in the canon is the requirement that the inventory be updated when changes are made to the ecclesiastical goods of the public juridic person. This would include the purchase of additional goods and the alienation or disposition of goods. The administrator of the ongoing inventory as prescribed by the canon should also note the enhancement or disposition of goods that are part of the patrimony of the public juridic person.

Canon 1284 identifies the responsibilities of the administrator as they relate to the care of ecclesiastical goods and the requirement that temporal goods be safeguarded according to civil law and that the intention of the donors or founders be given special care.[7] The canon begins with a foundational principle and reflects the teaching of the Second Vatican Council.[8] The reference to the good householder parallels that of the steward in canon 1273. The canon articulates practical applications for good stewardship that should be employed by the administrator in carrying out the responsibility of administrating the temporal goods of the public juridic person.

---

[6] Velasio DePaolis, *I beni temporali della chiesa* (Bologna: Edizioni Dehoniame, 1995) 166-167.
[7] See canon 1284. The canon specifies that administrators are bound to fulfill their office with the diligence of a good householder. In addition, the canon requires that the administrator care for the property, safeguard it through methods valid in civil law and take care that the intentions of founders and donors are honored
[8] See *Presbyterorum ordinis* 17.

APPLICATION

Canons 1282-1284 place on the ordinary and the administrator certain obliga-tions that are essential to the proper care and administration of the temporal goods of the Church. Within the context of these canons the diocesan bishop or religious superior is required to perform two distinct tasks. The first is to draw up the oath that is required of all administrators (Formulary 7) and second, to see to it that the administrator completes the inventory. While on a practical level these tasks may be delegated to other persons (e.g., vicars general, episcopal vicars, deans), the ulti-mate responsibility to see to it that these tasks are fulfilled pertains to the diocesan bishop or religious superior. In addition, the ordinary might develop property and inventory guidelines (Formulary 8) and the format for the inventory (Formulary 9) so that all administrators use a uniform document. Additionally, it would seem that the ordinary would want to make a review of the inventory an integral part of his personal or delegated visit of the public juridic person so as to ensure that it has been completed and is updated according to the norms of law.

The duties of the administrator of the public juridic person are critical to the fulfillment of the requirements of these canons. The administrator:

- must conduct the inventory;
- must seek an estimation of the value of the property;
- must submit the results of the inventory to the curial office;
- must update the inventory;
- must ensure that the stipulations of any donors or founders are pro-tected;
- must protect the goods from damage;
- must ensure that civil law is respected where applicable.

These responsibilities are imperative since the canons place upon the adminis-trator of the public juridic person the obligation of protecting the goods of the Church.

An aspect, which must be considered as the goods are inventoried, is civil laws, which might be applicable to church property. Part of the inventory should include any notations relating to either civil law requirements or limitations which may have been placed on immovable or moveable goods. For example, a church building might have been designated a National Historic Landmark or the goods which have been given to the church may have restrictions attached to their use or disposition by the donor of the goods. Such a designation or restriction places limitations on the goods and the inventory should note the limitation.

Finally, it is important to ascertain the ownership of property in the parish. The administrator might examine the checkbook of the parish or other financial records to determine who owns goods that are located on parish property.

CONCLUSION

It is rather clear that in the case of Father Peter Paul (case 22), newly appointed Pastor of Mary, Mother of the Hills Parish, an inventory of the goods of the parish should have been completed by the previous pastor. In order to correct this problem in the future it is important that diocesan policies be established and procedures developed to ensure that an inventory of ecclesiastical goods be done in every parish and institution of the diocese or if it is a religious congregation by the religious superior.

Canons 1282-1284 are relatively self-explanatory. The obligations placed upon the ordinary and the administrator of the public juridic person are well defined. The canons desire to ensure the protection of ecclesiastical goods and the patrimony of the juridic person. In addition, the canons also desire to protect the free will offerings of the Christian faithful who support the public juridic person and who have assisted in the development of the patrimony. To this end, while these canons have not always been employed, care needs to be taken that the canons be part of the ordinary responsibilities of administrators.

FORMULARY 7:
Sample Oath of an Administrator

I_____, having been appointed Parish

Priest/Administrator of _____ by the Most Reverend

Bishop of the Diocese of Heaven/Major Superior of the Congregation

for Goods Works, do hereby affirm that:

(1) I will faithfully execute my office as Parish Priest/ Administrator of _____;

(2) I will comply with the norms of the *Code of Canon Law*, especially in the area of the temporal goods of the Church;

(3) I will conduct and inventory all of the real property of the public juridic person under my care and will comply with the other prescriptions of law and;

(4) I will adhere to the policies and procedures which have been established by the diocese/religious institute in matters pertaining to the temporal goods of the public juridic person, especially those which relate to the alienation of that property and the ongoing inventory and enhancement of the property.

So help me God and God's holy Gospels on which I place my hand.

_____
Parish Priest/Administrator

_____
Delegate of the Bishop/Religious Superior

_____
Date

FORMULARY 8:

Sample Property Inventory and Disposition Guidelines Operating Norms

Introduction

Canon 1283 requires that each administrator of a public juridic person draw up a clear and accurate inventory of the real property of every public juridic person. Since a parish is a public juridic person by law, the following guidelines are established to assist the pastor/administrator in fulfilling the responsibility of preparing an inventory of the parish property.

In addition to the Church's interests in this regard, specifically with a view to ensuring its ability to pursue its "proper objectives" as referred to above, canon law has laid down certain conditions to govern any act of alienation. Alienation is the traditional and technical term used to indicate any act by which ecclesiastical property or rights over property are transferred from its present ownership to some other (cf., c. 1254). One of these conditions is the requirement of prior permission by the competent ecclesiastical authority. The present guidelines live as their purpose to assist alienation but they are not intended as a complete statement of all the issues raised in canon and civil law. It is important to recognize that without the permission of the competent authority, the alienation would be invalid (cf., c. 1291).

Guidelines

1. The Pastor/Administrator/Team must complete an inventory of all immovable and movable goods located in the buildings, including the rectory and convent, which are part of the parish. The Office of Parish Services will provide the necessary forms for this inventory. The completed forms are to be signed and must be submitted to the Office of Parish Services by _____.

2. One copy of the completed inventory will be kept in the administrative office of the parish and one copy sent to the Diocesan Archives (Office of the Chancellor).

3. All property – real estate, buildings, furnishings, equipment, etc.- are part of the assets of the parish. The Pastor/ Administrator/Team is responsible for determining the needs of the parish and the property to be retained. The only exceptions are furnishings, equipment, and/or supplies in convents or religious houses, which were provided by religious orders and can be appropriately documented.

4. No property, either real estate or movable is to be disposed of or sold without the appropriate permission.

5. A. The appointed Pastor/Administrator/Team may use discretion in disposing of movable property (that is NOT either precious or of significant cultural value) less than $2,500. (Unneeded rectory furnishings, for example, can be donated to the St. Vincent de Paul Society, distributed to the needy through the parish social service program, or sold, etc.)

   B. Disposition of movable property is to follow the appropriate diocesan policy if any individual sale is more than $2,500.

   C. All real estate transactions (renting, selling, leasing, etc.) are acts that can be sanctioned only upon observance of the formalities of law and therefore are to follow the appropriate diocesan policy.

6. Ecclesiastical and liturgical appointments (chalices, ciboria, tabernacles, monstrances, vestments, statues, candlesticks, etc.) are to be stored in a secured central parish location. NOTE: These items should be carefully inventoried, an estimate of their value determined and records kept (especially for insurance purposes).

7. Ecclesiastical and liturgical appointments may be donated to another parish (not private persons) only when the prescriptions of both canon and civil law or those imposed at the time of donation by the founder, donor or legitimate authority are observed. Records must be kept of what is given to whom, and a copy sent to the Office of Property Planning and Development.

8. Some documents, artifacts, furnishings/equipment are rather valuable, i.e., old photographs, church bulletins, minutes and documents of various parish organizations, newspaper clippings, antiques, artwork, oriental carpets, etc. Disposition of these movable precious goods (objects that have historical or artistic value) regardless of the value of these materials must be approved through Diocesan Archives (checklist attached) and Office of Property Planning and Development.

9. Significant relics or those greatly revered are subject to the restrictions of canon 1190 and must be safeguarded.

FORMULARY 9:

Sample Inventory form for church administrators

Parish _____

Building _____

Room: _____

Item	Number	Description	Condition (Excellent, Good, Fair, Poor)	Comments

FORMULARY 9:
continued

CATEGORIES OF PARISH INVENTORY

A. CHURCH/SANCTUARY

Table
Screen
Chair
Rack
Musical Instruments
Banner Standard
Free Standing Kneeler
Painting
Rug
Statue
Crib Set
Chalice
Tabernacle
Monstrance
Candle Holder/Stand
Ciborium
Paten
Thurible
Boat
Cruets
Processional Cross
Pyx
Hymnal
Portable Sound System
Vestments (list)
Oil Stock
Other

B. PARISH OFFICE

Desk
Chair
Table
Lamp
Typewriter
Calculator
File Cabinets
Computer
Printer
Scanner
Mimeograph
Copy Machine
Bookcase
Other

C. PARISH RECTORY

1. Dining Room (Area)
Dining Table
Chair
China Closet
Buffet
Rug
Other

2. Living Room
Sofa
Chair
Table
Lamp
Rug
Television
Radio
Bookcase
Fireplace Fixtures
Other

3. Kitchen
Stove/Range
Refrigerator
Dishwasher
Microwave Oven
Freezer
Dishes
(Place Settings over 4)
Silverware
(Place Settings over 2)
Appliances (List)
Other

4. Bedroom
Bed
Chest
Desk
Chair
Rug
Table
Lamp
Dresser
Bookcase
Other

5. Bathrooms
Towels
Other

6. Miscellaneous
(Closets, Hallways,
Entryways,
Basement, Etc.)
Vacuum Sweeper
Floor Polisher
Table
Lamp
Bench
Chair
Washing Machine
Dryer
Patio/Porch
Furniture
Other

FORMULARY 9:

continued

FINANCIAL RECORDS

PROPERTY RECORDS

- ❑ Architectural drawings
- ❑ Construction Files
- ❑ Deed Files

CEMETERY RECORDS

- ❑ Burial Records (record of interments, date of burial, funeral director, lot number, etc
- ❑ Lot Map
- ❑ Financial Record
- ❑ Cemetery Rules/regulations

PUBLICATIONS

- ❑ Anniversary Books
- ❑ Annual Reports of Parish
- ❑ Parish Bulletins

SCHOOL RECORDS

- ❑ Annual Reports
- ❑ Architectural drawings
- ❑ Calendar (school events)
- ❑ History File
- ❑ Permanent Student Cards
- ❑ Financial and School Fund Account Books
- ❑ Photographs
- ❑ Reports to Diocesan Office of Education
- ❑ School Board Minutes
- ❑ Student Publications (Yearbooks, etc.)

DIOCESAN ARCHIVES

Name of Parish

In addition to Parish Sacramental Records (obtain form from Canonical Services Office) the following parish records should be retained for their historical significance.

FORMULARY 9:
continued

Administrative Records
- ❏ Announcement Books (Record of parish activities)
- ❏ Annual Report of the Parish
- ❏ Appointments File (Documents concerning appointment of pastors and parochial vicars)
- ❏ Articles of Incorporation (of the Church corporation and parish organizations)
- ❏ Census Records
- ❏ Constitution and By-laws (for parish organizations)
- ❏ Correspondence – official (administration, parish policy, diocesan directives)
- ❏ Parish Council Minutes (older Church Committee Minutes should be included here if they exist)
- ❏ Parish Organizations Records (Holy Name Society, Ladies Altar Society, Legion of Mary, etc.)
- ❏ Parish History File (Historical sketches, newspaper clippings, photographs, etc.)
- ❏ Photographs of moveable items.

CHAPTER FOURTEEN

FINANCIAL REPORTS TO THE FAITHFUL

ROYCE R. THOMAS

CASE 23

The parish of St. Elizabeth Seton is relatively young. It started as a mission of a larger parish in town and has grown rapidly over the past ten years. There have been a series of priests who have come to say Mass and administer the sacraments but none stayed very long. The pastor of the mother church always took care of the money. Now, the parish has a resident pastor who comes with many good intentions. The parish needs to build a parish activities or family life center. They do not know whether they need to have a pledge drive, borrow from the diocese or a combination of these and other means for raising funds. They are not sure what has happened in the past financially. They believe people have been generous with cash and sometimes securities. But, they do not really know. The pastor of the mother church believed the people would give more if they did not know how much they had in the bank. He also detested the diocesan assessment, which was based on gross income. Therefore he had a variety of accounts so he could consistently underreport the parish income. Professional fund-raisers tell the finance council the parishioners will actually be more generous if they see their contributions are being handled responsibly. If they seek money from foundations in the way of grants then they will need reports, which are professionally prepared and complete.

Although in American civil law church property may be owned by a corporation sole vested in the bishop or the diocese or as separate corporations, canonically ecclesiastical property does not belong to any individual but to a public juridic person, in this case the parish. Therefore, the pastor or administrator holds a position of trust both toward the church universal and the local parish community. Traditionally, canon law has emphasized upward accountability. The parish is accountable to the diocese and the diocese is accountable to Rome. However, since Vatican II, the role of the laity in the Church is becoming more and more collaborative. According to canon 1287, §2 and the principles of stewardship and effective leadership, the laity are to be informed concerning the financial status of the parish, at least in respect to what they have contributed and how these funds have been utilized.

The pastor is responsible not only for the bishop but to the laity as well. More importantly there should be a relationship of trust which urges him to be efficient and faithful in his administration of church goods especially since they are held for the benefit of others. With the increasing need for specialization and the higher levels of education among the laity, it is more than advisable the laity not only be informed but consulted.

The financial reports necessarily depend on the integrity of the people handling the money and those assembling and preparing the information. Auditors and accountants can suggest ways to enhance reliability of behavior. This assurance usually involves separating tasks. The person who writes checks should not be the one who reconciles the checkbook. Such protective measures may not always practical in a one or two person office. But some controls are advisable.

The first task for the new pastor at St. Elizabeth (case 23) will be to discover what assets and liabilities the parish has and how the money has been spent or managed. These assets can be cash, buildings, land, machinery, stocks, bonds, etc. Regarding cash, the discovery can be done by checking local banks for the accounts. This will also help to discover any outstanding debts. Some parish organizations such as the Altar Society or Men's Club may have their own checking accounts. The pastor should ask each of the parish organizations for a financial report. These funds too should all be counted as assets of the parish. For the general income and expenditures of the parish, the pastor may have to go through the check book and bank statements looking at the stubs and canceled checks. A check written regularly to a business may indicate a debt to the business. As unlikely as it may seem in this case, there may even be some money on deposit with the diocese.

MASS OFFERINGS

Offerings for Masses are traditionally kept in a completely separate account and are not to be commingled with parish funds. These are not counted as assets of the parish and do not appear on the financial report. The reason for this is that Mass offerings are given to the priest who will satisfy the obligation of saying the Mass. Therefore this offering goes to the priest and not the parish. The Internal Revenue Service (IRS) considers these offerings as taxable income.

PERSONAL FUNDS

A common problem or occurrence in many parishes and schools is the use of personal or "slush" funds. Such accounts are private and many times unknown to anyone except the user. These will be more difficult to discover. Oftentimes, there is no oversight or accountability of such money. Major purchases are sometimes made from these funds which are never placed on the books. All funds should be subject to the oversight of the pastor and the finance council. Granted, some levels of trust may need to be developed before the individuals or organizations will turn their monies over to the pastor but it is still a goal for all to work toward.

STOCKS AND BONDS

Some people donate stocks and bonds instead of cash. When people donate securities they prefer to donate them in "street name." A local broker may have an account in the parish's name. These financial instruments have also been found in file cabinets in the parish office or the parish vault. The parish might own stocks and/or bonds and hold them for maturity or appreciation. Many dioceses have specific policies on who should hold these securities or who should have custody of them and who should vote the proxies.

ENDOWMENT FUNDS

Many endowment funds today are encouraging people to buy insurance policies, which will then belong to the Fund. Parishes can also benefit from these. These too are to be considered and listed as assets. Does the parish have any patrimony with a significant artistic or historic value? The parish insurance policy should list these or an appraiser will need to be consulted. This can be the first step in preparing a realistic inventory of the parish, which is useful for insurance purposes especially if the policy is for replacement value.

If, in addition to securities, the parish has been given property through bequests or other means, professional advice may be needed. It is true the church does not generally pay income tax. This is not the case, however, when the income is obtained from a non-religious activity; e.g., operating a winery. The IRS even considers income from bingo in areas where bingo is illegal to be unrelated business income. Certain tax reports will then be required. The church does pay property tax on property that is not used for religious purposes. If the parish owns rental property, or even land, which is not being used at all, there is probably some tax liability. This needs to be addressed lest the local government take it over for nonpayment of taxes. In any event, the property should be listed as an asset. The parish might consider whether the property will ever be used in their planned growth and expansion. If the property will not be used by the parish, the wiser course of action would be to sell it to help finance the new building.

Another potential asset of the parish is an endowment. The parish may have an endowment for a cemetery or a school. People hope their contributions are tax exempt. If the endowment is listed in the *Official Catholic Directory*, it is tax exempt. The chancery can help with obtaining a listing. A few years ago when the United States Catholic Conference's tax status was being challenged because of its pro-life advocacy, some institutions and organizations decided to obtain their own tax exempt status from the IRS. These have the same reporting requirements as other not-for-profit organizations. An endowment also has a special obligation to make an annual report to its donors and contributors.

Once the information concerning the finances and property of the parish has been obtained, the reports can be prepared. In the case study presented at the beginning of the chapter, it would appear that reports will need to be made to the parish, parish council, parish finance council, diocese, IRS, banks, foundations, and contributors to endowments. There will also be non-financial reports of meetings in which these matters were discussed and the reports might include audits or reports from outside agencies. Thus, the financial reports, which the pastor of St. Elizabeth Seton will have to make will have a variety of formats. These will depend on the audience or the readership of the respective report.

PARISH FINANCIAL REPORTS

Financial reports to the parish can be very simple. It might be the publication in the weekly bulletin of the amounts collected in the previous week's collection(s). There might be some comparison to the amount budgeted and maybe a year to date figure for both. From time to time a specific expense might be noted such as "last month we paid $1800 for electricity." Many would expect something more, at least annually. This could be a listing of major sources of income and expenses and a narrative by the pastor, business manager or chair of the finance council. Sometimes the report is given in both oral and written form.

PARISH PASTORAL COUNCIL AND FINANCE COUNCIL

The parish pastoral council and the parish finance council would see more detailed financial reports at their meetings. The financial report should tell how much income was received and how it was spent. It can then be compared with what was forecast and what was done in the past. Thus, it is useful for both planning and accountability purposes. The accountability is to the parishioners and to the diocese. The report also helps the pastor in his oversight role of the internal business operations of the parish.

The budgeting process is an important part of gaining an accurate overview of the financial health of the parish. It forces the parish and its organizations to do planning. What programs will they attempt? What activities will be sponsored? Some say that by listing the parish's goals and priorities the budget becomes something of a theological document. The financial report should report to the pastor, the pastoral council and the parish in such a way that they can compare how the money is being raised and spent; and how it was intended to be raised and spent. With an accurate budget process and reporting keyed to the budget, the pastor and his advisory groups can begin to estimate how much of a debt they can realistically service. A parish without a budget will run a greater risk of getting into financial trouble than one, which keeps track of how well it is doing.

The finance council will usually have as its members people who are accustomed to reading financial reports even though there may be some on such a council because of their expertise in other areas. The parish pastoral council may have members who are unfamiliar in reading financial reports. Therefore, the reports will have to be presented in such a way as to give them the information in, what is for them, a readable form. Many standards for financial reporting are set for the sake of consistency. For example, many dioceses prescribe which computer software its parishes will use to manage census and financial data. The systems can be refined to a certain extent so they produce and process varied information in varied formats. One of the more common formats is for the information to be given in columns expressing the year to date actual (actual income or expense), the year to date budget and the year to date actual of the preceding year. The diocese will also suggest a chart of accounts, which will be adopted by each parish depending on how much detail it wishes for each category. For example, one parish may want to separate the telephone expenses into local, long distance and fax. This would give it three different entries under "telephone." Another parish may decide its fax expenses are negligible; it knows how much local calls are; therefore, it is easy to determine the long distance amount by quick subtraction. So, it will have only one entry for telephone expenses.

FINANCIAL SOFTWARE PROGRAMS

There are a number of financial software programs on the market today. They can produce databases and spreadsheets in a quality fashion. Since a picture is worth a thousand words, pie charts and bar graphs are also extremely helpful in making reports. They convey a lot of information quickly.

The pastor has options as to how he will report to the parish and his advisors. However, he often has no such flexibility when he reports to the diocese. The diocese will have its own forms. The report will be required on a regular basis. These reports may be expected on an annual, semi-annual, monthly or even weekly basis. The report does not always follow the format of the financial chair's computer or even of the diocesan system itself. The pastor, who likely has little formal training in finances, will then be preparing three different reports (parish, finance council, diocese) all giving basically the same information.

FUNDING SOURCES

The parish may obtain financing for its planned building through the diocese or through a bank. The rates offered by the diocese are often much more favorable than those from a local thrift. If the diocese as a policy requiring parishes to borrow money from it or through its good offices, St. Elizabeth Seton will be expected to provide some financial history and projections. These will be based on many of the reports already prepared and processed. In addition, some information about demographics will also usually be requested.

If the parish discovers that it must seek funding from a bank, it will need to present financial statements for the previous years. These would probably be the same as required by the diocese. This will give the bank an indication of whether the parish will be able to service the proposed debt. Of course, if the property is held by the bishop as "corporation sole" the bank may be more optimistic. The more professional the reports' preparation and appearance, the more credibility they will have.

If building the new parish activities center will require a debt too large for the parish to service from its general revenues, a pledge or fund drive may be needed. In a building drive the diocesan authorities will also look at the pledges both long and short term. How well are they being collected? How many parishioners are participants? What are the forecasts for the future? Private foundations might also be solicited. The accuracy of the reports take on increasing importance.

If the parish is going to deal with a commercial lending institution, the IRS or a foundation, it will need financial statements, which conform to a format approved or recommended by one of the accounting institutions: Generally Accepted Accounting Principles (GAAP); American Institute of Certified Public Accountants (AICPA); Financial Accounting Standards Board (FASB), etc. Depending on the rules of the bank or foundation, the financial statement may need to be reported by external accountants. Thus, the pastor's sister may be a CPA and would gladly give help and advice in bookkeeping and charting various expenditures. However, she would not be considered independent for the purpose of preparing a report on the financial situation of the parish. The reports are classified as compilation, review, or audit depending on the degree of examination expended by the external accountants. A compilation is the lowest level of assurance; an audit is the highest. A compilation is merely the placing of the numbers into the professionally appearing format using GAAP. It does not attempt to disclose errors, irregularities or illegal acts such as fraud that may exist. There is no attempt to identify significant deficiencies or material weaknesses in the controls of the organization. If something is obviously wrong the compiler will note it and follow up on it. An audit is much more extensive and complete. It is designed to express an opinion regarding the institution's financial statement as a whole. The auditors will look for irregularities and possible illegal activities. A review is more formal than a compilation but less than an audit.

FINANCIAL ACCOUNTING STANDARDS BOARD (FASB) REGULATIONS

In recent years, those who have a familiarity with financial reports have noticed that FASB has made some changes in the ways the reports are presented or they have issued regulations calling for consistency in the reports. Some of these will be listed below. The numbers represent the number of the pamphlet published with the change.

Number 93 calls for computing depreciation on the reports. Prior to this, many organizations did not depreciate their buildings and equipment because there was no tax advantage and no perceived benefit in doing so. Nonetheless, the machinery and buildings are wearing out and will someday need to be replaced or receive major repairs. Therefore, it is less an asset than before.

Number 116 requires that contributions, or legally enforceable instruments (pledges), must be recorded as income at the time the pledges are made. Thus a $300 pledge payable over three years would be recorded as $300 in the year the pledge is made rather than reporting $100 each year for three years. In order for contributed services to be reported, they need to be tasks requiring specialized skills and performed by an individual possessing those skills; and typically they would need to be purchased if not donated. This is very important for planning purposes. An example of its application would be when religious are employed by a school or parish but not paid as laity doing the same work. Some day the religious may go elsewhere, and then the parish would not be ready to pay what the person was really worth on the open market.

Number 117 states that all not-for-profit organizations are to provide a statement of financial position, a statement of activities and a statement of cash flow. It requires classification of the organization's net assets and its revenues, expenses, gains, and losses based on the existence or absence of donor-imposed restrictions. It requires the amounts for each of three classes of net assets – permanently restricted, temporarily restricted, and unrestricted – be displayed in a statement of financial position and the amounts of changes in each be displayed in a statement of activity. Some unrestricted funds can be designated by the parish for a certain use i.e., all memorials go into the building fund. Internally, there may be an understanding to this effect, but it will not be listed that way on the financial report. Since there are no longer any interfund loans, some say this marks the end of fund accounting. However, fund accounting is still being used by many organizations.

Number 124 requires that investments must be listed at their fair market value. In the past, some institutions listed their securities at cost and others listed them at market value. This caused confusion in interpreting the financial statements. In October 1987, the stock market plummeted. It is known as Black Monday. Some say money is neither gained nor lost on an investment until it is sold. However, if a parish, or endowment fund, were listing its holdings at cost, the assets were worth considerably less on the Tuesday after Black Monday. The statement of financial position would reflect a loss of net worth. For the sake of the reports being the same and therefore useful for comparison purposes, FASB requires the investments to be reported at fair market value.

ECCLESIASTIAL TERMINOLOGY

In dealing with property and finance in the Church, some words, which the law on temporalities traditionally uses may be unfamiliar to the lay person. For instance, property may be called corporeal, incorporeal, moveable, immovable, precious, historical, artistic, etc. These distinctions are now found in the context of ecclesiastical goods, which is the primary term for understanding Book V. In the language of accounting, there is only real and personal property. Granted the ecclesiastical system has a long and proud tradition, but the American Church must operate in the Anglo American system; and, therefore, must understand and speak its language when necessary.

Whenever one builds or does significant remodeling, civil authorities will have to be contacted as to building codes and zoning regulations. In historical districts, these can be restrictive or confining. Therefore, the plans should be reviewed in their early stages by an architect or professional engineer. Further reports will be required which are non-financial in nature. These may prove to be more onerous than those reporting financial conditions.

CONCLUSION

Unfortunately, some priests, like the previous pastor at St. Elizabeth Seton, think that being less than candid on financial statements is wise. Professional accountants and fund-raisers would disagree. Those who would be deceptive believe people will not give as much if they see the parish with money in the bank. In addition, the diocesan tax, which they are trying to avoid, is often based on parish income and therefore the less reported the better for the parish. Of course, there are ways a financial statement can be constructed so the uninitiated will not understand it. Practices like expensing capital investments; capitalizing expenditures to inflate assets, and netting out expenses against income often mask some assets and expenses. These approaches are not acceptable accounting practices. Fraud, or outright lying, can never be condoned.

In canon law, the administrator of a public juridic person (in this case, the pastor of the parish) cannot perform acts of extraordinary administration without the consent of his financial advisors and the ordinary. The pastor will have to present the need for a parish activities center to the bishop. The bishop will probably delegate the review to others. They will expect the pastor to present the above mentioned information, especially the diocesan reports and any audits from years past. They will also expect to see the minutes of meetings of the pastoral council and the finance council at which these matters were discussed. Naturally, at those meetings the financial concerns will have been addressed by the respective groups. Although not canonically required, the diocese will normally expect some parish participation beyond the pastoral council in the decision making process. With all the facts in order and mutual trust and respect in evidence, the permission should be granted.

The parish of St. Elizabeth Seton was primarily interested in obtaining permission to build a much needed building. However, in the process of obtaining the necessary permissions and licenses, as well as the funding, they have learned and begun many other positive things as well. They now have a realistic inventory of their assets. They have a system of reporting to the parishioners and other stakeholders. They have developed more professional ways of dealing with their finances, and subsequently there is more trust, communication and consultation between the pastor and the parishioners which will enable them to do even more things in the future.

CHAPTER FIFTEEN

ANNUAL REPORT TO THE DIOCESAN BISHOP

THOMAS J. PAPROCKI and RICHARD B. SAUDIS

CASE 24

Because of the rapid growth of the Diocese of Magnus Auctus, the Holy See has recently split the diocese in two and created a new diocese, Nova Terra, with territory apportioned from the Diocese of Magnus Auctus. The freshly appointed bishop of the newly established Diocese of Nova Terra is wondering what his authority and responsibilities are for supervising the various entities in the diocese. He also wishes to know if these entities can be or should be held accountable to him through annual reports. If so, he wants to know what these reports should contain.

According to the Decree on the Bishops' Pastoral Office in the Church (par. 11), the bishop is called to devote himself to his apostolic office as a witness of Christ to all people. This means that he must know something about those entrusted to his pastoral care if he is to teach, to sanctify, and to govern them. It is an awesome responsibility, but not an impossible one, since the Holy Spirit guides the Church in this ministry. While we want a holy charismatic brother as our bishop, we also want that brother to be a wise and knowing leader. If a bishop is to be bishop, he is to be overseer, *episkopos*. His role of oversight is spelled out in the canon law on governance. One way for a shepherd to know his flock is by personal contact and one way to know about all the juridic persons that constitute the local Church is to hear from them.

CANONICAL AUTHORITY AND RESPONSIBILITY TO SUPERVISE ADMINISTRATION

Several canons treat of reports to be made to the bishop. In the terminology of organizations in the United States, the diocesan bishop is the chief executive of an enormous not-for-profit corporation which involves a large work force, millions of dollars in property, with a multiplicity of social, educational and health services, as well as parish operations. All of which call for very good internal controls.

Canon 1276 establishes in law the authority of the ordinary regarding temporal goods of the Church. It states:

§1 It is for the ordinary to exercise careful vigilance over the administration of all the goods which belong to public juridic persons subject to him, without prejudice to legitimate titles which attribute more significant rights to him.

§2 With due regard for rights, legitimate customs, and circumstances, ordinaries are to take care of the ordering of the entire matter of the administration of ecclesiastical goods by issuing special instructions within the limits of universal and particular law.

While our concern in this chapter is the responsibility of the diocesan bishop, it is to be noted that this canon refers to all ordinaries, to pontifical right major superiors, as well as those who possess ordinary general executive power, such as vicars general and episcopal vicars (c. 134). The role of the ordinary is supervisory; and does not necessarily entail any intervention in the immediate governance of juridic persons, unless he is the immediate superior of them (c. 1279). Although the bishop, with all his duties, cannot and should not become involved in all the details of the internal operation of every juridic person subject to him, still he is the only person who can ensure that every part of the diocese is functioning as it should. Because of the complexity of a diocese and its organizational structure, this supervision may take place through various delegates of the bishop and through consultative bodies, such as the finance officer, the moderator of the curia, the chancellor, or through vicars, finance councils, consultors, pastoral councils, or priests councils, etc. (see chapters eleven and twelve). How these delegates and consultative bodies participate in the role of the bishop is spelled out in other canons.

As part of his supervision, the ordinary should provide instructions in more detail than these canons, because of the need to respect not only church law, but also civil law, local circumstances and all lawful customs.

This supervisory function is a matter of jurisdiction which enables the ordinary to require a full accounting and, if necessary, to introduce corrective measures (c. 1279). The canon notes that the ordinary may also have further rights over juridic persons, e.g., from special delegation of the Holy See or by statutes.

The public juridic persons subject to the diocesan bishop in a large diocese will be, first of all, the parishes and schools, then cemeteries, and social agencies such as Catholic Charities (if the latter are separately constituted as public juridic persons), etc. Various agencies are directly operated by the central administration of the bishop's office and are, therefore, part of the diocesan juridic person itself.

Until very recently, most apostolic works and the religious mission of a diocese were carried out by juridic persons established by the law itself, such as parishes (c. 515, §3), seminaries (c. 238, §1), and schools operated by religious institutes as the sponsoring juridic person (cc. 634, §1 and 803, §1.) Now, as many religious institutes are divesting themselves of their hospitals and schools and turning them over to the management of lay boards, it is becoming more common for diocesan bishops to create public juridic persons to carry on the mission of education and health care formerly carried out under the sponsorship of religious institutes. Such juridic persons in a diocese are constituted by a special grant through a decree of the diocesan bishop (cc. 114 and 116, §2). They are public juridic persons if the task entrusted to them is fulfilled in the name of the Church (c. 116, §1). The temporal goods owned by public juridic persons are considered ecclesiastical goods (c. 1257, §1). While private juridic persons have the power to acquire, retain, administer and alienate temporal goods according to the norm of law (c. 1255), the temporal goods of a private juridic person are normally governed by its own statutes and not by canon law unless expressly provided otherwise (c. 1257, §2).

Some entities within the diocese, such as religious houses, hospitals, and schools, may belong to an exempt religious community or an institute of pontifical right and thus be under the direct supervision of other superiors. Those juridic persons who are not subject to the direct vigilance of the diocesan bishop must render an account to their own proper authorities. Nevertheless, all religious in a diocese, exempt or not, are accountable to the diocesan bishop in public worship, the care of souls, the public exercise of divine worship, preaching, catechetical instruction and education, and other apostolic works and activities of religion and charity (cf., cc. 678-683). Furthermore, canon 615 calls for "special vigilance of the diocesan bishop" in regard to certain autonomous monasteries, and canon 637 states that such monasteries "must render an account of their administration to the local ordinary once a year. Moreover, the local ordinary has the right to be informed about the financial reports of religious houses of diocesan right." Use of the term special vigilance in this context seems to refer primarily to pastoral concern. Therefore, in regard to autonomous monasteries subject to such vigilance, the local ordinary and the monastic superior should work in concert to determine the details of this accounting. Presumably, it would normally include a statement of income and expenses for the year as well as a report on the financial condition and important transactions of the house.

Concerning religious houses and other institutes of diocesan right, the local ordinary has the right to be informed of their financial affairs, although the law does not specify in what way or how often such information is to be supplied. This right to information concerns the house within the local ordinary's diocese, not the financial affairs of the whole institute, since the autonomy of the institute and the responsibilities of the bishop of the principal house of a diocesan institute are to be respected.

In paragraph two of canon 1276, the ordinary is directed to use special instructions regarding the entire administration of ecclesiastical goods. He is not only to require an accounting but also to provide help by detailed and specific direction. Rights and legitimate customs and special privileges, as well as universal and particular law should be made clear. Relevant civil legislation should certainly be brought to the attention of the concerned juridic persons. Local regulations on the administration of ecclesiastical goods should clearly define what is required. Many dioceses have issued books of policies and procedures concerning temporal goods; other dioceses send bulletins, as needed, in their regular mailings to the clergy and agencies of the diocese.

In this matter, there are various agencies today which can be of great help to the ordinary, to parishes and other public juridic persons. The Committee on Budget and Finance of the NCCB, the Accounting Practices Committee of the USCC, the Diocesan Fiscal Management Conference, the National Association of Treasurers of Religious Institutes, and the Statements of Financial Accounting Standards for Non-Profit Organizations of the American Institute of Certified Public Accountants are some of the resources that are available to help church administrators.

Requirements of the Annual Report

Canon 1284 briefly treats of annual reports. It states:

§1 All administrators are bound to fulfill their function with the diligence of a good householder.

§2 Consequently they must: ... 8° draw up a report of the administration at the end of each year; ...

§3 It is strongly recommended that administrators prepare annual budgets of incomes and expenditures each year; it is left to particular law, however, to require them and to determine more precisely the ways in which they are to be presented.

All administrators of church goods are bound by this canon. Therefore they should interest themselves in their personal responsibilities of administration. It is not enough to entrust the supervision of church goods totally to another who does not have the canonical position of administrator. Unfortunately, fraud and embezzlement have become an acute problem, not only in the business world, but sadly also in church administration, so much so that the NCCB felt urged in 1995 to issue a document on Diocesan Internal Controls which alerted bishops to take steps to monitor financial reporting more closely.

The content of the annual report is left to local determination. It will necessarily vary according to the nature and activity of the particular agency involved. The most common document, the parish annual report, at the minimum should detail ordinary and extraordinary income, ordinary and extraordinary expenses, savings and loans, bank accounts, property sales and purchases, construction, demographic and sacramental statistics. A very similar but separate form could be used for the schools in the diocese.

The agencies that come under the central administration of the diocese should complete an annual program report. They need not use separate financial reports, but the entire diocesan pastoral center should have an external audit made by an independent auditing firm, detailing the financial activities of the various diocesan agencies. Hospitals and schools which belong to religious communities need not file a comprehensive annual financial report with the diocese since they have their own separate external audit. As a matter of information, however, such institutions could provide the diocese with a copy of their own annual report.

The third paragraph of this canon introduces a new element concerning an annual budget by way of suggestion, not as a strict requirement. Other than this, the provisions of the former code about administration are basically repeated here in the new code. The recommendation is made that an annual budget be submitted of anticipated revenues and expenses. It is left to regulations on the local level to indicate whether or not it is to be required, what data is to be supplied, or how it is to be reported. One suggested approach is that the form sent to parishes and schools regarding a proposed budget be a mirror-image of the annual financial report for the past year.

ACCOUNTABILITY OF ADMINISTRATORS TO THE DIOCESAN BISHOP

Canon 1287 treats of the accountability required of all administrators. It states:

§1 Both clerical and lay administrators of any ecclesiastical goods whatever which have not been legitimately exempted from the power of governance of the diocesan bishop are bound by their office to present an annual report to the local ordinary who is to present it for examination by the finance council; any contrary custom is reprobated.

§2 According to the norms to be determined by particular law, administrators are to render an account to the faithful concerning the goods offered by the faithful to the Church.

As stated before, institutes of consecrated life which are not subject to the direct governance of the diocesan bishop are specifically excepted from this requirement to account to the diocesan bishop. They account to their own appropriate authorities in accordance with their constitutions.

Public associations established by the Holy See, or an episcopal conference, are obliged to render an account to their appropriate superior. Other public juridic persons, not only parishes, are to render an annual account of their administration. The ordinary in turn is required to present such reports to the diocesan finance council. However, in the matter of annual reports to the bishop, it is to be noted that canon 1287 gives the finance council the responsibility of reviewing the various reports which have been submitted. The finance council also examines the annual report which canon 494 directs the diocesan finance officer to submit. The diocesan financial report is presumably prepared by the finance officer and his staff together with outside professional auditors. Upon approval by the finance council, it is sent to the diocesan bishop. The completed financial statement should consist of a review by an independent accounting firm of the consolidated financial statements of the various diocesan agencies. The financial statements should be in accordance with the Statements on Standards for Accounting and Revenue Services issued by the American Institute of Certified Public Accountants and in keeping with established reporting standards for non-profit organizations in the United States.

Canon 493 obliges the finance council in turn to submit a budget of the entire diocese for the coming year. The bishop, of course, presides over the diocesan finance council, either directly or through his delegate.

Canon 1287 goes on to say that any contrary custom is reprobated. As provided by canon 5, therefore, any universal or particular customs existing prior to the 1983 code involving situations where the annual report, now mandated by canon 1287, was previously not required to be presented "are entirely suppressed, nor are they permitted to revive." Since diocesan finance councils are significantly different from the administrative councils of the former code, and since the role of the finance officer is a new and important one in the diocesan structure, it is emphasized that practices from the days of the former code which do not take into account these offices are no longer to be maintained or substituted for the new mandated offices.

After requiring the annual report to the diocesan bishop, canon 1287 in a second paragraph directs all administrators to give yet another accounting, this time to the faithful. Only donations of the faithful are mentioned as the subject of the report, and not all investments, sales of property, or other economic matters. However, the spirit of the canon is clearly a call for accountability of stewardship, both to the ordinary and to the faithful. The canon does not specify the means, the frequency, or the detail of that report to the public. It leaves all those matters to be determined by particular legislation. In many dioceses, the publishing of financial reports is usually accomplished in parishes by printing a copy of the report to the bishop either in full or more commonly in summary in the weekly parish bulletin. The diocesan report to the public is made in the diocesan newspaper, and it is composed of the annual consolidated audit of all the parishes and agencies of the diocese with an accompanying explanatory text from the diocesan bishop.

OBLIGATION OF THE DIOCESAN BISHOP TO REPORT

It can be noted that the code does not call for financial reporting by the diocese to be made to an external authority. While canon 399 requires the diocesan bishop to present a quinquennial report concerning the "state of the diocese" in conjunction with his *ad limina* visit every five years (unless the year set for presentation of this report falls entirely or in part within the first two-year period of his governance of the diocese), the canon does not specifically ask for any financial information, but leaves the form of the report to be determined by the Apostolic See. In practice, the current form for the quinquennial report issued by the Congregation for Bishops contains a section which asks for statistics and a narrative description of the financial state of the diocese. In addition, the Holy See requires dioceses to file annual statistical reports.

While there is no mandate for an external audit, the code sets up the diocesan finance committee as the internal auditor, requiring a careful review of all reports submitted to the diocese and by the diocese. Beyond this, civil law also has many things to say about financial responsibility and accountability.

An important area where the federal government has, in effect, delegated authority to the Church is the Group Ruling of the Internal Revenue Service, whereby tax exempt status is automatically granted to entities listed in the *Official Catholic Directory*. There are detailed rules from the IRS and instructions from the United States Catholic Conference which must be followed to ensure the tax exempt integrity of the listings in this book. An annual report to the diocesan bishop could be a helpful means to ascertain that organizations listed in the directory have maintained their tax-exempt characteristics. This is particularly crucial when entities such as schools and hospitals reorganize. For example, if such an organization is transferred from the canonical sponsorship of a religious institute to a self-governing lay board through a legitimate act of alienation, provision must be made for the new entity's relationship to ecclesiastical authority, such as through the establishment of a new public juridic person.

Canon law and civil law are not always totally in harmony with each other in the matter of ownership and accountability, in the concept of governance and the nature of religious authority. Different states see the diocese and its bishop in different ways. In some states, for example, the diocese is a corporation sole; in another state, it would be a corporation aggregate; in another, there is fee simple ownership; in another there is not civil incorporation but association status.

With two separate law systems that demand compliance, frequently more careful attention is paid to the civil laws regarding financial accountability, since there are civil consequences to consider. Therefore, reports to the federal and state government regarding taxes may be a greater concern to the administrator. Presumably the contentious atmosphere of the American legal system will not be as prevalent in the church's juridic structures.

In today's Church in the United States, the status of Catholic universities, colleges and hospitals vis-à-vis the diocesan bishop can get confused as religious orders change their manner of participation in those institutions – with obvious consequences regarding the accountability of those institutions.

While the relationship of public juridic persons and the diocesan bishop is carefully defined in canon law, in life that relationship is affected not only by the human individuals involved but also by federal and state laws and local ordinances, by civil law regarding contracts, imputability and oversight. The few canons in the code regarding reports to the diocesan bishop are important matters in the governance of the Church. They are, it is hoped, not obstacles but rather aids to bishop and administrator both in the fulfillment of their duties.

CHAPTER SIXTEEN

ORDINARY AND EXTRAORDINARY ADMINISTRATION

DAVID J. WALKOWIAK

CASE 25

The Diocese of Metropolis has an opportunity to buy an office building and its underlying parcel of land adjacent to the Diocesan Pastoral Center in downtown Metropolis. Office and meeting room space in the Diocesan Pastoral Center has been inadequate for a number of years not to mention the acute shortage of parking spaces for those who have business to conduct at the Pastoral Center.

CASE 26

The parish of Sacred Heart has experienced steady growth in the last twenty years. Parish leadership now wants to raise $2.5 million for the construction of an expanded worship facility, additional parish school of religion classrooms, meeting space, administration area, and expanded parking facilities.

The above initiatives may indeed present a unique opportunity, but also an extraordinary one, canonically speaking. Both the diocese and the parish are contemplating acts of extraordinary administration.

ACTS OF ADMINISTRATION

Canon law distinguishes three types of acts of administration: acts of ordinary administration; more important acts of administration; and acts of extraordinary administration. The canons of the *Code of Canon Law* do not define in detail, or describe, these categories. Acts of ordinary administration involve transactions and expenditures, which are considered to be necessary for the daily and routine operation and maintenance of the property, or work of the juridic person.

In the course of their duties, administrators generally perform routine ordinary acts of administration. In canonical tradition, commentators have understood ordinary administration to include actions, which occurred regularly, such as collection of debts, rents, interest, dividends; ordinary maintenance of church buildings, paying salaries, paying taxes, opening regular checking accounts, acceptance of ordinary donations; and leasing or renting church property for relatively short periods of time (fewer than nine years).[1]

More rarely, administrators perform acts, which are not ordinary, regularly occurring events and which of their nature are of greater importance. Significant actions exceeding routine administration and maintenance are considered to be of extraordinary administration. On July 21, 1856, the Sacred Congregation for the Propagation of the Faith issued an instruction listing acts which would be classified as exceeding the limits of ordinary administration. The listing included the following items:

- ◆ the acceptance or refusal of an inheritance or gift;

- ◆ the purchase of immovable property;

- ◆ the sale, exchange, or mortgage of immovable church property, or its subjection to any other servitude or burden;

- ◆ the sale, exchange, or mortgage of objects of art, historical documents or movable property of great importance;

- ◆ borrowing large sums of money as a temporary loan or entering into onerous contracts;

- ◆ building, tearing down, or rebuilding any church building or making extraordinary repairs on them;

- ◆ establishing a cemetery;

---

[1] John J. Myers, "The Temporal Goods of the Church," in *The Code of Canon Law: A Text and Commentary*, ed. James A. Coriden et al. (New York/Mahwah: Paulist Press, 1985) 874.

- the establishment or suppression of any parochial institution which is parish property;
- entering a lawsuit as litigant or defender.[2]

Although the list remains instructive even today, some of these actions would now be classified as acts of alienation and not of administration. The 1983 code would generally protect the sale, exchange, or the mortgaging of immovable church property or encumbering it in any way, under the procedures of alienation.

Canon 1277 states that "more important acts of administration" refer to transactions on behalf of the diocese. More important acts pertains to acts of administration for the juridic person of the diocese. Acts of administration of more importance are to be determined by the diocesan bishop in light of the economic condition of the diocese.

THE JURIDIC PERSON OF THE DIOCESE

Acts of Administration

1. Acts of Ordinary Administration

Canon 1277 deals with acts of diocesan administration but does not expressly speak of acts of ordinary administration. The canon's reference to acts of extraordinary administration, however, implies the existence of acts of ordinary administration, which canon 1281 expressly mentions. As implied above, ordinary administration involves actions, which are necessary for the day-to-day life of a juridic person and for the routine maintenance of its property. Acts of ordinary administration are considered a regular part of an administrator's responsibilities. The diocesan bishop, who is the canonical administrator of the juridic person of the diocese, does not need any authorization or the counsel nor consent of others in order to carry out such acts.

2. More Important Acts of Administration

Canon 1277 distinguishes a category of administrative acts known as more important acts of administration, which are not to be equated with acts of extraordinary administration: "The diocesan bishop must hear the finance council and

---

[2]S.C. de Prop. Fide, July 21, 1856 (Coll. S. C. P F., no. 1127; Fontes, no. 4841), cited in John A. Abbo and Jerome D. Hannan, *The Sacred Canons: A Concise Presentation of the Current Disciplinary Norms of the Church*, (St. Louis: B. Herder Book Co., 1952) 2: 731.

college of consultors to place acts of administration which are more important in light of the economic condition of the diocese." The criterion for determining such an act is the economic condition of the diocese. Actions, which are of more importance for one diocese may not necessarily be classified as such for another diocese, due to factors such as size and resources and the nature of the transaction. For example, the economic circumstances of a very populous diocese within a small geographic area will undoubtedly lead to a list of more important acts of administration which differs from the list for a territorially vast, sparsely populated diocese with far fewer financial resources.

The code does not specify the manner for determining which acts of administration are the more important ones. Nevertheless, the law expects that this determination will be made. The diocesan bishop, ideally with the assistance of his advisors, for example, the diocesan finance council and the college of consultors, must determine precisely what these more important acts are.

To carry out a more important act of administration, the diocesan bishop must consult the diocesan finance council (c. 492; see chapter twelve) and the college of consultors (c. 502). While the diocesan bishop is not obligated to follow the advice given by these groups; nevertheless, he should not act contrary to their recommendation, especially when there is unanimity or a consensus, without a compelling reason to do so (see c. 127, §2, 2°).

Failure to consult the diocesan finance council and the college of consultors regarding a more important act of administration would render the action invalid. Such canonical invalidity could have repercussions in the forum of civil law. It is not uncommon today for juridic persons and their sponsored institutions to be civilly incorporated with guarantees that canon law will be observed in all their activities.

3. Acts of Extraordinary Administration

The diocesan bishop needs the consent of the diocesan finance council and that of the college of consultors in order to perform acts of extraordinary administration besides cases specifically mentioned in universal law or in the charter of a foundation (c. 1277).

Three types of acts require the diocesan bishop to obtain the consent of the diocesan finance council and the college of consultors before he can perform them:

1) acts of extraordinary administration;

2) cases specifically mentioned in universal law; and

3) cases mentioned in the charter of a foundation.

Regarding the first set of actions, it belongs to the competence of the conference of bishops to define for its territory what is meant by acts of extraordinary administration. As examples of acts of the second type, although they are not acts of administration (where the universal law requires the consent of these two diocesan groups), one could mention acts of alienation (c. 1292) and any transactions, which could worsen the patrimonial condition of a juridic person (c. 1295). As for acts of the third type (cases mentioned in the charter of a foundation where consent is required), such requirements would be found in the statutes governing each foundation.

4. The Conference of Bishops and Complementary Norms Regarding Canon 1277

The conference of bishops determines acts of extraordinary administration for the dioceses within its territory as stated in canon 1277. On June 27, 1986, the National Conference of Catholic Bishops (NCCB) promulgated for the United States its complementary norms in accordance with canon 1277. The norms list six things to be considered as acts of extraordinary administration for the diocesan bishop.[3] One could note that four of these actions are already covered in the code under the title dealing with contracts and alienation – actions, which technically are not acts of administration. The 1986 complementary norms can now be seen to have been preliminary in nature and stand in need of reformulation. Moreover, since the NCCB decree apparently did not obtain the *recognitio* (review) from the Holy See, currently in the United States there are no complementary norms to implement canon 1277.

---

[3]The 1986 complementary norms listed as acts of extraordinary administration for dioceses the following transactions:

1) to alienate (in the strict sense, convey or transfer ownership) goods of the stable patrimony when the value exceeds the minimum limit (c. 1292, §1);

2) to alienate goods donated to the Church through a vow, or to alienate goods that are especially valuable due to their artistic or historic value regardless of the appraised value (c. 1292, §2);

3) to incur indebtedness (without corresponding increase in the assets of the diocese) that exceeds the minimum limit (c. 1295);

4) to encumber stable patrimony the value of which exceeds the minimum limit (c. 1295);

5) to lease church property when the annual lease income exceeds the minimum limit (c. 1297);

6) to lease church property when the value of the leased property exceeds the minimum and the lease is for more than nine (9) years. National Conference of Catholic Bishops, *Implementation of the 1983 Code of Canon Law: Complementary Norms* (Washington: United States Catholic Conference, 1991) 21. **Editors' Note:** The issue of whether or not the complementary norms for extraordinary administration have been approved by the Holy See has been debated by many canonists. The editors wish to state that while some authors indicate that the complementary norms have not received the *recognitio* of the Holy See, the National Conference of Catholic Bishops General Secretariat indicates that the complementary norm are approved where required and are the norm of law in this Episcopal Conference.

PROCEDURES

Ordinary Administration

The diocesan bishop needs no explicit permission to perform acts of ordinary administration.[4]

More Important Acts of Administration

Before proceeding with an act of administration of more importance, the diocesan bishop must convene the diocesan finance council and the college of consultors and seek their advice (c. 1277).

Extraordinary Administration

The Holy See has not given the *recognitio* for any complementary norms to be issued by the NCCB setting forth what is meant by acts of extraordinary administration for dioceses in the United States. If, however, such complementary norms did exist, before proceeding with an act of extraordinary administration, the diocesan bishop would be required to convene the diocesan finance council and the college of consultors and obtain their consent (c. 1277).

---

[4] What is stated of the diocesan bishop can be delegated to the diocesan finance officer for acts of ordinary administration.

FORMULARY 10:
Suggested Checklist: The Juridic Person Of The Diocese

More Important Acts of Administration

1. Notice of meeting should be sent to each member of the consultative groups whose advice must be obtained.

2. Documentation to be submitted to the consultative groups (in advance of the meeting at which the matter will be discussed):

    ◆ Description of the proposed transaction: the parties involved; explanation of the reasons for the proposed transaction
    ◆ Copy of the legal instrument/contract (if applicable)
    ◆ Appraisals of the value of the property in question (if applicable, at least two)
    ◆ Statement regarding civil law aspects of the proposed transaction
    ◆ Assessment of transaction upon the stable patrimony of the diocese
    ◆ Financial statement of diocese

3. Since consultation is required, the diocesan bishop must convene the appropriate groups (e.g., diocesan finance council and consultors) and seek their advice. For the validity of the proposed action, the counsel of all who are present must be obtained (cc. 127, §1 and 166, §3).

4. As proof of consultation, a copy of the minutes of the meeting where the matter in question was discussed will verify that the consultative groups were called and gave their advice.

5. If the diocesan bishop decides to proceed with the proposed act of administration, he must carefully preserve the documents and records surrounding the transaction process in the archive of the diocesan curia (cc. 486, §4; 1284, §2, 9°).

Acts of Extraordinary Administration

The checklist remains the same as above, except that the appropriate groups must give their consent rather than advice.

CASE STUDY APPLICATION AND SAMPLE DOCUMENTS

At present, the NCCB has not issued complementary norms implementing canon 1277, which determine acts of extraordinary administration for dioceses in its territory. Therefore, for the purpose of the case study found at the beginning of this chapter, the diocese of Metropolis has determined that the following are to be considered as more important acts of administration in light of the economic condition of the diocese, as understood in canon 1277:

♦ The purchase of real estate

♦ All acts which involve an expenditure in excess of $250,000.

JURIDIC PERSONS SUBJECT TO THE DIOCESAN BISHOP

Acts of Administration

Unlike the juridic person of the diocese, only two categories of acts of administration exist for public juridic persons subject to the diocesan bishop: ordinary and extraordinary.[5]

1. Acts of Ordinary Administration

Canon 1281 speaks of acts of ordinary administration but does not define them or give any criteria for determining which actions of an administrator are of an ordinary nature. As noted above, ordinary administration involves actions, which are necessary for the day-to-day life of a public juridic person and for the regular maintenance of its property. The administrator of a juridic person subject to the diocesan bishop does not need any special authorization in order to carry out such acts.

2. Acts of Extraordinary Administration

"Without prejudice to the prescripts of the statutes, administrators invalidly place acts which exceed the limits and manner of ordinary administration unless they have first obtained a written faculty from the ordinary" (c. 1281, §1).

Administrators cannot act on their own authority when they propose to go

---

[5] Other public juridic persons might provide otherwise, such as a religious institute in its constitutions.

beyond the limits and procedures of ordinary, day-to-day administration.[6] They need the prior written permission of the appropriate ordinary. Failure to obtain prior written permission renders invalid the proposed act of extraordinary administration. The ordinary mentioned in canon 1281, §1 primarily refers to the diocesan bishop but also includes the vicar general or an episcopal vicar who has been entrusted with this area of administrative oversight (see cc. 134, §1; and 479).[7]

The acts which go beyond the limits and procedures of ordinary administration are to be defined in the statutes of the juridic person (c. 1281, §2). Acts of extraordinary administration for juridic persons other than the diocese are determined by means of their statutes (c. 94). The statutes identify those acts, which are to be considered as of extraordinary administration. It is important that all juridic persons should have approved statutes, which refer to matters of ordinary and extraordinary administration. Transactions which are ordinary for one juridic person would not necessarily be ordinary for another juridic person, depending on the size of the juridic person or the nature of its activities. For example, should wealthy and poor parishes have the same standards for acts of extraordinary administration? Parishes could have individual statutes reflecting the reality of their economic condition.

The 1983 code states: " … if the statutes are silent in this regard, however, the diocesan bishop is competent to determine such acts for the persons subject to him, after having heard the finance council" (c. 1281, §2). When the statutes of a juridic person fail to determine which acts are of extraordinary administration, the diocesan bishop is competent to decide (in consultation with the diocesan finance council) what constitute acts of extraordinary administration for public juridic persons subject to him. Acts of extraordinary administration are those which because of the nature or importance of the act itself, or its financial value, require the permission of a higher authority. Examples of extraordinary acts include those acts which do not occur on a regular basis, such as purchase of land, construction of new buildings or extensive repair of buildings, expenditures over a designated financial amount, refusal of major bequests, purchase or replacement of major equipment, and the dedication of surplus funds. The list of acts con-

[6]Every public juridic person has an administrator responsible for the management of its affairs and the administration of its property (c. 1279, §1). Administrators of juridic persons subject to the diocesan bishop include figures such as pastors, the moderator of a team of priests entrusted with the care of a parish, the priest supervisor of parishes without a pastor, and moderators of public associations of the Christian faithful (cc. 532; 543, §3; and 517, §2).
[7]The term *ordinary* can also include, for example, the major superiors of clerical religious institutes of pontifical right and societies of apostolic life and pontifical right.

tained in the 1856 instruction of the Sacred Congregation for the Propagation of the Faith could prove to be helpful in making such a determination.

A parish is a familiar example of a juridic person, which is subject to the diocesan bishop. In many dioceses, the diocesan bishop has established a monetary limit for authorized expenditures for parishes. Such a determination functions as the bishop's provision when the statutes referred to in canon 1281 do not specify matters.

PROCEDURES: THE PARISH

For the sake of illustrating the procedures to be followed by a public juridic person which is subject to the diocesan bishop in an act of extraordinary administration, we will use the juridic person of the parish.

Ordinary Administration

Before proceeding with an act of administration, the pastor needs to determine whether the parish has statutes, which determine the limits of ordinary administration, or whether the diocesan bishop, after consulting the diocesan finance council, has set the limits of ordinary administration for parishes in the diocese.

The pastor needs no explicit permission from the diocesan bishop to perform acts of ordinary administration, provided the other relevant diocesan norms have been observed.

Extraordinary Administration

The pastor needs written authorization from the competent ordinary to proceed with an act of extraordinary administration. Administrators act invalidly if they perform acts of extraordinary administration without prior written permission of the ordinary. Without this permission, the action is null and void, and perhaps also in the civil forum as well.

Before the pastor seeks this permission, he may have to convene the parish finance council and seek its advice regarding the proposed action.[8] For example, the bishop could determine cases in which the pastor needs to consult the finance council for the validity of a particular act of administration. The finance council's competency, then, could well include advising on all acts of extraordinary administration.

---

[8] The parish finance council assists the pastor in the administration of the parish property (see chapter twelve). The duties of the parish finance council should be spelled out by norms issued by the diocesan bishop (see c. 537).

Diocesan statutes may additionally require the pastor to consult with the parish pastoral council. Generally speaking, consulting the parish pastoral council regarding a presumably important matter such as an act of extraordinary administration might prove both prudent and beneficial. In fact, a parish-wide consultation may at times be very helpful in enlisting support for an administrative matter of great importance.

PERMISSION OF THE ORDINARY

The ordinary must give his permission for a parish to perform an act of extraordinary administration (c. 1281, §1). He may turn over such a request to his legal, financial and canonical advisors and receive from them a recommendation, which he can freely accept or reject. When the ordinary has given permission to proceed, he communicates this permission to the pastor by means of a letter notarized by an ecclesiastical notary.

CASE STUDY APPLICATION AND SAMPLE DOCUMENTS

In the case study proposed at the beginning of this chapter, the proposed act of administration involves the raising of a large sum of money to build new buildings and expand existing facilities. For the purposes of the case study, the following diocesan norms will be operative.

For the Parish

The following norms pertain to acts of extraordinary administration:

> The pastor should write to the diocesan bishop requesting preliminary approval to initiate a consultation process with appropriate parish groups regarding any major parish project.

> Expenditures in excess of a specified amount are to be considered acts of extraordinary administration for parishes and other entities subject to the diocesan bishop. At present, the pastor must obtain the permission of the diocesan bishop when the proposed cost for capital purchases, leases and contracts exceeds $10,000 or 1% of the total parish gross income, whichever is greater.

For the Parish Finance Council

The pastor is to consult with the parish finance council on matters of major financial and legal concern.

1. Consultation is required with the finance council for the proposed acquisition or alienation (transfer of ownership) of parish property.

2. Consultation is required with the finance council when the proposed cost for capital purchases, leases and contracts exceeds $10,000 or 1% of the total parish gross income, whichever is greater.

3. Consultation is required with the finance council regarding the financial feasibility of proposals and projected resources to support the projects and the expected support of the parish pastoral council and other parish groups.

For the Parish Pastoral Council

The pastor is to consult with the parish pastoral council concerning the pastoral aspects of matters of major financial concern.

Sample letters will illustrate how to proceed with the set of circumstances found in this case study (see Formularies 11, 12, 13, 14).

Civil Law Considerations

The legal office of the diocese or its attorneys should examine for its civil law implications every proposed act of extraordinary administration for the diocese and its parishes (plus any other juridic persons subject to the diocesan bishop). Examples of possible kinds of legal concerns include zoning issues, environmental regulations, ensuring that proper building permits are obtained, health and safety regulations, and examination of legal instruments for completeness and accuracy.

FORMULARY 11:

Sample Letter Setting up Meetings for Required Canonical Consultation

To: The Members of the Diocesan Finance Council
           The Members of the College of Consultors

From: Diocesan Finance Officer

Date: _____, _____

Re: Notice of meeting to discuss the purchase of real property
           located at 123 Main Street

The members of the respective consultative groups are hereby requested to attend a meeting to discuss a proposal, which requires their advice.

The Diocesan Finance Council will discuss this matter at its next meeting at 7:30 p.m., on Tuesday, September 29, 1998, in Meeting Room A of the Diocesan Pastoral Center.

The College of Consultors will discuss this matter at its next meeting at 7:30 p.m., on Thursday, October 1, 1998, in Meeting Room A of the Diocesan Pastoral Center.

Please make every effort to attend this important meeting. If you have any questions or need additional information, please do not hesitate to call the Diocesan Finance Office.

****

The following information is provided to assist the Diocesan Finance Council and the College of Consultors in their deliberations regarding the purchase of the real property at 123 Main Street, Metropolis, State.

The Diocese of Metropolis intends to purchase the Gordon Office Building and its underlying land parcel located at 123 Main Street, Metropolis, State. Pursuant to the provisions of canon 1277 and in light of determinations made by the diocesan bishop, the purchase of the real property in question is to be considered a more important act of administration. The Bishop of Metropolis must seek the advice of the Diocesan Finance Council and the College of Consultors.

The seller of the real property is the Keenan Company, a corporation, which buys and sells real estate.

There are good reasons for purchasing the land and building. Office space and meeting room facilities are badly needed. Moreover, the parking spaces avail-

FORMULARY 11:
continued

able on the property will increase the number of spaces available for Diocesan Pastoral Center visitors and employees.

The terms of the sale are delineated in the purchase agreement, a copy of which is attached as Exhibit A. The purchase price is $ 2,220,000.

The relevant value of this property in this determination is the fair market value. The relevant portions of an appraisal of this property are attached hereto as Exhibit B, and indicate an estimate of the fair market value. A second appraisal is included herein and labeled as Exhibit C. Inspection of the building found it to be in good condition.

A careful study of these appraisals in view of the economic condition of the Diocese of Metropolis suggests that the purchase will not endanger the stable patrimony of the Diocese. The financial statement attached as Exhibit D indicates that the Diocese is in sound financial condition. The Diocese has sufficient funds on hand to cover this purchase.

FORMULARY 12:

Sample Letter of Pastor to Bishop Requesting Permission to Initiate Consultation Process

Most Reverend Bishop
Bishop of Metropolis

May 27, 1998

Dear Bishop,

I am writing to request permission to initiate a consultation process with the appropriate consultative groups and parishioners of Sacred Heart Church regarding the following project.

Sacred Heart Church needs to expand its facilities. As you know, the parish has experienced tremendous growth in the last twenty years. To address current and future needs, the parish leadership has begun to consider plans for the construction of an expanded worship facility, additional parish school of religion classrooms, meeting space, administration area, and expanded parking facilities. A preliminary estimate of the amount of money needed to complete this project, amounts to roughly $2.5 million.

If this initiative meets with your preliminary approval, I will begin meeting with the parish finance council and the parish pastoral council. At the appropriate time I will publish bulletin announcements regarding the details of the expansion project. Finally, I would schedule a parish "town hall" meeting to give parishioners an opportunity to voice their opinions. It is my belief that the parish community will enthusiastically embrace this proposal after all the formal information has been gathered and reviewed.

Please let me know if you need any further information at this time. I would be happy to meet with you if you would find it to be helpful. Thank you for your consideration of this request.

Sincerely yours in Christ,

Reverend N.
Pastor
Sacred Heart Parish

FORMULARY 13:

Sample Memorandum of Pastor to Consultative Groups

To: Members of the Parish Finance Council;
Members of the Parish Pastoral Council
From: Your Pastor
Date: December 22, 1998
Re: Notice of Meetings to Discuss "Building in Faith Together" Project

The following information is provided to assist you in your deliberations regarding the parish expansion project as described below. Diocesan regulations require that I, as your pastor, must formally consult with you, the members of the parish finance council and parish pastoral council, about the final outline of this important project.

I ask you to review the enclosed material and be prepared to share your opinions at the following meetings.

The Parish Finance Council will discuss this matter at its next meeting at 7:30 p.m., on Tuesday, September 29, 1998, in the meeting room in the basement of the rectory.

The Parish Pastoral Council will discuss this matter at its next meeting at 7:30 p.m., on Wednesday, September 30, 1998, in the meeting room in the basement of the rectory.

Please make every effort to attend this important meeting. If you have any questions or need additional information, please do not hesitate to call me. Thank you very much for your attention to this matter of great importance for the financial well being of our parish.

The Proposal

The Building in Faith Together Campaign

There are good reasons for expanding Sacred Heart's facilities at this time. Eighteen years ago Sacred Heart Parish started with 200 families worshipping in the gym of the local middle school. Today the parish numbers more than 1300 families and is still expanding. Currently there are twenty-five parish organizations serving the needs of the parishioners and others in the neighborhood. Quite simply, the existing facilities cannot meet the increased demands of parish life.

FORMULARY 13:

continued

The parish community plans to raise $2.5 million through the *Building in Faith Together Campaign* for the construction of an expanded worship facility, additional parish school of religion classrooms, meeting space, administration area, and expanded parking facilities. After contacting three fundraising companies, the parish finance council has recommended that ABC Company, a nationally known fundraising firm, be selected to work with the Sacred Heart Parish community over the next three years to raise the necessary funds. It is projected that sufficient funds will be raised to complete the project.

The major portion of the campaign will help expand the church's worship and educational facilities. Plans for the church include the renovation and expansion of existing space to create a larger sanctuary and gathering place after Mass. The larger church will increase its seating capacity from 400 to 700 people. There will be a new Eucharistic chapel for reservation and adoration of the Blessed Sacrament, while the choir area will be expanded to include 50 new seats. A permanent baptismal font is also planned, as well as a new sound system and additional parking.

The parish school of religion now numbers more than 250 children. Nine new classrooms will be created by renovating, and expanding the current lower level of the existing building. These classrooms will be used for religious education and as meeting rooms for other ministries and community activities.

A public meeting for all parishioners was held on Friday, August 14th. Those in attendance were quite supportive. A few concerns were raised concerning some aspects of the church renovation, but the architect was able to give satisfactory answers.

The attached financial statement of the parish indicates that the parish financial condition is sound. It can be projected that the parish will be able to mount a successful fundraising campaign and that parishioners will be able to pay down their pledges in a timely manner without jeopardizing the financial condition of the parish.

The Diocesan Legal Office and parish attorney have reviewed the legal aspects of the proposed renovation and building plans and have offered an opinion that all legal requirements can be successfully fulfilled.

FORMULARY 14:

Sample Letter of Pastor to Bishop Formally Requesting
Permission for Act of Extraordinary Administration

Most Reverend Bishop
Bishop of Metropolis

October 3, 1998

Dear Bishop,

I am writing formally to request your permission to proceed with the following act of extraordinary administration.

Sacred Heart Parish community plans to raise $2.5 million through its *Building in Faith Together Campaign* for the construction of an expanded worship facility, additional parish school of religion classrooms, meeting space, administration area, and expanded parking facilities. The parish finance council has selected the ABC Company, a nationally known fundraising firm, to work with the Sacred Heart Parish community over the next three years to raise the necessary funds.

In accordance with diocesan procedures, Sacred Heart Parish sought and obtained permission to initiate a consultation process within the parish regarding this proposal (see Exhibit A, Letter from Bishop to Pastor, June 1, 1998, prot. no. 445/1998).

The attached financial statement of the parish indicates that the parish financial condition is sound. It can be projected that the parish will be able to mount a successful fundraising campaign and that parishioners will be able to pay down their pledges in a timely manner without jeopardizing the financial condition of the parish.

In regard to civil law considerations, our parish attorney, in consultation with the Diocesan Legal Office, has carefully studied the issues arising from the proposed renovation and building expansion. They have given a positive legal opinion regarding the project.

The documentation included in this file was sent to the members of the finance council and parish pastoral council in advance of the meeting at which this proposal was discussed. The Parish Finance Council discussed this matter at its

FORMULARY 14:

continued

meeting on Tuesday, September 29, 1998. The Parish Pastoral Council discussed this matter at its meeting on Wednesday, September 30, 1998. Both groups shared their opinions openly and recommended proceeding with the Building in Faith Together Campaign. A copy of the minutes of these meetings where the matter was discussed the required consultation given is included as Exhibits C and D.

On Friday, August 14th, a public meeting was held for all parishioners and other interested parties. Those in attendance were very supportive. Copies of the bulletin announcements are included as Exhibit E.

After carefully weighing the information received from these consultations and other sources, I now formally request your permission for Sacred Heart Parish to begin its Building in Faith Together Campaign. Please do not hesitate to call me if you have need of further information.

In the name of the people of the Sacred Heart Parish, I thank you for your consideration of this request.

Sincerely yours in Christ,

Reverend N.
Pastor
Sacred Heart Parish

*Sample Letter of Bishop to Pastor Giving Permission
for an Act of Extraordinary Administration*

Most Reverend Bishop
Bishop of Metropolis

Reverend N.
Pastor
Sacred Heart Parish

October 10, 1998
Protocol Number

Dear Father N,

I have received your letter requesting permission for Sacred Heart to begin a major fundraising campaign for the renovation and expansion of the parish facilities. It is my understanding that the ABC Company will assist you in running the Building in Faith Together Campaign, whose goal is to raise $2.5 million.

I have reviewed with my financial, legal, and canonical advisors the very complete and helpful documentation, which accompanied your petition. In view of the information received and the advice given, I hereby grant Sacred Heart Parish permission to inaugurate its Building in Faith Together Campaign for the purpose of renovating and expanding the existing parish facilities. I ask you kindly to remain in close communication with the Diocesan Legal Office throughout the length of this project.

Wishing you and your parish community every success in this endeavor, I am

Sincerely yours in Christ,

Bishop of Metropolis

Notary

FORMULARY 16:

Suggested Checklist: The Juridic Person of the Parish

1. The pastor writes to the diocesan bishop, outlining the shape of the proposal and requesting preliminary permission to continue to explore the proposal and to initiate a consultation process with appropriate parochial groups. (This first item is not a canonical requirement, but it may be a prudent measure, especially if the proposed act may be somewhat controversial.)

2. The pastor must follow the statutes or diocesan norms established for parishes, parish finance councils, and parish pastoral councils.

3. Notice of the meeting should be sent to each member of the consultative groups who must be heard or whose consent must be obtained (if applicable).

4. Documentation should be submitted to the consultative groups in advance of the meeting at which the matter will be discussed:

   ♦ Description of the proposed action: the parties involved; rationale for the proposed action;

   ♦ Copy of the legal instrument/contract (if applicable);

   ♦ Written appraisals of property involved in the transaction (if applicable);

   ♦ A statement regarding civil law considerations for the proposed action;

   ♦ Projected impact of the action on the patrimonial condition of the parish;

   ♦ Financial statement of the parish;

   ♦ A statement of how other requirements prescribed by particular law have been observed.

5. If consultation or consent is required, the pastor must convene the appropriate groups (e.g., the parish finance council) and seek their advice or obtain their consent. For the validity of the proposed action, the counsel or consent of all who are present must be obtained (cc. 127, §1; 166, §§1 and 3).

6. The consultation process might include announcements in the parish bulletin regarding the details of the proposed act of extraordinary administration. Depending upon the transaction in question, it might be prudent to conduct an open meeting to give parishioners an opportunity to voice their opinions.

7. After carefully weighing the information received from these consultations, the pastor decides whether to petition the diocesan bishop for permission to proceed with the proposed action.

8. The pastor must prepare and forward to the diocesan bishop documentation concerning the proposed action (c. 1281, §1). The documentary file for the diocesan bishop includes all of the above information. Required consultation or the consent of the relevant consultative groups should be verified by a copy of the minutes of the meeting where the matter was discussed.

9. If the diocesan bishop gives permission for the act of extraordinary administration, the pastor must carefully preserve the documents and records of the transaction process in the parish archive (cc. 535, §4; and 1284, §2, 9°).

CHAPTER SEVENTEEN

LEASING ECCLESIASTICAL GOODS

NICHOLAS P. CAFARDI

CASE 27

When St. A's inner city parish was founded, it held all of its religious services in a rehabilitated theater. Eventually the parish, as it grew and became more established, raised sufficient funds to build its own church structure. When it moved into the new church, it did not divest itself of ownership of the old theater building, but kept it for parish activities and for rental purposes as a way to make some additional cash for the parish.

In 1996, the pastor rents the theater, on an exclusive long-term, five-year lease to a national film distributing organization for one hundred thousand dollars a year. The first two years of the lease go well; the film company shows mostly PG movies and pays its rent on time. In the third year of the lease, the film company starts to show mostly PG-13 and R-rated films. One particular R-rated movie about a priest losing his vocation causes an uproar in the parish. The pastor writes to the film company complaining about their choice of films. The film company responds to the pastor that, if the company is to pay their rent, they must show movies that sell tickets. The pastor says, over my dead body, and rips up the lease. What permissions did the pastor need to enter into the lease? Can he legally tear up the lease?

CASE 28

St. B's Parish is a brand-new suburban parish with a very attractive physical plant, encompassing a new church and rectory, a school building and a parish activities center. The parish activities center has become a very popular place to hold parish weddings. The parish rents out the center, only to parishioners, for this purpose. The parish does not provide food or drink, but does provide a list of "approved" caterers who are permitted by the parish to provide these services. Parishioners using the center for weddings must separately contract with one of these caterers for their food and drinks at the wedding.

At the O family wedding, a guest is served too much alcohol. On his way home from the wedding, he collides with another car when he ignores a stop sign. The people in the other car are severely injured. In their suit for damages, they name the driver, the catering company and the parish? Is the parish liable?

WHAT IS A LEASE?

A lease is a contract from an owner of property to another party that grants *exclusive* possession of the property to the other party for a specified period of time in exchange for some consideration or payment. At the end of the lease, the exclusive right to possess the leased property reverts to the owner unless otherwise specified.

In the American legal system, we can lease both real and personal property. In the lease of real property, the owner is called either a landlord, rentor or lessor and the other party is called the tenant, rentee or lessee. In the lease of personal property, it is inappropriate to use the terms landlord and tenant, since they refer specifically to interests in real estate. So when we are referring to leases of personal property, we are limited to the terms rentor/rentee or lessor/lessee.

CANONICAL PRINCIPLES

In the 1983 *Code of Canon Law*, there are two canons on leases: canons 1297 and 1298, which specify, respectively, that it is for the national bishops' conference to establish norms for the leasing of church goods (c. 1297) and that, except for objects of little importance, no church goods are to be leased out to their own administrators or close relatives of those administrators (up to the fourth degree), unless a higher authority has approved.

Although we are used to thinking of leases only in terms of real estate, the code does not limit the term to that usage. In both canons 1297 and 1298, the object of the lease is referred to as *bona ecclesiastica*, church goods, a term that is broad enough to cover both real estate and personal property. As a result, the canonical norms on leases are applicable whether the church property being leased is real estate or personal property. In other words, the canonical language is broad enough that the rules on leases could cover both the rental of a building or the rental of computers or the rental of computer programs.

A lease is not a form of alienation. Nor is a lease considered as a canon 1295 transaction (one capable of worsening the patrimonial status of a juridic person). Leases are characterized and treated differently from both these transactions in the 1983 code, and the rules for these transactions do not normally apply to leases. Some canonists might disagree that a lease is not a canon 1295 transaction on the grounds that leases are capable of worsening patrimonial condition, and therefore could be covered by canon 1295. However, in canons 1297 and 1298, the code puts leases into a separate category that is to be covered by legislation established by national episcopal conferences.

In the former code, leases were also distinguished from alienations, and the former code had an extensive set of norms for leases. These norms are not carried over into the present code which replaces the prior detail in the universal law with canon 1297, that simply empowers the national bishops' conference to create leasing norms for its territory. Unfortunately, in the United States, the NCCB has yet to act on this mandate concerning the establishment of national norms. As indicated above, the language of the universal law is such that when it does come to issuing its norms on leases, the NCCB would be within its authority to issue norms that cover both real estate and personal property.

The NCCB has dealt with leases in another area, however. In issuing norms pursuant to canon 1277, which allocates to episcopal conferences the right to define acts of extraordinary administration for its territory, the NCCB has specified that leases of church property in which the annual lease income exceeds the minimum amount ($500,000) and leases of church property whose value exceeds the minimum amount and whose term is for more than nine years are to be considered acts of extraordinary administration. Moreover, the *recognitio* (review) of the Apostolic See has yet to be received for the NCCB's action on canon 1277. To date, however, there are no NCCB norms specifically on leasing, and the canon 1277 norms have not themselves received the *recognitio* of the Holy See.

Pursuant to the NCCB's canon 1277 norms (whose legal effect is in doubt, given the lack of the Holy See's *recognitio*) leases of church property where the annual lease income is more than $500,000, and leases of church property valued at more than $500,000 for periods of more than nine years would be considered acts of extraordinary administration. According, to canon 1277, an act of extraordinary administration by the diocese, or any public juridic person subject to the authority of the diocesan bishop, e.g., parishes, requires the consent of the diocesan finance council and the consent of the college of consultors.

SOME CIVIL LAW ISSUES

Since a lease is a form of contract, canon 1290 is also applicable to all leases. That canon specifies that whatever the civil law of a country specifies about contracts will be given the same effect by canon law, unless the civil law is contrary to divine law or canon law. Canon 1290 in effect makes American civil law applicable to all leases of church property. Since property law is normally a question of state and not federal law, this means that leases of church property must conform to the law of the state where the property is located unless state law is contrary to canon law or divine law.

This presents some interesting possibilities. For example, a lease of real estate for more than thirty years (the term will vary by state, but most states have similar laws) is treated as a conveyance in Pennsylvania. It must be recorded as a deed, and the transfer tax must be paid just as if title has passed. Does this civil law make a lease of real estate for more than thirty years into a canonical alienation? A good argument could be made that it does, in which cases alienation approval (depending on the value of the real estate) must be sought.

While it is difficult to think of many situations where a state law might be contrary to church law or divine law, there are a number of civil law cases in states with fair housing ordinances where the lessor's religious beliefs were not a viable defense when fines were levied against the lessor for failure to lease property to unmarried or homosexual couples, groups that were protected by the local fair housing ordinance. There are no instances of a Church, as opposed to individual lessors, being held liable for fair housing violations when it refused to lease property to unmarried or homosexual couples, and the one case that is of record upheld a Midwest archdiocese's decision to evict Dignity, the Catholic homosexual group, from its Newman Center, on religious grounds.

Federal law, to the extent it is applicable to leases, will impact in this same area of non-discrimination, since there are federal laws prohibiting discrimination in housing rentals on the basis of race, sex (but not sexual orientation), ethnic origin, age, religion and handicapped status. The 1964 Federal Civil Rights Act, which is the source of this prohibition, however, exempts churches from its coverage. Church-related institutions do not share this blanket exemption, however.

One area of the law common to all states is that leases of real estate for more than a certain period of time must be in writing to be enforceable. By virtue of canon 1290, this type of requirement has canonical force as well. The common law rule (called the Statute of Frauds) specified that this requirement of a written lease applied to all leases of real estate for periods of more than one year. Some states have simply repeated this requirement in their statutes; other states have lengthened it, for example, Pennsylvania, which requires leases of real estate for three years or more to be in writing, signed by both parties, to be legally enforceable. Since this is a matter of local law, this is a question for local legal counsel.

Of course, every well-drafted lease, whether for real estate or personalty, will include a clear statement of the length (term) of the lease, together with a clear identification of the parties, lessor and lessee, a clear description of the leased property, a clear statement of what the lease payments are and where, when and how they are to be paid, a clear statement of how the leased property will be used by the lessee, how and by whom it will be maintained, where the risk of loss (duty to insure) lies for a partial or total loss of the property, which party is responsible for the maintenance, utilities and property taxes. A tax clause placing the burden of local real estate taxes on the lessee is very important in leases of church property because typically church property, prior to the lease, when it is being used only by the Church, is in the tax exempt category but its use by a non-church party, the lessee, will place it in the taxable category. If this happens, the lease should make it clear that such tax burden falls on the lessee as a cost of leasing the property.

The lease should also state what the parties' remedies are if the other side fails to perform, if, for example, the landlord does not provide habitable premises or if the tenant does not pay the rent. In respect to leases of real estate, especially dwelling places, all of the states have legislation covering the types of available remedy and how procedurally they are to be obtained. Again, this is a matter for local legal counsel.

In leases where the Church is the lessor, it is also prudent to include language that the lessee is mindful of the religious nature of the lessor and that it agrees to use the property in such a way that it will not cause public harm to the good religious name of the lessor. The lease should specify that should such an eventuality come to pass a material breach has occurred and, in the lessor's sole discretion, the lease may be terminated by the lessor. Leases tie two completely unrelated parties together for the term of the lease, and when one of these parties is the Church it makes sense that the terms of the lease allow the Church to protect its good name in the community. It could happen, for example, that a parish allows a local theater group to use the parish school gym for its summer theater season. This transaction would normally take the form of a lease. The lease should have language that allows the parish to immediately end the lease, without any further liability to the lessee, if the theater company, the lessee, begins performing plays that cause damage in the local community to the parish's good name. This language should be up-front, should be specific, should be brought to the attention of the lessee as part of the negotiation process, and should be non-negotiable. Such language might read as follows:

> Lessor and Lessee hereby acknowledge the fact that Lessor is, and always has been identified as, a nonprofit entity operating within the Roman Catholic tradition of charitable works, and that Lessor's reputation as such is of primary importance to it. As a result of the importance of this reputation to Lessor, Lessee agrees that, as a material term and condition of this lease, it will not act in any way, either within or without the lease relationship herein established, to cause damage to Lessor's religious reputation. If, in Lessor's reasonable exercise of its sole discretion, Lessee does act in such a way that its association with the Lessor, through this Lease Agreement, causes public damage to Lessor's religious reputation, within the community served by it, Lessor may terminate this Lease Agreement as if a material breach has occurred.

Obviously, local legal counsel must be consulted in drafting any lease, and the above language is not offered as legal advice but simply as something to discuss with potential lessees of church property and with local counsel.

LICENSES, NOT LEASES

Most leases of church property are not really leases because they do not involve the exclusive use of the church's property by the lessee for an extended period of time. The wedding party that rents the church hall, the local dance club that rents the parish gym, the Boy Scouts or Girls scouts that meet in the school after school hours, the local little league or soccer league that uses the parish ball field are not leasing the property. Their use of the property is not exclusive – that is to say they are not the only ones entitled to use the property – and the use is not for an extended period, but only for a few hours for a single occasion or perhaps repeated occasions.

In such situations, the party using the church premises should not be granted a lease, but rather a license. A license is simply permission from the owner to another party to enter onto the owner's premises and to use the property for a limited period of time, without any exclusive possessory interest being granted to the user. A license is simply permission to enter and use. Since licenses are not leases, they are not covered by the code's language on leases. A license is a contract, however, and as such is covered by canon 1290, which requires conformity to the civil law in contractual matters.

While licenses may be oral, and very often are, the prudent steward of church property will put all licenses into a writing signed by both parties. The license will have many of the details of a lease as specified above. Perhaps the most important part of any license agreement involving church property will be the insurance provisions. Weddings where alcohol is served, athletic activities in church school gyms or ball fields are inherently risky activities. As a result of these risks, some dioceses have enacted statutes prohibiting such activities on diocesan or parish premises. Dioceses and parishes that allow such activities on their premises must take steps to protect their patrimony from unintentional loss through their potential liability for such activities when they are permitted or licensed. The best way to do this is through some form of insurance provided by the user to the property owner. This insurance coverage should be required in the license agreement, whether the license agreement covers a one time use or a repeated use. Of course, the actual language requiring this type of insurance should be drafted by local legal counsel.

A CONSIDERATION OF THE CASE STUDIES

Without any specific NCCB legislation on leases themselves, the only canonical legislation may be considered to become applicable is the NCCB's legislation on canon 1277 which specifies that leases of church property for which annual lease income exceeds $500,000 are to be treated as acts of extraordinary administration. Realizing that the NCCB's canon 1277 legislation lacks the Holy See's *recognitio*, but applying that legislation for purposes of analysis only, in case 27, neither the total lease amount ($500,000) nor the annual amount ($100,000) exceeds $500,000. As a result, this is not an act of extraordinary administration as defined by the NCCB. The diocesan bishop, however, may by local statute, once he has heard the diocesan finance council, define acts of extraordinary administration for juridic persons subject to him (c. 1281, §2), which acts require his written permission (c. 1281, §1). Depending on whether or not this particular type of transaction was defined as an act of extraordinary administration, then, the written permission of the local ordinary may or may not be required. All things being equal, it would seem that a transaction that legally encumbered parish property for five years, or that dealt with property of the evident value of the former theater, is matter for a local statute.

The pastor will have to turn to civil law to determine whether or not he can void the lease. Absent some type of "Catholic reputation" clause in the lease itself, the film company would not appear to have violated the lease. As long as the company pays its rent on time, the parish must keep its part of the bargain.

Case 28 is really a question of civil liability, without any canonical component. Normally, in this situation, the parish would not be liable for the injuries caused by the drunk driver, even though the driver was served the alcohol on parish premises. This is because the caterer is an independent contractor, and not agent of the parish. The case study makes this issue a bit interesting by saying that the parish has authorized only a small group of caterers. The fine legal issue that must be dealt with is whether or not this authorization of a caterer might somehow make the caterer, who did serve the liquor, the parish's agent. Since there was a list of possible caterer's, not just limited to this one, the best analysis is that the caterer's being on the approved parish list does not make it an agent of the parish for whose injuries the parish is liable.

Although the parish probably escapes liability here, it will have to defend itself in the legal action brought by the injured parties. In most situations, diocesan insurance will provide a defense, but the parish might want to consider language in its license agreement with the parishioners using the center (and there should be such a written agreement, and it is a license, not a lease) that requires the parishioners to carry their own insurance on which the parish is an additional insured and to indemnify the parish from any losses it may suffer as a result of the license agreement.

CHAPTER EIGHTEEN

INSURANCE AND ECCLESIASTICAL GOODS

JOSEPH A. FRANK

Although the purchase of insurance policies is specifically referenced in the code on one occasion (c. 1284, §2, 1°), issues of insurance and the larger issue of risk management are closely related to the administrator's responsibility to protect and preserve the Church's resources.

In discussing the responsibility of administrators to protect ecclesiastical property other chapters have presented and discussed the principles of canon 1284. It is worthwhile to summarize the principles applicable to this chapter:

- ◆ Administrators have an obligation to care for the goods of the Church;

- ◆ Ecclesiastical property can include not only the invested and purchased assets of the Church, but also the good name of the ecclesiastical entity and the church at large;

- ◆ The duty of the administrator is to protect entrusted goods with the diligence of a good householder.

Insurance is just one part of risk management and it is the responsibility of church administrators to be good risk managers.

RISK MANAGEMENT

By one definition, risk management is a discipline for dealing with the possibility that some future event will cause harm. The Nonprofit Risk Management Center[1] advances the more simplified position that risk management is a decision making process that seeks answers to three questions:

- ♦ What could go wrong?
- ♦ What will we do?
- ♦ How will we pay for it?

Administrators of ecclesiastical property must seek answers to these same questions if they are to "take care that none of the goods entrusted to their care is in any way lost or damaged ...."

The process begins with the identification of risks or exposures that can cause loss or damage to ecclesiastical goods. Common exposures that come to mind are the physical loss or damage to church property such as those caused by fire, lightning or windstorm. Other threats of loss to property could include unauthorized use of funds, or theft of equipment or supplies. Beyond damage to property or to contents, the organization can face the risk of legal responsibility for the action, or inaction, of its administrators for causing injury to its members, employees, or the public at large. Likewise, certain activities can cause damage to the organization's reputation, inhibiting the ability to raise funds and interfering with the fulfillment of its mission.

In determining how to manage the risks faced by the organization, there are two primary objectives to consider: what can be done to prevent loss; and if a loss occurs, what can be done to minimize the harmful effects or severity of the loss?

Lastly, because no amount of planning can eliminate the occurrence of all losses, risk management seeks to finance losses through the purchase of insurance coverage or other funding methods.

---

[1]Nonprofit Risk Management Center, 1001 Connecticut Avenue, NW, Washington, D.C. 20036, www.nonprofitrisk.org.

Insurance

Insurance provides a safety net protecting the organization from the financial consequences of loss. Canon 1284, §2, 1° specifically authorizes administrators to take out insurance policies for the protection of goods against loss or damage. The purchase of insurance coverage is intended to assure the availability of funds for the restoration of an asset or to pay for amounts due because of a liability settlement or judgement. The task of making certain that the proper coverage for an organization is provided can be a complex undertaking. The purchase should be undertaken by an individual familiar with the organization's exposure to loss and should be accomplished with the assistance of knowledgeable professionals. In order to take advantage of the expertise of the finance council, as well as the economic advantages that come from the pooling of insurance, most if not all dioceses in the United States have created comprehensive insurance programs. These programs seek to cover all parish and all other organizations and typically offer very little in the way of choice to the local administrator.

Purchasing Issues

Whether a central administrative authority purchases insurance coverage, or if it is done at the local level, the issues are the same. The purchaser must select a competent insurance agent or broker and with their assistance go about the task of defining the organization's needs for insurance coverage.

With the assistance of the insurance professional, the organization will need to determine:

- what to cover (building and contents, fine arts, financial assets, earnings, vehicles, personal effects of priests and religious);
- for what value;
- who to cover (employees, volunteers, students, professionals, boards);
- what limits of coverage to purchase;
- what coverage forms (property, business income and extra expense, boiler and machinery, general liability, auto liability, auto physical damage, professional liability, crime, umbrella and excess liability).

Care must be taken to review policy terms and conditions, exclusions, coverage dates and triggers. Levels of retention or self-insurance must be properly matched to the organization's loss expectancy and financial capabilities. Program funding and accounting requirements must be determined. Insurance carriers should be selected in consideration of their financial stability as well as their record for claims settlement.

While this is by no means an exhaustive list, it is reflective of the nature of decision making that is required and why as a practical matter insurance coverage purchasing decisions are best conducted at the diocesan level.

In purchasing insurance, it is extremely important to provide accurate and truthful information. The parish or organizational administrator can support the purchasing effort through the identification of significant or unique exposures or any changes in the exposure base. The administrator should report in accordance with established practices the addition or deletion of parish facilities. Fine arts or other items of significant value should be brought to the attention of the program administrator. Coverage should be verified for any program or undertaking that is innovative or untried.

Many diocesan programs utilize elements of retention or self-insurance as a way to control and stabilize the cost of risk. Funds are typically established for the payment of claims, the purchase of excess insurance policies and the payment of administrative expense. Insurance program participants are required to pay into the fund their allocated portion of the identified costs. The fund is ecclesiastical property that is then subject to the administration of the ordinary.

PREVENTION OF LOSSES

The best way to care for any organization's goods is to implement practices designed to prevent losses from occurring. Having identified the organization's exposure to loss, the organization can begin to address ways in which loss can be avoided or controlled.

Administrators need to evaluate activities in light of their relationship to the organization's mission as well as their loss causing potential. An administrator may determine that it is best not to undertake the activity. For instance, utilizing the school gymnasium for a rollerblading party may seem like a good idea to some; the administrator has to ask if the potential for injury outweighs the anticipated benefit? In practice, risk avoidance, or not undertaking a loss causing activity, is the one certain way to prevent loss.

A second loss prevention technique that can be employed in the organization is risk modification. In considering the potential for harm to the goods of the Church arising from an activity, the administrator can consider what requirements the prudent householder might consider when carrying out the activity. Examples of controls include:

- financial controls which restrict access to funds and audit controls which assure that financial controls are working; and

- written personnel policies and procedures and their communication and enforcement, identifying who has permission to drive a vehicle, use a facility or sign a contract.

Another technique for mitigating the financial harm of losses is to transfer responsibility for losses to another party. In order to protect church property effectively from harm the administrator must take special care in making certain that contracts are entered into when required and that the terms of the contract address the responsibility for loss and indemnification. If an outside party is using organizational facilities, it is prudent to require that they be responsible for any injuries or damages that arise out of their occupancy. Using contractors without a contract or the knowledge that they are not insured, can recklessly expose property to loss.

CASE 29

St. Joseph parish is looking for an amusement company to provide games and rides for its annual carnival. The ABC Amusement Company responds with a quotation and submits for signature the standard agreement that it requires for all orders. The pastor, noting that the contract includes a waiver of any and all liability against the amusement company, contacts the diocesan insurance office to confirm that the parish's insurance will cover any claims if participants are injured on the carnival rides. After discussion with the Risk Manager, the pastor tells the ABC representative that he is very interested in purchasing their services but that the agreement must be changed to include terms that are more favorable to the parish. The pastor wants the amusement company to acknowledge responsibility for injuries to participants, agree to indemnify and defend the parish for any claims that it might receive from injured parties and provide the parish with proof that it can pay for claims by providing an insurance certificate which names the parish as an additional insured on the amusement company's policy. The amusement company agrees.

The pastor has recognized that the activity, in this case rides and games at a parish carnival, has loss causing potential and that there is a need to make certain that funds, through insurance coverage, are available to pay for the financial consequences of a loss. In this case, control over the activity rests with the vendor and not with the parish. If a loss were to occur, it would not be a prudent use of parish, or diocesan funds, to pay for damages arising out of some one else's negligence. Since the vendor has control of the activity, payment for losses arising out of the activity should be the responsibility of the vendor.

It should be noted that requiring the vendor to assume this responsibility is not unreasonable. While a vendor may attempt to shift risk and its financial consequences to another party, a responsible vendor will agree to be responsible for his or her own actions and will have insurance coverage to pay for losses. The risk manager has properly identified that the proper method for assigning financial responsibility is by way of the contract and that a certificate of insurance is required to document the purchase of coverage.

By identifying what could go wrong and how losses will be paid, the parish has diligently cared for its household. The diocese, moreover, might also require that the vendor's insurance names not only the parish but also the diocese as insured against liability.

DUTIES IN THE EVENT OF A LOSS

Recalling that it is the duty of the administrator to protect entrusted goods with the diligence of a good householder, the administrator must assume responsibility to minimize the financial impact of loss. The administrator should be familiar with the necessary steps to be taken when a loss or an accident or event that can result in a claim for damages occurs. These requirements are typically outlined as part of the loss and claim reporting procedures of the insurance program in which the entity participates. Responsibilities that should be common to all administrators include:

- protection of persons and property from harm or further damage. Examples of appropriate action are obtaining immediate medical care for injuries or removing standing water from a building or securing a facility;

- contact claims personnel as soon as possible and cooperate as required;

- do not admit liability or make promises of payment;

- preserve all evidence;
- obtain detailed information regarding injured persons or any witnesses;
- obtain and submit detailed estimates of actual damages;
- make all necessary repairs to restore the asset as quickly as possible.

All events that have loss causing potential, i.e., harm to persons, property or reputation are opportunities for administrators to exercise their responsibility to protect and preserve the church's resources. Risk management enables an organization to identify risks, prevent losses from occurring, to control the impact of losses that do occur and to fund for the payment of losses through the purchase of insurance or other funding mechanisms.

In practice, the insurance purchasing function has been centralized in most if not all dioceses. While a central authority can support risk management, it remains the responsibility of the administrator of ecclesiastical property to care for the goods of the Church. Risk management is an effective discipline that can be employed in the fulfillment of that obligation.

FORMULARY 17:
Risk Management Policy Statement Example

(Each diocesan entity should adopt this statement or a similar version.)

_____(Location) is committed to personal safety and to preserving the property which allows us to provide for the spiritual, educational, and social needs of our people in a community setting. Safety is a major priority, and expresses our dedication to the health, well being, and security of our community and our awareness of our responsibility to serve.

The generosity of those whom we serve made the construction and operation of our facilities possible. Reducing the financial strain from losses, allows us to improve our stewardship and use temporal resources for the greater needs of our community.

With the goal of optimal safety, our policy is as follows:

- We will incorporate safety concerns into our planning, building maintenance, security procedures, employee training, parish activities and school operations.

- Our safety team will administer the safety policy, establishing means for eliminating hazards and improving conditions.

- We will train and support our employees and volunteers in safe work practices, knowing that their cooperation is essential to this program.

- Our administration will support and direct everyone in fulfilling our safety policies.

- All will observe the laws of our state and city, and the directives of our archdiocese, which are essential to safety and the preservation of property.

CHAPTER NINETEEN

ADDRESSING IRREGULARITIES IN THE ADMINISTRATION OF CHURCH PROPERTY

ELIZABETH McDONOUGH, O.P.

CASE 30

For the better part of a decade Father Viginti, a diocesan priest, was (for all practical purposes) the apparently able and generally liked pastor of a somewhat small, relatively rural parish. But over the years Fr. Viginti had developed the habit of removing (and keeping for his own personal use) any $20 bills that happened to be in the Sunday collection. This was never a large amount, perhaps $60 or $80 a week and it was quite easy for him to remove the few $20 bills between Sunday afternoon and Monday morning because Sunday collections were brought to the celebrant at the offertory and placed in the rectory safe after Mass until the regular volunteers counted and recorded the weekly collections on Monday before depositing them at the local bank. A new volunteer, Nan, joined the group of Monday morning collection counters and happened to notice after a few months that there were never any $20 bills in the loose cash. At first she thought nothing of it, but eventually decided to put a $20 bill in the collection herself to see if it appeared on Monday a.m. It did not. She then did the same for three more weeks, and when no $20 bill appeared in the loose cash on Monday morning for the fourth week in a row she called the chancellor of the diocese to tell him something seemed amiss.

CASE 31

For some years, Father Edificium was pastor of a once quite well built, nicely decorated church which had begun to deteriorate somewhat from age and use. When he came into a very significant monetary inheritance, Fr. Ed (as he was fondly called by parishioners) decided to use his windfall to re-decorate the church (with a view to being remembered fondly forever by the parishioners therein). He had what he thought were wonderful plans for new marble statues, for multi-color refinishing of the columns, and for gold leaf highlighting the vaulted ceiling. The diocese required that all major renovations be approved by the bishop, but the bishop – though not at all unhappy that Fr. Edificium was willing to fund 80% of the renovation with his own money – simply did not approve of Fr. Ed's choices for the renovation. Since Fr. Ed had most of the money, however, he simply told the parish council, finance council and parishioners that he had consulted the diocese (which, indeed, he had) and then proceeded to hire contractors for the renovations he had in mind. Several months passed before word trickled into diocesan headquarters that Fr. Ed's church was being renovated in a fashion that appeared rather extravagant and not entirely in keeping with what the diocese usually approved. Shortly thereafter, the bishop's secretary drove out to see what was happening and noted that the non-approved church renovation as planned by Fr. Ed was well under way. In fact, it had progressed to such a degree that it could not be terminated without great loss of investment and could not be altered without even greater expense.

Both of the above scenarios are actual cases but employ obviously fictitious names and somewhat altered circumstances in order to protect the guilty. They occur in what is perhaps the most common day-to-day context for administration of ecclesiastical goods, namely, within the pastoral responsibility of a local parish. However, comparable behaviors can occur, *mutatis mutandis*, at almost any level in the administration of church goods. Although the monetary values involved are very different, these cases deal with two key areas wherein irregularities frequently occur, that is, the misuse of income and the misuse of expenditures.

Transgressions – such as the above – of the long standing canonical norm that the temporal goods of the Church are to be obtained, possessed and used for divine worship, for the honest sustenance of clergy and other ministers, and for charitable and apostolic works (c. 1254, §2) do occur. And, as happens with most such irregularities, it is not always simple to address them from a canonical perspective, while it is generally not advisable to deal with them in a civil legal forum.

At issue in this chapter is not what the pastors in question (or comparable church authorities at some other level of administration) would have done had they been properly fulfilling their obligations or complying fully with diocesan policies. What is at issue is precisely what can and should be done in a constructive manner in order to address the fact that these irregularities have occurred. The basic principles governing pastoral fiscal responsibility, as well as those for ordinary or extraordinary administration, have been treated in chapters ten and sixteen, and will be mentioned only in summary fashion here. The most fundamental and most important element of advice, however, is that in all fiscal matters the best protection against any irregularities is to have enacted, before the fact, thorough and accurate policies which are well communicated and are consistently applied.

On the one hand, whatever comes to a parish or to any other juridic person whether in money or in kind belongs by law to the parish unless the contrary is established (cc. 515, §3 and 1267, §1). Offertory collections clearly fall within this norm, even if – as in the case of Fr. Viginti – the amount skimmed off may be judged as small in any one instance. While restricted gifts – as could be applied in the case of Fr. Edificium – must be used for the purpose(s) for which they have been given (c. 1267, §3), the permission of the ordinary is required before such gifts can be accepted if they entail burdens or conditions for the beneficiary (c. 1267, §2). And, though pastors are responsible for the ecclesiastical goods and the business transactions of the parish entrusted to their care, they are also bound to follow canons 1281-1288 in carrying out these responsibilities. In addition, pastors also always administer the goods of the parish (c. 532) under the jurisdiction and vigilance of the local ordinary (c. 1276).

On the other hand, the principle of subsidiarity as included in the revised code within the context of temporal goods can lead to certain areas of legal *lacunae* wherein transgressions, such as the above, are either difficult to detect (as in collection skimming) or exceedingly difficult to remedy (as in non-approved renovations). While parishes must have a finance council, its composition and operation are governed, for the most part, by diocesan regulations (c. 537 as a specification of c. 1280); and these regulations may or may not require consent of the council before a pastor can make certain expenditures. Further, though it is clear that administrators invalidly place acts beyond those of ordinary administration unless they have written faculties from the ordinary to do so (c. 1281, §1), both the matter of and the procedures for extraordinary administration must be specifically delineated in appropriate statutes (c. 1281, §2). It is canonically clear that a juridic person is not responsible for an invalid act when the matter and procedures for ordinary/extraordinary administration are articulated but an administrator, nevertheless, acts beyond or in violation of these (c. 1281, §3). In parallel fashion, it is canonically clear that the juridic person is responsible for those acts of financial administration, which meet the established requirements for validity but are carried out illegally. Nevertheless, in such cases, there is provision for possible corrective action against the errant administrator who places valid but illicit acts of administration (c. 1281, §3). To be clear about this last point, an action is illegal in canon law if it fails to fulfill each and every legal norm pertaining to it; but an action is only considered invalid – that is, it is considered as not having taken place – if it fails to fulfill what is expressly required for validity (c. 10). Finally, if the financial transactions of the pastor can be judged to be harmful to the patrimonial condition of the juridic person of the parish, then these actions are subject to the canons on alienation (c. 1295). This means that civilly valid actions for which the required canonical solemnities have not been observed can be addressed through corrective canonical measures as provided by canon 1296 in order to vindicate the rights of the Church.

In relation to the above cases, both pastors could be subject to the procedure for formal removal from office as pastor (cc. 1740-1747). Since pastors are required to file an annual report of income and expenditures (c. 1287, §1), Fr. Viginti's practice of skimming $20 bills from the offertory collection would render this report a false document for which delict he could be subject to a just penalty (c. 1391). Note that submitting the false report would constitute a valid but illicit act on his part. If the matter were pursued in the civil arena, Fr. Viginti could also be subject to the civil penalty for theft. Depending to a great extent on diocesan regulations and particular statutes, Fr. Ed's actions could be both canonically illicit and invalid or they could be valid but illicit. In any case, both pastors could be judged guilty of the delict of abusing the ecclesiastical office entrusted to them (c. 1389). And both pastors could certainly be required to make financial restitution to their respective parishes – Fr. Viginti for the estimated amount he has stolen from parish coffers over the years and Fr. Edificium for the other 20% of the non-approved renovation costs which had to be paid by the parish. In order to take any of these corrective actions, however, canonical procedures must be carefully followed.

Basically there are three courses of action available for addressing irregularities in the administration of temporal goods as noted in the cases presented here, but these would also apply, *mutatis mutandis*, to addressing irregularities in other realms of responsibility in the Church. One course of action is the use of a penalty, strictly speaking. The other two are non-penal, administrative actions which either remove the person from office or impose on the person a precept (even, possibly, a penal precept) in order to correct the harm that has been done by the initial irregular action insofar as this is possible. These three basic courses of action–with some variations in particular instances – could be applicable to anyone, whether clergy or laity, who hold an office which includes responsibility for ecclesiastical goods or who are delegated such responsibility in a particular matter. It is important to note, however, that some penalties – such as suspension (c. 1336) – can apply only to clerics. Further, there is also the possibility – which applies for the most part only to clerics – of administratively removing the faculties which are granted by the local ordinary for them to function in public ministry.

First, however, it is important to be aware of what procedures apply to which circumstances. In this regard, note that if the law grants someone a faculty or ability to act in a particular situation, and there is no provision anywhere within the law itself for removing or for restricting that faculty or ability, then such removal or restriction is technically in the category of a penalty and must follow all the required procedures for application of canonical sanctions. For example, by the very fact of ordination itself the law gives clerics the faculty to preach everywhere unless the competent ordinary restricts or revokes that faculty (c. 764). Therefore, a competent ordinary can restrict or revoke the preaching faculty of a priest or deacon for an adequate cause by issuing a decree to that effect while following the norms for decrees (cc. 48-58, especially 48-52 and 58). However, when the law grants some faculty or ability to act by reason of office and makes no provision for the restriction or revocation of that faculty or ability, then the competent ordinary is basically imposing a penalty by doing so. For example, by law a pastor can validly assist at the marriages of his parishioners as well as of non-parishioners within the parish boundaries provided at least one party is of the Latin rite (c. 1109). Moreover, assisting at marriages is one of the many specific responsibilities entrusted to pastors (c. 530). Therefore, to restrict, or to remove the faculty of a pastor to assist at marriages, the ordinary would not only have to follow the procedures for application of penalties (cc. 1341, 1717 and following) but would also have to provide specifically *ad interim* for that aspect of pastoral care to be fulfilled within the parish. In the arena of temporal goods, the pastor by law has the function of acting on behalf of the juridic person that is the parish (c. 532). However, that pastoral function is not legally unrestricted and is, in fact, circumscribed by requirements for ordinary or extraordinary administration as established by the ordinary. To place additional restrictions on the ability of a specific pastor to act in a particular manner regarding ordinary or extraordinary administration would not constitute a penalty but would merely be an administrative action for which the ordinary need employ only the procedures for issuing the appropriate decree. Similarly, if a provision already exists in law for a specific action – such as removal of a pastor (cc. 1740-1747) – then carrying out such provisions is not technically a penalty. So, for example, in cases such as those presented here, only the procedures for removal of pastors, not those for the imposition or declaration of a penalty, need be observed.

Second, once the proper category of procedure is identified, it is imperative to follow each step of that procedure exactly, issuing and retaining copies of adequate and accurate documentation for each step. Explanations and suggested documentation for each of the procedures mentioned above have been explicated in previous publications of the Canon Law Society of America. For example, procedures and sample documents for the application of penalties appear in their *Clergy Procedural Handbook*,[1] as do procedures for removal from ecclesiastical office,[2] for issuing individual decrees or precepts,[3] for removal of a pastor,[4] and for removal of faculties.[5] While it is neither necessary nor possible to replicate all those procedures and documents in this limited space, mention of some key areas of difficulty and a few cautionary comments are in order.

Although it is possible that some bishops may not ordinarily take corrective action for irregularities of financial administration unless these happen to be extreme or long term, it can also happen that some bishops may seek immediate and definitive remedies, which occasionally ignore or circumvent various requirements of canonical procedure. Perhaps the most common error in this regard is the attempt to impose a penalty when, in fact, no delict has been committed.

[1] Randolph R. Calvo and Nevin J. Klinger, eds., *Clergy Procedural Handbook* (Washington, DC: 1992). Hereafter, cited as *Clergy Procedural Handbook*. For penalties, see therein Gregory Ingels, "Processes which Govern the Application of Penalties," 206-230, with sample documentation, 231-237.
[2] James F. Parizek, "Ecclesiastical Office," in *Clergy Procedural Handbook*, 121-123 and 131.
[3] Craig A. Cox, "General Principles Governing all Administrative Processes," in *Clergy Procedural Handbook*, 59-62.
[4] Parizek, in *Clergy Procedural Handbook*, 123-127 and 139-141.
[5] James H. Provost, "Effects of Incardination," in *Clergy Procedural Handbook*, 45-47, and "Faculties," 98-102.

A delict is the technical, canonical term for an external and morally imputable violation of a law or precept to which at least an unspecified sanction is attached.[6] There simply can be no penalty if there is no law or precept, which says there is penalty for this or that behavior. And no one is liable to the penalty that is indicated in a law or precept unless the violation is seriously imputable from a deliberate intention to violate the law or precept, that is, from *dolus* or from omission of due diligence in order to keep from violating the law or precept – that is, from *culpa* (c. 1321). Furthermore, a number of excusing and mitigating circumstances render penalties non-applicable (c. 1323) or require them to be tempered when they actually do apply (c. 1324). But, as it happens, there are very few penalties that concern the administration of temporal goods in the first place. Among these, the abuse of ecclesiastical office (c. 1389) or the falsification of ecclesiastical documents (c. 1391), as in the examples given, could probably be invoked in most cases. Depending upon specific circumstances, however, it is possible that simony (c. 1380), trafficking in Mass offerings (c. 1385), or the exercise of business by clergy (c. 1392) might also be applicable.

Another all too common error in attempting to employ penalties is not paying adequate attention to the preliminary steps that are required in order to avoid penalties if at all possible. At the very least these should include various efforts to correct the difficulty by pastoral solicitude (c. 1341) and preliminary discussion of the difficulty with the offender in the form of a *monitio* or *correptio* (c. 1339). These should then be followed by the preliminary investigation of canons 1717-1719. Among other things, these canons require formal decisions by the competent ordinary concerning circumstances and imputability, as well as about the type of process (judicial or administrative) to be employed. Each step or decision in this preliminary investigation should have separate and appropriate documentation. Some of these can be in the form of memoranda or formal letters communicating the results of preliminary assessments (c. 1717). Others must be in the form of decrees with a seal and notary signature which indicate: the matter at hand, the decision rendered, and the reasons for the decision (cc. 48-51 and 1718). When these decrees concern cases involving a priest, it is good to remember that the notary must also be a priest. No canon in the procedures for penalties requires this, but canon 483, §2 states in part that: "In cases in which the reputation of a priest can be called into question, the notary must be a priest." Since

---

[6]The definition of a delict is not contained as such in the revised code, but all its elements as specified in 1917 code c. 2195 are basically contained in 1983 code c. 1321. See Elizabeth McDonough, "A Gloss on Canon 1321," *Studia Canonica* 21 (1987) 381-390.

the declaration or imposition of a penalty would ordinarily fall within this description, priest notaries should be used for those decrees, which are issued even in the initial stages of the process.[7]

PRACTICAL GUIDELINES

Because the procedures for imposing or declaring penalties are not contained in one section of the code and because their proper sequence is important, an appendix to this chapter lists the various canons for penal procedure in the order in which they might be most helpful if and when a penalty does, indeed, apply. That re-ordering of the canons attempts to present them in such a way that one can find out what needs to be done roughly in the order in which the competent authority needs to do it. In carrying out these steps, the following guidelines or suggestions may also be of practical assistance:

1. Each separate instance of information offered on the matter at issue should be noted with a memorandum or letter by the key person(s) involved. These should be accurately dated and signed (or initialed). They should also be both brief and precise in relation to the alleged irregularity and the circumstances surrounding it, excluding any superfluous information or gratuitous comments. Whenever possible, it is helpful to have corroborating information from separate sources; but as a general rule, the offer of information from anonymous sources should not be entertained. An exception to this general rule would be formal documentary evidence (such as a receipt or a canceled check) which could be verified and admitted on its own merit.

2. It is the responsibility of the competent ordinary, or someone delegated by him, to ask the person whose actions are in question to come to a meeting for the purpose of discussing the issue(s) raised. Commonly this can be arranged by a simple phone call (with the caller keeping a record of the conversation), but scheduling such a meeting might also require a contact by mail. If the latter is necessary, ordinary mail may be used for the first contact if the situation does not necessitate a meeting immediately. However, if there is no

---

[7] Ingels, 214, in the *Clergy Procedural Handbook* section on penalties (see above, note 1), mentions this requirement in the narrative section, but does not indicate this restriction in the sample documents which show possible signatures by either the chancellor or a notary, neither of which need be a priest in the ordinary course of events under the revised code.

response and phone contact is not successful, then certified/return receipt mail should be used. In either case the letter should indicate precisely by what date the addressee should contact the sender, as well the possible means for making such contact should be quite clear (by mail or phone or FAX, etc.). Obviously, any subsequent contact by the addressee should be immediately acknowledged.

3. The actual meeting (if it takes place) could suffice for the *monitio* of canon 1339, §1, which is helpful if it becomes necessary to move to imposition or declaration of a penalty. Such a meeting could also constitute the *correptio* of canon 1339, §2, but ordinarily some appropriate amount of time, depending on the circumstances of the particular case, should elapse between these two actions. As required by canon 1339, §3, the *monitio* and/or *correptio* are to be recorded by appropriate documentation in the secret archives. What transpires at these meetings depends to a great extent on whether the person whose actions are in question is disposed to cooperate and desires to amend the behavior(s) at issue and/or to make amends for whatever harm may have occurred.

4. Depending on what transpires at the initial and/or subsequent meetings (as indicated above), the ordinary may move to a penal precept (c. 1319) by following the rules for precepts, which are a special form of decree (cc. 48-52, especially c. 49). This may be done as a precautionary measure to preclude similar behavior in the future even if the person involved is cooperative and contrite. However, whatever is commanded or forbidden in the precept must be expressed in such a way that it is actually "do-able." It must also be possible, practically speaking, to assess whether or not what has been commanded or forbidden is being done or omitted in the external forum

5. If the person in question admits to having acted irregularly (or illegally or invalidly), resignation from office may be in order and, if so, should be requested immediately. Resignation from office must be submitted in writing, or in the presence of two witnesses, and must be accepted by the person who is competent to confer the office (c. 189, §1).

6. Once a resignation from office has been submitted and accepted, or once someone is removed from office (if that becomes necessary), any faculties that might have previously been granted by

the competent ordinary should be removed. This can be done administratively since faculties are given only for the purpose of ministry, and the ministry of the person in question has basically ceased.

7.   If the person to whom the *monitio* or *correptio* is addressed does not admit to the irregularities of behavior at issue, the ordinary may still move to an administrative and non-penal removal from office (cc. 192-195) if he judges that circumstances warrant such action. Recall, however that there is a special procedure, which must be employed for removal of pastors (cc. 1740-1747), and that the requirements therein must be meticulously followed. Also, since administrative recourse (with non-suspensive effect) is possible against any non-penal removal from office (cc. 1734 ff), the ordinary who does issue a decree removing someone from ecclesiastical office must be certain that he can demonstrate (and vouch for) an adequate, non-arbitrary cause for his action. The cause(s) must be expressed at least in summary fashion in the decree of removal itself.

8.   Faculties can be withdrawn as an administrative act by the ordinary who has granted them even if the person involved in irregular behavior has not resigned. As noted above, however, certain faculties, which are granted by the law itself and for which there is no legal provision for restriction or removal, cannot be withdrawn without employing a penal procedure.

Please note that the steps suggested above as a responsible course of canonical action are able to be employed for almost any problem or irregularity that may be called to the attention of the ordinary. Also note that, if these steps are carefully observed, the entire sequence also suffices to fulfill most of the requirements for initiating a penal process (as in cc. 1717-1718) should that be necessary.

PRACTICAL REMEDIES AND POSSIBLE CIVIL ACTION

After having considered the basic canonical procedures for dealing with irregularities in the administration of ecclesiastical property, it is important to point out that several canons concerning temporal goods refer to the observance of civil law in connection with canonical requirements. With certain restrictions, canon 22 requires that civil law be followed for any instance wherein canons remit matters to it. Among these, canon 1284 requires civilly valid methods for safeguarding ownership of ecclesiastical goods (2°), as well as vigilance in order that harm not result from non-observance of civil laws (3°). Canon 1286 requires compliance with civil laws pertaining to labor and social policy (1°). And, with some exceptions, canon 1290 defers to civil law regarding contracts and payment of debts. Thus, civil law is important for proper administration of the temporal goods of the Church, and it can – or, perhaps, should – be invoked in some circumstances. However, it is generally not advisable that civil law should become the primary focus for guiding the acquisition, administration and alienation of church property or for correcting irregularities therein. Indeed, it is more fitting canonically and it is frequently more effective functionally to pursue correction of irregularities regarding temporal goods within the ecclesiastical arena, whenever this is possible, before seeking civil remedies.[8]

In Fr. Viginti's case, for example, rather than press charges for stealing, it would seem to make much more sense to ask him to resign as pastor (or remove him if necessary) and to mandate that he repay in full from his own income, over a specified period of time, the estimated amount he has gradually taken. Likewise, in the case of Fr. Edificium, removal from office and required reimbursement (from his future income) to the parish of the renovation expenses not covered by the restricted gift of his inheritance would seem a much more constructive approach than attempting to redress his transgressions in the civil arena. In short, it is proposed (without apology) that careful adherence to canonical norms and to the code's procedures for addressing irregularities in the administration of the church's temporal goods, including possible action for damages within a penal process (c. 1729), are actually better means for competent authorities to employ than are sometimes lengthy and frequently expensive civil procedures. Moreover, the canonical process is more likely to accomplish those significant results for which ecclesiastical sanctions are provided in the first place, namely, for repairing scandal, for restoring justice, and for reforming the offender (c. 1341).

---

[8] This is not, however, to suggest that clergy or other church personnel are or ought to be exempt from appropriate civil consequences of legal transgressions for which they are responsible when such is, indeed, warranted.

FORMULARY 17:
A Helpful Re-ordering of the Canons on Penal Procedure

Note that this re-ordering attempts to present the canons in such fashion that whatever needs to be done can be readily identified roughly in the order in which the competent authority needs to do it.

Initial Investigation

CANON 1717, §1 Whenever an ordinary has knowledge, which at least seems true, of a delict, he is carefully to inquire personally or through another suitable person about the facts, circumstances, and imputability, unless such an inquiry seems entirely superfluous.
§2 Care must be taken so that the good name of anyone is not endangered from investigation.
§3 The person who conducts the investigation has the same powers and obligations as an auditor in the process; the same person cannot act as a judge in the matter if a judicial process is initiated later.

CANON 1341 An ordinary is to take care to initiate a judicial or administrative process to impose or declare penalties only after he has ascertained that fraternal correction or rebuke or other means of pastoral solicitude cannot sufficiently repair the scandal, restore justice, reform the offender.

CANON 1339, §1 An ordinary, personally or through another, can warn a person who is in the proximate occasion of committing a delict or upon whom, after investigation, grave suspicion of having committed a delict has fallen.
§2 He can also rebuke a person whose behavior causes scandal or a grave disturbance of order, in a manner accommodated to the special conditions of the person and the deed.
§3 The warning or rebuke must always be established at least by some document which is to be kept in the secret archive of the curia.

CANON 1340, §1 A penance, which can be imposed in the external forum, is the performance of some work of religion, piety, or charity.
§2 A public penance is never to be imposed for an occult transgression.
§3 According to his own prudent judgment, an ordinary can add penances to the penal remedy of warning or rebuke.

CANON 1319, §1 Insofar as a person can impose precepts in the external forum in virtue of the power of governance, the person can also threaten determinate penalties by precept, except perpetual expiatory penalties.
§2 A penal precept is not to be issued unless the mature has been considered thoroughly and those things established in cann. 1317-1318 about paritcular laws have been observed.

CANON 1718, §1 When is seems that sufficient evidence has been collected, the ordinary is to decide:
1° whether a process to inflict or declare a penalty can be initiated;
2° whether, attentive to can. 1341, this is expedient;
3° whether a judicial process must be used or, unless the law forbids it, whether the matter must proceed by way of extra judicial decree.

CANON 1342, §1 Whenever just causes preclude a judicial process, a penalty can be imposed or declared by an extra judicial decree; penal remedies and penances, however, can be applied by decree in any case whatsoever.
§2 Perpetual penalties cannot be imposed or declared by decree; nor can penalties be so applied when the law or precept establishing them prohibits their application by decree.

CANON 1347, §1 A censure cannot be imposed validly unless the offender has been warned at least once beforehand to withdraw from contumacy and has been given a suitable time for repentance.
§2 An offender who has truly repented of the delict and has also made suitable reparation for damage and scandal or at least has seriously promised to do so must be considered to have withdrawn from contumacy.

CANON 1718, §2 The ordinary is to revoke or change the decree mentioned in §1 whenever new evidence indicates to him that another decision is necessary.
§3 In issuing the decrees mentioned in §§1 and 2, the ordinary is to hear two judges or other experts in the law if he considers it prudent
§4 Before he makes a decision according to the norm of §1 and in order

to avoid useless trials, the ordinary is to examine carefully whether it is expedient for him or the investigator, with the consent of the parties, to resolve equitably the question of damages.

CANON 1722 To preclude scandal, to protect the freedom of witnesses, and to guard the course of justice, the ordinary, after having heard the promoter of justice and cited the accused, at any stage of the process can exclude the accused from the sacred ministry or from some office and ecclesiastical function, can impose or forbid residence in some place or territory, or even prohibit public participation in the Most Holy Eucharist. Once the cause ceases, all these measures must be revoked; they also end by the law itself when the penal process ceases.

CANON 1348 When an accused is acquitted of an accusation or when no penalty is imposed, the ordinary can provide for the welfare of the person and for the public good through appropriate warnings and other means of pastoral solicitude or even through penal remedies if the matter warrants it.

CANON 1719 The acts of the investigation, the decrees of the ordinary which initiated and concluded the investigation, and everything which preceded the investigation are to be kept in the secret archive of the curia if they are not necessary for the penal process.

Judicial circumstances warrant it. Discretion

CANON 1342, §3 What a law or precept states about the imposition or declaration of a penalty by a judge in a trial must be applied to a superior who imposes or declares a penalty by extra judicial decree unless it is otherwise evident or unless it concerns prescripts which pertain only to procedural matters.

CANON 1343 If a law or precept gives the judge the power to apply or not to apply a penalty, the judge can also temper the penalty or impose a penance in its place, according to his own conscience and prudence.

CANON 1344 Even if the law uses preceptive words, the judge can, according to his own conscience and prudence:

1° defer the imposition of the penalty to a more opportune time if it is foreseen that greater evils will result from an overly hasty punishment of the offender;

2° abstain from imposing a penalty, impose a lighter penalty, or employ a penance if the offender has reformed and repaired the scandal or if the offender has been or, it is foreseen, will be punished sufficiently by civil authority;

3° suspend the obligation of observing an expiatory penalty if it is the first offense of an offender who has lived a praiseworthy life and if the need to repair scandal is not pressing, but in such a way that if the offender commits an offense again within the time determined by the judge, the person is to pay the penalty due for each delict unless in the interim the time for the prescription of a penal action has elapsed for the first delict.

CANON 1345 Whenever the offender had only the imperfect use of reason or committed the delict from fear, necessity, the heat of passion, or mental disturbance from drunkenness or something similar, the judge can also abstain from imposing any penalty if he thinks that reform of the person can be better accomplished in another way.

CANON 1346 Whenever the offender has committed several delicts, it is left to the prudent decision of the judge to moderate the penalties within equitable limits if the sum of the *ferendae sententiae* penalties appears excessive.

CANON 1349 If a penalty is indeterminate and the law does not provide otherwise, the judge is not to impose graver penalties, especially censures, unless the seriousness of the case clearly demands it; he cannot, however, impose perpetual penalties.

CANON 1326, §1 A judge can punish the following more gravely than the law or precept has established:

1° a person who after a condemnation or after the declaration of a penalty continues so to offend that from the circumstances the obstinate ill will of the person can prudently be inferred;

2° a person who has been established in some dignity or who has abused a position of authority or office in order to commit the delict.

3° an accused person who, when a penalty has been established against a delict based on negligence, foresaw the event and nonetheless omitted precautions to avoid it, when any diligent person would have employed.

§2 If the penalty established in cases mentioned in §1 is *latae sententiae*, another penalty or a penance can be added.

Statute of Limitations

CANON 1362, §1 Prescription extinguishes a criminal action after three years unless it concerns:

1° delicts reserved to the Congregation for the Doctrine of the Faith;

2° an action arising from the delicts mentioned in cann. 1394; 1395; 1397; and 1398, which have a prescription of five years;

3° delicts which are not punished in the common law if particular law has established another period for prescription.

§2 Prescription runs from the day on which the delict was committed or, if the delict is continuous or habitual, from the day on which it ceased.

CANON 1363, §1 Prescription extinguishes an action to execute a penalty if the offender is not notified of the executive decree of the judge mentioned in can. 1651 within the time limits mentioned in can. 1362; these limits are to be computed from the day on which the condemnatory sentence became a res iudicata.

§2 Having observed what is required, the same is valid if the penalty was imposed by extra judicial decree.

FORMULARY 17:
continued

Extra-judicial (Administrative) Procedure

CANON 1720 If the ordinary thinks that the matter must proceed by way of extra judicial decree:

1° he is to inform the accused of the accusation and the proofs, giving an opportunity for self-defense, unless the accused neglected to appear after being properly summoned;

2° he is to weigh carefully all the proofs and arguments with two assessors;

3° if the delict is certainly established and a criminal action is not extinguished, he is to issue a decree according to the norm of cann. 1342-1350, setting forth the reasons in law and in fact at least briefly.

Judicial Procedure

CANON 1721, §1 If the ordinary has decreed that a judicial penal process must be initiated, he is to hand over the acts of the investigation to the promoter of justice who is to present a libellus of accusation to the judge according to the norm of cann. 1502 and 1504.

§2 The promoter of justice appointed to the higher tribunal acts as the petitioner before that tribunal.

CANON 1723, §1 The judge who cites the accused must invite the accused to appoint an advocate according to the norm of can. 1481, §1 within the time limit set by the judge.

§2 If the accused does not make provision, the judge is to appoint an advocate before the joinder of the issue; this advocate will remain in this function as long as the accused does not appoint an advocate personally.

CANON 1724, §1 At any grade of the trial the promoter of justice can renounce the trial at the command of or with the consent of the ordinary whose deliberation initiated the process.

§2 For validity the accused must accept the renunciation unless the accused was declared absent from the trial.

CANON 1725 In the discussion of the case, whether done in written or oral form, the accused, either personally or through an advocate or procurator, always has the right to write or speak last.

CANON 1726 If at any grade and stage of the penal trial it is evidently established that the accused did not commit the delict, the judge must declare this in a sentence and absolve the accused even if it is also established that criminal action has been extinguished.

CANON 1727, §1 The accused can propose an appeal even if the sentence dismissed the accused only because the penalty was facultative or because the judge used the power mentioned in cann. 1344 and 1345.
§2 The promoter of justice can appeal whenever the promoter judges that the repair of scandal or the restoration of justice has not bee provided for sufficiently.

CANON 1728, §1 Without prejudice to the prescriptions of the canons of this title and unless the nature of the matter precludes it, the canons on trials in general and on ordinary contentious trials must be applied in the penal trial; the special norms for cases which pertain to the public good are also to be observed.
§2 The accused is not bound to confess the delict nor can an oath be administered to the accused.

Action for Damages

CANON 1729, §1 In the penal trial itself an injured party can bring a contentious action to repair damages incurred personally from the delict, according to the norm of can. 1596.
§2 The intervention of the injured party mentioned in §1 is not admitted later if it was not made in the first grade of the penal trial.
§3 The appeal in a case for damages is made according to the norm of cann. 1628-1640 even if an appeal cannot be made in the penal trial; if both appeals are proposed, although by different parties, there is to be a single appellate trial, without prejudice to the prescript of can. 1730.

CANON 1730, §1 To avoid excessive delays in a penal trial the judge can defer the judgment for damages until he has rendered the definitive sentence in the penal trial.

§2 After rendering the sentence in the penal trial, the judge who does this must adjudicate for damages even if the penal trial still is pending because of a proposed challenge or the accused has been absolved for a cause which does not remove the obligation to repair damages.

CANON 1731 Even if the sentence rendered in the penal trial has become a res iudicata, it in no way establishes the right of the injured party unless this party has intervened according to the norm of can. 1729.

Consequences/Observance of Penalties

CANON 1351 Unless other provision is expressly made, a penalty binds the offender everywhere, even when the authority of the one who established or imposed the penalty has lapsed.

CANON 1352, §1 If a penalty prohibits the reception of the sacraments or sacramentals, the prohibition is suspended as long as the guilty party is in danger of death.

§2 The obligation to observe an undeclared *latae sententiae* penalty which is not notorious in the place where the offender is present, is suspended totally or partially whenever the offender cannot observe it without danger of grave scandal or infamy.

CANON 1353 An appeal or recourse from judicial sentences or from decrees,which impose or declare a penalty, has a suspensive effect.

Remission of Penalties

CANON 1354, §1 In addition to the persons listed in cann. 1355–1356, all who can dispense from a law which includes a penalty or who can exempt from a precept which threatens a penalty can also remit that penalty.

§2 Moreover, a law or precept which establishes a penalty can also give the power of remission to others.

§3 If the Apostolic See has reserved the remission of a penalty to itself or to others, the reservation must be interpreted strictly.

CANON 1355, §1 Provided that the penalty has not been reserved to the Apostolic See, the following can remit an imposed or declared penalty established by law:

    1° the ordinary who initiated the trial to impose or declare a penalty or who personally or through another imposed or declared it by decree;

    2° the ordinary of the place where the offender is present, after the ordinary mentioned in n. 1 has been consulted unless this is impossible because of extraordinary circumstances.

§2 If the penalty has not been reserved to the Apostolic See, an ordinary can remit a latae sententiae penalty established by law but not yet declared for his subjects and those who are present in his territory or who committed the offense there; any bishop can also do this in the act of sacramental confession.

CANON 1356, §1 The following can remit a ferendae sententiae or latae sententiae penalty established by a precept not issued by the Holy See:

    1° the ordinary of the place where the offender is present;

    2° if the penalty has been imposed or declared, the ordinary who initiated the trial to impose or declare the penalty or who personally or through another imposed or declared it by decree.

§2 The author of the precept must be consulted before remission is made unless this is impossible because of extraordinary circumstances.

CANON 1357, §1 Without prejudice to the prescripts of cann. 508 and 976, a confessor can remit in the internal sacramental forum an undeclared *latae sententiae* censure of excommunication or interdict if it is burdensome for the penitent to remain in the state of grave sin during the time necessary for the competent superior to make provision.

§2 In granting the remission, the confessor is to impose on the penitent, under the penalty of reincidence, the obligation of making recourse within a month to the competent superior or to a priest endowed with the faculty and the obligation of obeying his mandates; in the meantime he is to impose a suitable penance and, insofar as it is demanded, reparation of any scandal and damage; however, recourse can also be made through the confessor, without mention of the name.

§3 After they have recovered, those for whom an imposed or declared censure or one reserved to the Apostolic See has been remitted according to the norm of can. 976 are also obliged to make recourse.

CANON 1358, §1 Remission of a censure cannot be granted unless the offender has withdrawn from contumacy according to the norm of can. 1347, §2; it cannot be denied, however, to a person who withdraws from contumacy.

§2 The person who remits a censure can make provision according to the norm of can. 1348 or can even impose a penance.

CANON 1359 If several penalties bind a person, a remission is valid only for the penalties expressed in it; a general remission, however, takes away all penalties except those which the offender in bad faith omitted in the petition.

CANON 1360 The remission of a penalty extorted by grave fear is invalid.

CANON 1361, §1 A remission can also be given conditionally or to a person who is absent.

§2 A remission in the external forum is to be given in writing unless a grave cause suggests otherwise.

§3 Care is to be taken that the petition of remission or the remission itself is not divulged except insofar as it is either useful to protect the reputation of the offender or necessary to repair scandal.

✛ ✛ ✛

CONVEYANCE OF
ECCLESIASTICAL GOODS

✛ ✛ ✛

CHAPTER TWENTY

ALIENATION OF CHURCH PROPERTY

NICHOLAS P. CAFARDI

CANONICAL CONCEPTS ON ALIENATION

All church property is subject to the canon law on the administration of ecclesiastical goods, but not all of church property is subject to the canon law on alienation. From the context of canon 1291, it is clear that the rules on alienation apply only to a very special type of church property that the *Code of Canon Law* refers to as "stable patrimony."

Stable Patrimony

Nowhere in the *Code of Canon Law* is the term "stable patrimony" defined. This means that we must look to sources external to the text of the law itself for an understanding of the notion of stable patrimony.

The Prior Law

In the 1917 code, the term "stable patrimony" does not appear. The term is new with the 1983 code. But the former code did have rules on alienation; it simply used a different terminology to specify the object of alienation. In the 1917 code, permission was needed to alienate *res ecclesiasticas immobiles aut mobiles, quae servando servari possunt* (1917 CIC c. 1530).

Res ecclesiasticas refers to "church property," or as the 1983 code identifies it, the property of a public juridic person.

Immobiles means "immovable property," and is a term widely used in European civil law to mean "real estate." Many European countries still speak of "immovable property" today, and what they mean by this term is what American usage would refer to as "real property" or "real estate," which in the US legal system refers to land and the permanent improvements to land, such as buildings.

Mobiles refers to "movable property," which is a term from the European civil law system. The comparable term in US civil law is "personalty" or personal property, which refers to any property that is not real property.

Quae servando servari possunt, means property which, by being cared for, is able to be preserved as "imperishable." "Imperishable" modifies both the terms "immovable" and "movable" property, but realistically has more applicability to movable property or personalty than to immovable property or real estate. Normally real estate is not considered as perishable or imperishable; however, personal property is considered this way.

In the former code, the object of alienation was real property or imperishable personal property that belonged to the Church. The unifying concept in this notion is permanence. Real estate has a permanent character to it. Imperishable personal property has a permanent character to it. The former code said that the permanent or enduring character of property placed it into the category of goods that are protected by the alienation process. The permanent property of public juridic persons needs to endure and be of use for the ages. For the alienation of enduring property, property with a permanent character to it, the law requires more than simply the decision of the present administrator of that property. This is the purpose of the alienation process.

The 1983 Code of Canon Law

There is an obvious carry over of this concept of enduring property in the term "stable patrimony." The word "stable" itself suggests the permanence and endurance of property.

The word "patrimony," another concept from European civil law, also implies property with a type of permanence to it. Patrimony refers to inherited property. It is the property that is passed on from one generation to the next, property that is not to be dissipated by an individual heir, but that is to be managed by him or her to generate income to support the family for his or her generation, leaving the main bulk of the patrimony to support future generations. The heir may live off of it, derive income from it, but must also preserve it for his or her heirs, just as prior generations preserved it for the current generation.

In the 1983 code, the term often has the meaning of "heritage." For example, the spirit, character and wholesome traditions of a religious institute are its patrimony or heritage (cc. 578; 586, §1; and 631, §1). In Book V, canon 1292 specifies that precious artwork and property with historical value are subject to the alienation process as well, thereby reinforcing this notion that patrimony refers to the property which is the heritage of a public juridic person.

The term "patrimony" is used two other times in Book V. In canon 1283, 3°, regarding the duties of administrators before taking office, patrimony refers to the list of property which would be included in an inventory, in other words, real estate and those elements of personal property which have a certain permanence and value (c. 1288, 2°). In canon 1285, administrators are permitted to make gifts from stable patrimony under certain limited circumstances. These parallel uses of the term "patrimony" or "stable patrimony" in the 1983 code are also a source for the meaning of the object of alienation.

A Definition of Stable Patrimony

Stable patrimony is the inheritance of a public juridic person – the permanent goods (real estate and imperishable personalty) that the current administrators have either received from prior administrators or have accrued themselves. Such goods are to be used by them to benefit the public juridic person and are to be preserved by them for the future benefit of the public juridic person.

Lawful Designation

The 1983 code requires that stable patrimony must be so *ex legitima assignatione* (c. 1291), by lawful designation. Under the prior code, property was considered the object of alienation simply by virtue of the kind of property that it was – real estate or imperishable personal property. The new code requires the administrators of the public juridic person to whom the property belongs take affirmative and lawful steps to designate the property as stable patrimony. It would seem that real estate and imperishable personal property, acquired by a public juridic person after the effective date of the 1983 code (November 27, 1983), does not qualify as stable patrimony and is not subject to the laws on alienation unless it was designated as stable patrimony by the lawful act of the administrator of the public juridic person.

The designation of particular piece of property as stable patrimony is not a normal occurrence. It is not something that canonical administrators do everyday, yet the 1983 code seems to imply that property, upon its acquisition, should be placed by the administrator into either the stable or non-stable categories, and that only stable patrimony is subject to the laws on alienation. The new law would seem to further imply that real estate and imperishable personal property are no longer *ipso facto* the object of the alienation laws; rather, real estate and imperishable personalty acquired after 1983 may or may not be subject to the alienation laws depending upon whether or not it was ever designated as stable patrimony by the lawful act of the administrator of the public juridic person who acquired the property. It would appear to be completely possible for a diocese, parish or religious institute to have acquired large parcels of real estate after 1983 and to sell them now without going through the alienation process on the grounds that the parcels were never designated as stable patrimony. The status of real estate or imperishable personal property acquired before this change in the code would still be covered by the prior law. It would be covered by the alienation laws based on the kind of property that it is, and not on whether or not the administrators of a public juridic person have lawfully designated it as stable patrimony. But this same distinction does not apply to property acquired after November 27, 1983. That property, regardless of whether it is real estate or imperishable personal property, is not subject to the laws concerning alienation unless it has been affirmatively designated as stable patrimony by the proper administrator.

Designation by Implication of Law

How does a canonical administrator designate property as a part of stable patrimony? Must the administrator expressly say: "This property is to be considered stable patrimony?" or can it occur by implication? This is an important question because, as noted above, even with the change in the new law, administrators are not in the habit of designating property as either stable or not. But the difficulty with an implied designation of property as stable patrimony, as opposed to an express designation, is that such a designation is restrictive of rights. Once so designated, the property is no longer freely alienable by the public juridic person. The principle of canon 18 (restrictive laws are to strictly interpreted) would seem to argue against a designation of stable patrimony that is implied and not expressed. Nonetheless, there are certain situations where, even without an express designation, property acquired after 1983 could be considered stable patrimony by implication of law.

For example, canon 1283 requires canonical administrators to keep an inventory of the property of the public juridic person whose property they are in charge of. Certainly placing property on this list indicates that the property is considered a part of the stable patrimony of the public juridic person. This would be a type of designation by implication of law.

The code also requires that, prior to the establishment of a public juridic person, the competent ecclesiastical authority must ascertain that the potential juridic person has the assets necessary to achieve its designated end. Newly created public juridic persons, after 1983, by placing assets on the list of those resources which will enable them to meet their goals are designating by implication such assets as their stable patrimony. But this applies only to those public juridic persons created after 1983, and will be a rather rare occurrence.

Whenever property is given to the Church by a donor who specifies that the goods so given, usually money, are to be restricted to use for a particular purpose, then this gift, if properly accepted by the public juridic person, assumes a stable or fixed character. This happens by operation of law, even if the expressed designation of the gift as stable patrimony is not used. Similarly, the administrator of a public juridic person could stabilize certain funds of the juridic person, for example, whenever a diocese or religious institute sets up a pension fund with the duly noted intent that the fund be permanent. The administrative act which restricts such funds on a permanent basis constitutes them as a stable asset of the public juridic person in the law, whether or not the phrase "stable patrimony" is ever used, though it is to be noted that such a stabilization is an act of extraordinary administration which must be done with the approval of the competent superiors. This is not a reference to "fund accounting" where, for accounting purposes only, and with no intent to create a stable fund that would require the permission of higher authority to invade or change, some funds of public juridic persons are labeled as "retirement," "missions," "formation," etc.

Perhaps the most determinative fact about whether or not the property of a public juridic person is implicitly designated as stable patrimony is the manner in which the property is used by the public juridic person. For example, if a parish buys a piece of real estate and proceeds to construct a grade school on it, no one would doubt that this property is part of the parish's stable patrimony, even though it was never so formally designated and even though the pastor did not keep the inventory required by canon 1283. If a diocese purchases property and then erects a seminary on it, even though the lands and buildings were never formally designated as stable patrimony by the bishop and even though the diocese does not keep the inventory required by canon 1283, no one would doubt that the seminary property was a part of the diocese's stable patrimony. If a religious institute in the health care apostolate acquires a new health care facility, no one would doubt that the facility becomes a part of the religious institute's stable patrimony, even without a formal designation as such or including an inventory.

The basis for this determination is the property's use. If such property is not considered to be stable patrimony, then property that is required for a juridic person to meet its proper ends would be freely alienable, a result that would not make sense. By placing property into the category of what is necessary for the public juridic person to achieve its ends, the administrator has, by the lawful act of so designating the property, designated it as stable patrimony whether that term is used or not in the designation. It has been the consistent praxis of canon law that those assets that are necessary to a public juridic person in order to accomplish the ends for which it was established are a part of stable patrimony of that juridic person and may not be freely alienated.

THE CONCEPT OF ALIENATION

Reading the alienation canons in light of their introductory canon 1291, the transfer of any interest in stable patrimony would be considered alienation. This interest can be a *complete interest* in which case the alienation would be a sale; if it is for a consideration or a price, or a gift, it is done without consideration. Or the interest transferred could be a *partial interest*, such as is conveyed by a lease or mortgage. In both leasing and mortgaging, the owner has retained legal ownership of the property, but has transferred a less than complete interest, such as a leasehold interest or a security interest (mortgage) in the property to another party. The American legal system recognizes many ways to transfer an interest in property to another. In addition to a sale, gift, lease or mortgage, interests in property may be transferred through options to purchase, through the creation of an easement or the granting of a lien. All of these are types of alienation because, according to canon 1291, alienation is the transfer of *any* interest in stable patrimony to another party.

One of the most difficult types of potential alienations to analyze involves corporations, which are owned (in a canonical sense) or sponsored by public juridic persons. Very often these corporations are highly structured health care or educational corporations (see chapter four). The public juridic person who founded them originally structured them in such a way that ultimate corporate authority within these sponsored health care or educational corporations was with the administrators of the founding public juridic person. Over the years, the role of the sponsor within the corporation may have changed as educational or health care delivery activities became much more complex. There is no doubt that the surrender of corporate authority within a corporation performing an important part of the apostolic activity of a public juridic person is a type of alienation. It is the loss of an interest in property – but not just any property. Because the performance of apostolic activity (education, healthcare) is the reason for the very existence of the public juridic person (c. 114), these incorporated apostolates are unquestionably a part of stable patrimony. The performance of the apostolic activities that they carry on is the reason why their sponsor was given life by the law of the Church. Property that has been designated for a use that is essential to the purpose of a public juridic person is stable patrimony.

Today, these incorporated apostolates, health care delivery corporations especially, are undergoing immense corporate transformations as mergers and affiliations become the rule. All of these types of transactions must be closely looked at for their potential alienation possibilities, which will invariably involve a complex analysis of what legal authority the sponsoring public juridic person will maintain and what it will surrender in the corporate changes that are proposed. A surrender of too much legal authority within the incorporated apostolate results in the alienation of stable patrimony; and depending upon the asset value, must be reviewed by the competent ecclesiastical authority. Since, when dealing with large educational or health care delivery corporations, the values are in the many millions of dollars, this authority is normally the Holy See.

A Canon 1295 Transaction

Canon 1295 says that the alienation process applies not just to the alienation of stable patrimony but to any transaction by which the patrimonial condition of a juridic person can be worsened. Oddly enough, this canon omits the word "stable" in referring to patrimonial condition, but the term must be implied from the context. (The canon also omits the word "public" in referring to juridic persons, even though we know from canon 1257, §2 that these canons on alienation refer only to the property of public juridic persons.) It would make little or no sense to apply the alienation procedures to a transaction, which jeopardized or worsened the condition of non-stable assets. The very nature of non-stable assets is that they are transitory. Some commentaries have referred to a canon 1295 transaction as alienation in the broad sense, limiting alienation in the narrow sense to those transactions described in canon 1291. However, canon 1295 is not defining a new type of alienation. It is simply saying that in transactions where the stable patrimony of a public juridic person may be jeopardized or placed in danger of loss – where the condition of the public juridic person's stable patrimony is worsened – then the alienation procedures must be followed; it is not redefining alienation in a broader sense. As a result of canon 1295, the procedures for alienation must be applied not only to transactions where the stable patrimony of a public juridic person is alienated (c. 1291) but also to those transactions where the condition of a public juridic person is jeopardized or placed at risk (c. 1295). For the sake of both clarity and exactness, the transfer of any interest in stable patrimony as described in canon 1291 will be referred to as an alienation, and an act which places stable patrimony in potential jeopardy or at risk of loss will be referred to as a canon 1295 transaction.

The Alienation Process

Alienations of stable patrimony and transactions that have the potential to worsen the stable patrimonial condition of a public juridic person must be approved by the competent ecclesiastical authority. This authority is defined in canon 1292, and who is competent authority depends on the value of the stable patrimony being alienated or placed in jeopardy.

Values at or Below the Minimum

If the value is at, or below, the minimum amount set for a territory by the conference of bishops, (approved by the Holy See) the authority is determined by the public juridic person's own statutes. In the United States, the minimum amount has been set at $500,000. This means that for stable patrimony worth $500,000 or less, under the 1983 *Code of Canon Law*, the authority who can approve the transaction will be determined by the statutes of that juridic person itself. Normally for parishes in the United States, the applicable statutes are promulgated by the diocesan bishop and specify an amount somewhere between zero and $500,000 at which the pastor can act, with or without the approval of the parish finance council or pastoral council – again that is a matter for local diocesan statutes. But at some point between zero and $500,000, diocesan statutes will require the approval of the diocesan bishop for the alienation of parish property. This amount differs from diocese to diocese. In some dioceses, it is as small as $5,000 while in other dioceses the amount may be as much as $150,000.

These same rules will in general hold true for religious institutes as well (see chapter four). Below the minimum amount for a territory, the competent authority to approve a transaction either alienating or jeopardizing stable patrimony will be determined by the institute's own statutes. Very often, a similar process to that described above for parishes will be the case. There will be an amount between zero and the minimum amount (which has not yet been established for pontifical institutes of consecrated life or societies of apostolic life in the United States) at which the local house itself can act; and beyond that, approval must be obtained from the next level of authority, usually the provincial superior and council.

Values Above the Minimum But Not In Excess of the Maximum

For the alienation of stable patrimony whose value is above the minimum amount, but not in excess of the maximum amount set for a territory by the episcopal conference and approved by the Holy See for parishes and for dioceses themselves, the competent authority is the diocesan bishop, with the consent of the diocesan finance council, the college of consultors and the "parties concerned." That last phrase is troublesome. Who are the parties concerned when parish or diocesan property is being alienated? This phrase is definitely not a reference to parishioners, since they have no canonical right to act on behalf of the parish. The same would be true for members of a diocese. They have no canonical standing to act on behalf of the diocese. Many canonists believe that this refers to property given to the Church for a particular purpose by donors who reserved certain rights under canon 1300, which reservation of rights was accepted by the Church at the time of donation. This phrase is thus a reference to donors who reserved certain rights with the approval of the donee parish or diocese pursuant to canon 1300.

Since in the United States the maximum amount has been set at $3,000,000, canon 1292 would require that, for the alienation or placing in jeopardy of parish or diocesan patrimony whose value was more than $500,000 but not in excess of $3,000,000, the transaction would have to be approved by the diocesan bishop, with the consent of the diocesan finance council and the diocesan college of consultors.

For religious institutes who are alienating property above the minimum amount set forth for a territory (not yet established in the United States), but not in excess of the maximum amount ($3,000,000 in the United States), the competent authority will be determined by the institute's own statutes. Normally those statutes will divide the responsibilities for approval between the province or equivalent geographic division of the institute, and the generalate. At some point between $500,000 and $3,000,000 the province will be able to act on its own authority; but beyond the amount set by the religious institute's statutes, the approval of the next level of internal authority will be required, usually the generalate.

Values In Excess of the Maximum

For the alienation or jeopardizing of stable patrimony whose value is in excess of the maximum amount set for a territory by the episcopal conference and approved by the Holy See, the approval of the Holy See is required. This is the case whether the stable patrimony belongs to a parish, a diocese or a religious institute. As a result, anytime the stable patrimony of a parish, diocese or religious institute worth more than $3,000,000 is proposed, either to be alienated or to undergo a transaction where it will be subject to a possible loss of value (a worsening of stable patrimonial condition), the Holy See must approve. For dioceses and parishes, the competent authority is the Congregation for the Clergy; for religious institutes, the Congregation for Institutes of Consecrated Life and Societies of Apostolic Life.

Vowed, Artistic or Historic Property

Canon 1292 also sets forth another type of transaction that requires the approval of the Holy See. If a transaction involves either the alienation or jeopardizing of property given to the public juridic person as a result of a vow; or if it involves property that has a special artistic or historic value, then the approval of the Holy See is also required before the public juridic person can either alienate such property or place it in jeopardy of loss.

It may be rare, but possible, that parish, diocesan or religious institute assets have special historical or artistic value. And since the usage of vowed gifts is not common in the United States, there may be few opportunities concerning vowed property. The important thing to note is that there is no specification of monetary value on this particular type of property. All vowed property, all property of significant artistic or historical value, regardless of its value, is subject to the approval of the appropriate dicastery of the Holy See when it is either alienated or placed in jeopardy of loss.

The Alienation Petition

In seeking the approval of the Holy See for a proposed alienation, the petition should contain the following information:

- The identity of the public juridic person seeking the permission;
- A description of the property that is the subject of the proposed transaction. The description should be accurate and complete;
- The names of any parties in interest in the property in addition to the public juridic person seeking the permission, with a description of their interest;
- An explanation of how the property was originally obtained, e.g., purchased, gift, vow;
- The acquisition cost of the property, if it was acquired by purchase, together with a description and cost of subsequent improvements or additions not included in the acquisition cost;

- The appraised value of the property. Canon 1293, §1, 2° requires at least two estimates of value. These should be in writing and attached to the petition;

- The reasons or basis for the proposed transaction: why is it being done? Canon 1293, §1, 1° requires a just cause such as urgent necessity, evident utility, piety, charity or another pastoral reason;

- An assessment of the effect that the alienation of this property will have on the public juridic person's ability to carry on its ministry or to perform its apostolic activities;

- An identification of any other parties to the transaction, e.g. the buyer, the lending institution;

- Is there a broker or other commercial agent facilitating the transaction, and if so, what is the fee or commission, both as a percentage and in actual dollars?;

- A complete explanation of the financial terms of the transaction, e.g., down payment amount, the terms and length of the financing, the loan payment or mortgage schedule;

- A list of the protocol numbers of previous permissions granted by the Holy See to the public juridic person making the request;

- Have all other levels of approval required either by the *Code of Canon Law* or the statutes of the public juridic person been obtained? State what these are and how they were obtained;

- What is the opinion of the local ordinary in the diocese where the subject property is located? It is up to the public juridic person seeking the permission to ask for this from the local bishop. This *votum* may either be attached to the request or sent separately by the bishop;

- A statement of the current financial condition of the public juridic person seeking the permission. This can be answered by providing a summary financial statement such as a balance sheet showing both the assets and liabilities of the public juridic person.

Some Case Studies in Alienation

As we have seen, alienation typically occurs through the sale, gift or corporate transformation of stable patrimony. It is widely, but incorrectly thought that transfers within the Church, from one juridic person to another, are not considered alienation and need no permission. This is not the case. Transfers of stable patrimony from one juridic person to another are considered alienations and are subject to the same alienation procedures as would be the case were the transfer to be from a public juridic person to a non-church party. We must keep this principle in mind as well as we examine the case studies.

CASE 32

A parish closes its grade and high school. A developer wishes to purchase these properties to turn them into a shopping mall. The properties are valued at $600,000 dollars.

1. The Holy See

Since the property valued does not exceed the $3 million limit for the United States, this transaction does not require the approval of the Holy See.

2. National Conference

The National Conference of Catholic Bishops has no direct role in this transaction, but it has legislated, pursuant to canon 1277, that $500,000 is the minimum in the United States for acts of extraordinary administration. Therefore the consent of the diocesan finance council and the college of consultors is necessary for this transaction.

3. Diocese

As noted above, the diocesan finance council and the college of consultors must approve of (consent to) the transaction. In addition, the diocese may have its own statutes or internal procedures that require review by diocesan offices (property management, planning, finance, legal) with expertise in such transaction. While the consent of the diocesan finance council and the college of consultors are necessary for the validity and liceity of this transaction, these expert opinions are not. The opinions of such experts, however, are helpful in making such important decisions.

4. Parish

The consent of the parish financial council may be necessary according to local statutes for acts of extraordinary administration by the parish. This consent is not required by universal law. In addition, local statutes may require the consent or participation of other parish bodies, e.g., parish pastoral council.

CASE 33

> The American province of a religious institute of pontifical right has been operating a high school for one hundred years and can no longer afford to do so. It is located on a ten acre parcel next to the downtown area of the major city in the diocese. The land and buildings, which include a large auditorium, fields for football, soccer and baseball are valued at $7,000,000. The diocese wishes to take over ownership of the high school and to continue operating it as a Catholic high school. The diocese cannot afford to pay the religious institute $7,000,000, however, and it has offered $2,000,000 which the institute has accepted. What approvals are necessary?

1. The Holy See

Since the property is valued at $7,000,000, the approval of the Holy See is necessary for this transaction because $7,000,000 is above the $3,000,000 limit for the United States (c. 638, §3). A petition for alienation must be prepared by the religious institute and submitted to the Congregation for Institutes of Consecrated Life and Societies of Apostolic Life. Note that the amount that indicates the need for the Holy See's approval is not the actual sales price ($2,000,000, which is below the national limit) but the actual value of the property.

2. The Religious Institute

The code specifies that for all transactions in which the patrimonial condition of the institute can be adversely affected, the written permission of the competent superior with the consent of council is required (c. 638, §3). In our example, there are two competent authorities, the provincial superior and council and the general superior and council. Both would have to grant approval.

3. The Diocese

Since the diocese is acquiring and not divesting itself of this property, there is no need for the diocese to obtain any form of alienation permission. This transaction could, however, qualify as an act of extraordinary administration for which the diocese should obtain the consent of the diocesan finance council and the college of consultors (c. 1277).

CASE 34

Fifty years ago a farmer in a country parish donated a ten-acre parcel of land to his parish which was located about five miles from the parish church with the intent that the church lease the land to provide income. As the city near the farm grew, the bishop decided that the land owned by the country parish was the perfect place to establish a new parish. The diocese asked the parish to sell the parcel of land to the new suburban parish established by the bishop. The country parish engaged in a consultation process and agreed to sell the land to the new parish. The price was set at $100,000, which all agreed was a fair price. What approvals are required for this transaction?

1. The Holy See

Since the value of the property to be conveyed is less than $3,000,000, there is no requirement to forward this transaction to the Holy See for approval.

2. The National Conference

According to the norms established by the Conference for alienations, this transaction is below the minimum amount ($500,000), for which the consent of the diocesan finance council and college of consultors would be necessary, thus leaving the issue of the appropriate approvals to local diocesan legislation.

3. The Diocese

Diocesan statutes could give a role (consultative or deliberative) on this matter to a number of diocesan bodies or offices, e.g., the diocesan finance council, the college of consultors, the diocesan property management, planning, finance, or legal offices. This is purely a matter of local law.

4. The Parish

It is likely that diocesan statutes will require the consent of the parish pastoral and finance councils. The parish itself may have its own norms requiring the participation of other parish bodies.

CASE 35

A diocese in a large urban area owns and operates three nursing homes which it built in the 1920s and 1930s. Due to the complex nature of modern health care delivery, the diocese no longer has the expertise to operate these homes out of the diocesan social services office, and it wishes to turn them over to a new corporation with a primarily lay board that the diocese will create in order to manage these homes on a more professional basis. This new corporation is also meant to act as a shield for the diocese for liability purposes in regard to the high-risk activities of the homes. The nursing homes have assessed values of $1.1, $1.3 and $1.5 million dollars, respectively. What approvals are necessary?

1. The Holy See

If these transactions were considered individually, that is, three separate conveyances, the approval of the Holy See would not be necessary. Individually, none of the homes has a value in excess of the national maximum. However, if considered together, and that is the preferable characterization (c. 1292, §3) since the alienation covers the diocese's entire nursing home ministry, then the value does exceed the national maximum and the approval of the Holy See is required. The petition for alienation should be submitted to the Congregation for the Clergy.

2. The National Conference

The National Conference of Catholic Bishops has no direct role in this transaction, but it has legislated, pursuant to canon 1292, §1, that $3,000,000 is the maximum amount in the United States for alienations of stable patrimony. Therefore, the consent of the Holy See is necessary for this transaction, as noted above.

3. The Diocese

The diocesan finance council and the college of consultors must also approve this transaction (c. 1292, §1).

SOME FINAL CANONS ON ALIENATION

Those persons who have the ability to consent to an alienation should not do so unless they are fully informed (c. 1292, §4) and the purpose of an alienation petition is to fully inform the Holy See about the essential details of a transaction. This same requirement, that those who must consent to an alienation be fully informed, also applies at lower levels of approval as well – on the diocesan or religious institute level – although in these situations, since the persons whose consent is sought are usually closer to the transaction, the same level of detail may not be necessary. In addition, when the property being alienated is worth more than $500,000, the ecclesiastical authorities who must give their approval to the alienation are able to set whatever conditions on the alienation they believe are necessary to prevent harm to the Church. In the case of a parish or diocese, this would be the diocesan bishop, who could specify conditions for the proposed alienation above the minimum but not in excess of the maximum amount. For transactions in excess of the maximum, it would be the Holy See who could set such conditions. For transactions involving the stable patrimony of a religious institute, those persons, determined by the institute's statutes, who have the right to approve transactions above the minimum but not in excess of the maximum, also have the right to set conditions as does the Holy See for transactions in excess of the maximum amount. Once an alienation is complete, the proceeds are either to be invested carefully or to be used for the purposes set forth in the request for alienation (c. 1294, §2). The final canon on alienation specifies that where stable patrimony has been alienated by its canonical administrators without obtaining the required canonical permissions, but where the alienation is valid in civil law, church authorities are to decide what action, real or personal, civil or canonical, are to be taken to vindicate the rights of the Church. It is also an ecclesiastical offense, to be punished by a just penalty, for someone to alienate ecclesiastical property without the necessary permission (c. 1377). The procedures described by canon 1296 to vindicate the rights of the Church or the infliction of a penalty as described in canon 1377 for improper alienations are rarely used.

PRESCRIPTION

The concept of prescription is defined in Book I of the *Code of Canon Law* in canon 197 as a "means of acquiring or losing a subjective right and of freeing oneself from obligations." In regard to temporal goods, ownership of which is established by a subjective right in the property, prescription can have the effect of either establishing or extinguishing ownership; and, normally, the establishing of the right in one party means the loss of the right to another. Prescription in regard to property does not only affect rights of ownership. It can also create or extinguish lesser property rights, such as a right to use the property in question without actually owning the property. In civil law, prescription has a parallel in the laws of adverse possession, sometimes referred to in legal shorthand simply as "adversity."

Prescription applies not just to stable patrimony, but to any and all ecclesiastical property and obligations. Canon 1268 recognizes prescription (adverse possession) as a means of both acquiring property and being freed from an obligation. That means that public juridic persons can both gain and lose property by prescription. Although prescription can, as we have noted, apply to non-property situations (i.e., obligations), this section is concerned only with property issues.

Canonical Principles on Prescription

Canons 197 to 199 describe the principles that govern prescription in the Church:

1. The Church recognizes the civil law of the jurisdiction where the property is located as governing the prescription of property (c. 197).

2. Good faith (i.e., a legitimate belief on the part of the occupier that the property is his/hers) from the start of the period of prescription until the end is necessary in order to claim an ownership right in property as a result of prescription (c. 198).

3. While there are a number of exceptions to the applicability of prescription in regard to certain rights and obligations, the only excep-

tion in property matters pertains to the certain and unchallenged boundaries of ecclesiastical territories. These cannot be changed by prescription (c. 199, 4°).

In addition to these general principles set forth in canons 197-199, 1269 provides that sacred objects may be acquired by prescription if they are already privately owned; however, if they belong to a public juridic person, they can only be acquired through prescription by another public juridic person. For example, a crucifix owned by a parish could not be acquired by prescription by an individual.

The code establishes time limits for prescription for immovable property, precious movable objects and rights in real property. When dealing with the immovable property, precious movable objects, or real rights of the Holy See, the prescription period is one hundred years. For most other public juridic persons, the time period for prescription is thirty years. Certain entities such as the Benedictines (sixty years) and the Franciscans (one hundred years) have had longer time limits set by earlier legislation that was not changed by the 1983 code.

The Civil Law

The civil law of each jurisdiction needs to be consulted to determine its application in each case. Since the canons govern cases involving church entities only, the civil law is relevant only where canon law has no provision. For example, if the civil law of a jurisdiction provides a twenty-one year time period in order to acquire property through adverse possession (the civil law equivalent of prescription), this period would not be applicable in a case involving two church entities, one claiming property from another through prescription. However, in cases involving non-church parties claiming ownership of the property of a public juridic person through adverse possession, the twenty-one year civil law period would apply, not the canons' thirty-year period. Besides simple possession for twenty-one years of the property being claimed, the civil law also typically requires that the possession be open, notorious, hostile, exclusive, continuous and under a claim of right or title. The code doesn't deal with such matters, requiring only good faith during the time of possession. These other matters, though, will be issues in the civil law adjudication of a claim of adverse possession.

CASE 36

Parish A has title to property for which it solicited donations for the construction of a Marian shrine. Use of the shrine by Parish A was inconsistent, however, and for one ten year period, the shrine lay dormant. It was then restored by a Marian Sodality from Parish B, which paid both for the restorations and the shrine's upkeep for the next thirty-five years. Parish A now has a new Marian group that wants to take the shrine back. The parishes cannot agree on joint operation of the shrine.

Parish B has filed a petition in the diocesan tribunal to claim title to the shrine, alleging that it both met the civil law and canon law requirements for prescription (adverse possession). In support of its claim, Parish B says the former pastor of Parish A gave it permission to use the shrine. This priest has been dead for over seven years, and there is no written record in the files of either parish of this permission.

Parish B's petition states that it meets the canonical requirements of good faith and continuity. However, Parish A claims that, according to civil law, if Parish B had permission to use the shrine, it cannot assert adverse possession since the civil law requires that adverse possession be hostile, without the consent of the owner.

The tribunal must make its decision based on the canon law, which is not entirely consistent with the civil law in this regard. The code's requirement of good faith and the civil law's requirement that the possession be hostile, without regard for the rights of the real owner do not quite jibe. If Parish B can factually prove its assertion that it believed, in good faith, that it was the owner of the shrine for the thirty-five year period that it operated it, then Parish B should prevail before the tribunal.

CASE 37

A diocese receives by bequest some 65 wooded acres located in a highly rural part of the diocese. The deed from the estate is properly recorded and the diocesan property manager goes out to walk the property, which is very hilly. Besides this, nothing is done with the property except every year to pay the property taxes, which are minimal due to the undeveloped nature of the land.

Well over thirty years later, the diocese gets a generous offer from a logging company to purchase the 65 acres. Preparatory to a sale, the diocese has the property surveyed and finds out, much to its chagrin, that on the eastern side of the property, adjoining a working farm, the neighboring farmer has approximately five of the diocese's acres under tillage. When questioned, the farmer says that he has been farming those five acres for the last twenty-two years, thinking that they were a part of his farm. The state has a twenty-one year statute for adverse possession. In a civil suit of adverse possession against the diocese, the farmer claims ownership of the five acres that he has farmed.

The civil law twenty-one year statute, and not the code's thirty-year statute, will be applied by the civil court.

In regard to claims made by individuals or groups claiming land by virtue of adverse possession, the administrators of public juridic persons must protect the property of the juridic person by means of thorough title searches, accurate surveys and title insurance (which can specifically cover adverse possession) on all property that they acquire, whether it be by purchase, gift or bequest. Such cautions are mandated by canon 1284.

CHAPTER TWENTY-ONE

PIOUS FOUNDATIONS

PATRICIA M. DUGAN

CASE 38

Kathleen Murphy emigrated to the United States from County Mayo, Republic of Ireland in 1939. Once in the United States, she met and married Andrew Dougherty. They had no children and worked hard all of their lives, saving something from every paycheck. Once she had emigrated, Kathleen never saw Ireland again. Andrew died ten years before Kathleen, who continued living frugally and saving from everything she earned. Mary Ellen Sweeney, her friend and the chef at her parish rectory, did a wonderful job of caring for Kathleen after her eightieth birthday. Mary Ellen was with Kathleen at her deathbed, when Kathleen told her to open her stongbox, which she kept under her bed. Inside was ten thousand dollars in cash, the deed to the cemetery plot with Andrew, and Kathleen's Last Will and Testament. Kathleen took the cash, handed it to Mary Ellen and told her it was a gift and that she hoped for her to use it for a trip to Ireland. The Will disposed of everything else Kathleen owned, a residuary estate with a net total of seven hundred and fifty thousand dollars in assets. The Will directed that one-third of the residuary estate go to the Shrine of Our Lady of Knock in Ireland. One-third of the estate was to be given to the Philadelphia parish of Saint Brendan, the Navigator and Discoverer of America, for the continuation of its weekly Mass in Gaelic. The final one-third was to be used for Masses at her parish of Saint Bridget for the repose of the souls of Kathleen and Andrew. The Will named Mary Ellen Sweeney as the Executrix of Kathleen's Estate.

The Archdiocese filed a protest against the trip money given to Mary Ellen; it wanted the gift declared invalid and the money to be distributed as part of the residuary estate. The Shrine at Knock began plans for an Imax theater to threedimensionalize the apparition with stereo sound and light show. Father Malachy, eighty-two years old, and the only Gaelic-speaking priest in North America, was so taken with the generosity of the gift that he suffered a fatal coronary. Saint Bridget's standard Mass stipend is ten dollars, and with two priests in residence, the pastor sought out the local ordinary concerning the acceptance of this bequest.

It is a tenet of natural law that a person is free to dispose of his or her goods in any way he or she wishes. Canon law specifically adds that a person can dispose of possessions for pious causes.[1] These gifts and bequests are very important assets to the Church's pursuing of its mission. Therefore, the individual must have the capacity to do so.[2] To perpetuate these gifts it is critical for the faithful to know that their wishes will be adhered to. The purpose of this section of the *Code of Canon Law* is to arrange for the orderly administration of any gifts, bequests or endowments, which are established to aid the Church's mission in a continual way.

There are two primary ways of transferring property to the Church. If the gift is given while the donor is still alive it is designated as a "gift *inter vivos.*"[3] If the gift takes place only after the death of the donor, it is designated as a "gift *causa mortis.*"[4] Canon 1299 holds that it must be initially and foremost, a voluntary act of the donor, who has the natural capacity to do so.[5] It could happen that a testator or donor is capable of giving something naturally and canonically, but not

---

[1] The pious causes referred to here are defined in canon 114, §2. Purposes mentioned are understood as those, which pertain to works of piety, of the apostolate or of charity, whether spiritual or temporal. These three have roots deep within the life of the worshiping community. These refer to personal sanctification and holiness, the proclamation of the gospel and the enhancement of public worship and the works of spiritual and temporal charities.

[2] This can be done orally or by written instrument. Civil laws, varying from jurisdiction to jurisdiction, may require a written instrument be used for different types of property. Civil laws always require that a written instrument be used to transfer real property.

[3] For the receiver of the gift, the acceptance is in some way presumed, that is, will not be refused and that it is able to be received in good faith.

[4] The effect of the gift in relation to the death is immediate.

[5] Such a gift cannot be legitimately made by a minor, or incompetent. In addition, canon law itself sets limits on some persons in religious institutes from freely disposing or their goods.

civilly.[6] Canon law would not recognize this civil incapacity and insist that there is at least a moral obligation to permit the execution of the will to the intention of the testator or donor. In the *Code of Canon Law*, the norms for contracts give precedence to the civil law binding in the jurisdiction. When it comes to gifts for pious causes however, the Church does not simply yield to the civil law as controlling. While gifts *inter vivos* and based on a contractual relationship must be in a civilly valid form to have canonical validity,[7] the Church insists that a person must be free to give gifts to pious causes in the Church in any humanly valid form. If a gift does not conform to civil law requirements, it would follow that it would not be possible to use the civil courts to ensure that the intention of the testator or donor is fulfilled.[8] This canon does encourage that where possible, the will respect all civil law formalities.[9] If this is not done, this canon calls for reminding the heirs of their obligation under this canon, to fulfill the last wishes of the deceased regarding the gifts to pious causes. The civil formalities must be adhered to as closely as possible as a protection to both the testator and the Church. Without a will, the ordinary has the obligation to see that the heirs are so advised. This is a mandatory act for the ordinary, not an option (c. 1301, §1).

It is frequently the case that a testator will attach conditions or other qualifications to the gift. Canon 1300 makes the purely moral obligation a canonical one as well. In such circumstances, the Church is to be protected from outside control, overly burdensome conditions, or bizarre qualifications placed on the gift (cc. 1267, §2 and 1304, §1). Gifts proffered with conditions connected to them must have the permission of the ordinary to accept the gift along with the conditions.[10] This canon does not imply that a testator of a pious will can automatically bind the Church to a way of acting. The Church is not bound until it accepts the will with its conditions. The Church can reject the will if it is found that the conditions attached to it cannot be observed.

---

[6] For example, if there were a civil law that prohibited gifts to the Church.

[7] See canon 1290.

[8] A major problem would be in determining the true intent of the donor. At what point would a gift under consideration become an actual gift or bequest? In civil law, the answer in many jurisdictions is only when it is written down.

[9] These could include specific recitations that what is being done is a "Will;" that there be a designated number of witnesses; and that signatures conform to a specific type of requirement set out specifically in the civil law.

[10] These are also frowned upon in civil law as a reaching out from the grave. One often seen case involves a condition that the surviving spouse receive a bequest only if the surviving spouse never remarries.

Taken as a whole, canon 1301 is designed to guarantee that the wishes of the testator will always be carried out. The ordinary has a right and a duty to make certain that this happens.[11] An executor in canon law is the person[12] responsible for the complete and orderly administration of the gifts and bequests.[13] In canon law, it is always the ordinary who is the executor of the will. Obviously, this could clash with the executor as named to satisfy civil law requirements. In this canon, the Church continues to subrogate civil law to itself by declaring null and void any instructions attached to bequests which contradict this right and duty of the ordinary to supervise their proper execution. The obligations of the ordinary are to be vigilant, even by inspection, to see that the bequest is fulfilled. If there are executors appointed by the will, other than the ordinary, they must give a full accounting of their stewardship to the ordinary as part of the course of their work.

TRUSTS

A trust is a gift of money, property or goods, which is given for a pious cause, but not given directly to any ecclesiastical entity. Rather, it is given to a private person, a third person.[14] When a person gives money to a pastor, it is a gift to the parish and not a trust (c. 1267, §1). If the money is clearly given to the trustee as a private person, it is a trust. When a gift is given via a trust, it is a grave obligation[15] for the trustee to inform the ordinary of such a trust for pious causes. Canon 1302 does not specify any time limit for such notification. In addition under this canon, all immovable goods must be indicated in the notice, along with any obligations such as liens or mortgages due and owing. If the testator specifically forbade the notification of the ordinary regarding the trust, the position of trustee should not be accepted.[16]

---

[11] See c. 134, §1. All ordinaries mentioned in this canon have this responsibility including: the Roman Pontiff, diocesan bishops, major superiors of clerical religious institutes of pontifical right, and of clerical societies of apostolic life of pontifical right.

[12] In civil law, this could be an institution such as a bank.

[13] In civil law, the executor has other responsibilities such as publishing the estate, paying all debts and satisfying all state and federal inheritance and estate taxes.

[14] In civil law, whenever a trust is established, a trustee is also named to administer the trust. Frequently it is the executor who is also named as the trustee. A trustee has to be specifically appointed.

[15] Use of the Latin word "*debet*" characterizes the obligation as such.

[16] "*Omnia*" in the Latin, makes the notification of the ordinary a *sine qua non* for the accepting of the fiducial mantle of trustee.

Along with the norms of canon 1301, the ordinary has a responsibility toward the trust. All of the assets of the trust must be assembled, identified, and accounted for, to aid the ordinary in his responsibility. An executor administers and disperses. A trust involves a holding and administering of the assets, or trust principal, often dispersing only the income on principal for the purposes of the pious causes. Therefore, the responsibility of the ordinary under this canon is to keep and safeguard the assets for as long as the trust exists.

When a trust is established with the principal being committed to a member of a religious institute or a society of apostolic life, the identification of the ordinary may become clouded. It depends on whom the trust assets are intended to benefit. If it is the diocese, a place, or a pious cause of either a diocese or place, the ordinary is the local ordinary or bishop. Otherwise, it is the major superior of either the religious institute or the proper ordinary in any type of institute.

WHAT ARE PIOUS FOUNDATIONS? – CANON 1303

There are two types of pious foundations: autonomous pious foundations and non-autonomous pious foundations.[17] For autonomous foundations, there are three conditions at the base of their existence. An autonomous foundation must consist of a collection of goods that has been erected into a juridic person by a competent authority.[18] The non-autonomous foundation involves goods given to a public juridic person,[19] that is, added to a public juridic person and not constituted in itself as a public juridic person.[20] Its purpose is for the celebration of Masses, for the carrying out of some ecclesial function or for the means mentioned in canon 114, §2. These purposes are regulated by particular law.[21]

---

[17] In the former code of 1917, only non-autonomous foundations were called foundations. An autonomous foundation was called a "benefice" (see c. 1493 of the CIC 1917). Today the concept of pious foundation has been enlarged from the 1917 code.

[18] The intervention of the authority is specific to each individual foundation and constitutes it as a juridic person.

[19] This is a foundation of goods themselves, which can be either collegial or non-collegial.

[20] The intervention of the authority here is simply according to the regulations of particular law which provide for the length of survival of the foundation and its disposition when the time runs out.

[21] "*Fundatio*" has many definitions. It could relate to the donor's proposal of a gift; to the act itself of giving the gift; to the goods themselves; to the total complex of goods. In the strict sense, it would relate to the goods themselves, once they have been received and accepted by the recipient, along with the juridical acts required for such acceptance.

There are common elements between the two types of foundations here. They are both a Mass of goods. They both are directed to certain ends consistent with the nature of the Church. Both require some sort of intervention by the competent authority. The difference between the autonomous and non-autonomous is based solely in the intervention of authority upon the foundation. The difference reflects the foundation's ability to stand on its own. In the autonomous foundation, the authority is specific to the foundation. In the non-autonomous foundation, the intervention is simply according to the regulations of particular law.

In comparing the 1917 code and the 1983 code, although autonomous foundations as juridic persons are by their nature perpetual, the current code no longer speaks of a perpetual foundation.[22] When a foundation is entrusted to a juridic person, even for a long time, it is not founded in an absolute sense, but rather with conditions; and it is different from a gift, which has no conditions attached. The "onus" cannot be separated from the foundation but is essential to it. Normally, this "onus" can last from thirty to fifty years, but it is determined by the particular law.[23]

The second paragraph of canon 1303, §2 answers a critical and related question. Where do the goods go after the foundation has expired? There are different possibilities. They may go to the diocesan fund.[24] These residue goods can go to another place specifically mentioned by the founder. Finally, they may go to the religious institute on which the goods are conferred.[25]

Canon 1304 clearly obligates the public juridic person to first seek the permission of the ordinary to accept the gift (c. 134, §1). This permission to accept must be in writing. Before giving a permission, the ordinary must exercise great care.[26] He must take special care to investigate all aspects of the gift in relation to the

---

[22] "*Cum onere.*"

[23] This is an area that could end in a conflict with civil law. In many jurisdictions, perpetual gifts are acceptable under civil law. If such a gift is made with a condition that knows no end, the gift may be void unless it can be accepted by the foundation without a time limitation.

[24] This is established by canon 1274, §1.

[25] This paragraph of the canon deals specifically with what happens at the end of the time of the allotted goods. The first two possibilities hold when the goods were initially entrusted to a public juridic person, subject to the diocesan bishop.

[26] The ordinary must be convinced first, that the foundation can in fact fulfill any condition attached to the proffered gift. There must be a consideration of any pre-existing obligations binding the foundation. This is especially true in regard to Mass foundations. Vice-versa, the ordinary must be convinced that the value of the gift is sufficient to support conditions attached to it. This again, is especially true in regard to Mass foundations.

conditions attached.[27] In an additional paragraph under this canon, further conditions on the acceptance of the gift can be defined by particular law, both for constituting and accepting a foundation or gift.[28]

Canon 1305 calls for the immediate[29] and prudential[30] safeguarding of assets, specifically movable goods.[31] Movable goods may be sold; but if they are sold, the money must be deposited.[32] It is not necessary that the goods, or proceeds be, "banked," but that they be held in a safe place, or with a safe person. Any such investment should have the permission of the ordinary for validity.

Canon 1306 is most practical. With the passage of time, oral agreements can be innocently altered, forgotten or misunderstood. This canon requires that the terms of the foundation are to be in writing. The terms are to state everything that is to be given. In this way, it has the same nature as a contract.[33] The writing of the foundation is part of the juridical structure of it and is necessary

---

[27] This fulfillment of conditions, as specified by the donor, is extremely important within the civil systems of law. Once an executor accepts the gift, failure to fulfill the gift can bring about litigation, a return of the entire gift and additional penalties that could go beyond the liability for the original value of the gift. If an executor or trustee under civil specifications were to fail to enforce the conditions in full, that fiduciary under the civil system could find himself liable personally for money damages to the estate of the donor.

[28] Referring back to the precedent paragraph, such additional conditions would be cognizant of local customs in the region or place where the gift is made.

[29] "*Statim*" translated as immediately, and within the commentaries usually means within three days. This is not always practical since the probate of an estate could certainly take weeks longer than that in certain jurisdictions. Until probate is completed, the movable goods can probably not be liquidated at all. In western countries, it is not practical to imagine that the funeral has even taken place within three days.

[30] This canon seems to presume that the movable good will be sold. The presumption is that the goods will be sold unless the goods themselves are precious and show some promise of increasing in value.

[31] Immovable goods are not mentioned as it was considered that they could not be taken or stolen. This does not necessarily imply that the principal value cannot decrease, and it would follow that they may also be subject to liquidation in order to preserve the original value.

[32] In this case, all of the laws regarding the alienation of goods in the code continue to control.

[33] In the United States, this would be very comparable to the statute of frauds, which very clearly requires writing of certain and most contracts in order for them to be enforceable. If they are not written, they are strictly barred from enforcement no matter what the factual basis or equitable nature of the underlying agreement.

for the validity of the foundation. In foundations that stretch over long periods of time, it is critical that written records be kept to document the events enacted to fulfill the conditions placed on the foundation.[34]

Canon 1308, §1 provides the general principle regarding reduction of Masses required by a foundation. This ability to reduce is reserved to the Holy See. If the appeal must be made in the internal forum, then it is to the Sacred Penitentiary that the reduction is directed. If the appeal is made in the external forum, it is made to the appropriate Congregations of Clergy, Religious, or Oriental Churches. There must be extremely stringent conditions to justify such a reduction.

One exception to reduction restricted to the Holy See is that the appropriate ordinary may reduce a Mass obligation on the ground of reduced income if the document of foundation specifically indicates that such can be the case. Such a dictation into the originating document would be of maximum benefit to the foundation as well as the intention of the donor. The present code tries to unify the system of obligations of foundations to include rosaries, novenas, etc. in addition to Masses. The general principle is that the founder gives permission for a reduction or change in the foundation.

A second exception occurs when there is no provision in the letter of foundation for a reduction, but a change in the foundation. Paragraph three of canon 1308 directs the elements necessary for liceity in doing so. This entire paragraph with all of its elements must be specifically followed. On the sole basis of diminution of income, the ordinary must consider the level of the offering lawfully current in the diocese (cc. 950 and 952). Such a reduction can only occur while the diminution of income persists. The ordinary can only take such action if there is no obligation to increase the offering in any mandatory way. Under paragraph four of this canon, the ordinary can do the same reduction for ecclesiastical institutes, such as Catholic hospitals.

Finally in canon 1308, §5, the supreme moderator of a clerical religious institute of pontifical right has the same powers as those given in paragraphs three and four.[35]

Canon 1309 characterizes changes to conditions other than a reduction in the number of Masses to be accidental. The competent authorities listed in the pre-

---

[34]Regarding Masses, one must refer to canon 958 outlining a special book, which lists the intentions, stipends, and dates of obligations being met, for each Mass offered. This book must be available for examination as it is considered to be a public book.

[35]The organization of this canon is specific to the various authorities discussed. Paragraph one relates to the Apostolic See; paragraph two to the ordinary; paragraphs three and four to the diocesan bishop, and paragraph five to the supreme moderator of a clerical institute of pontifical right.

vious canon may transfer Mass obligations to days, churches, or altars different from those designated by the foundation. These authorities may make such changes for suitable reasons.[36] As such, these types of changes can be made more readily than the reduction of Masses.

The final canon governing pious foundations is canon 1310. Again, it deals with changes to the foundation.[37] The ordinary can reduce,[38] moderate,[39] or commute[40] the wills of the faithful for pious causes. Such changes must be expressly permitted by the founder, and there must be a just and necessary cause for making changes. The ordinary must stay within the limits of the pious foundation's terms. The ordinary cannot act without discretion. He may only act on his power for a just and necessary cause.[41]

Paragraph two of canon 1310 deals specifically with the impossibility of fulfillment. If the impossibility is due to insufficient funds, or other reasons not attributable in specific fault to an administrator, the ordinary can act. First, he must consult with interested parties as well as with his own financial council. Throughout, the ordinary must attempt to preserve the will of the founder as far as possible.[42] This in turn means that the funds may be diverted into another work, which is similar to the intention of the founder, even if the original work may no longer be directly fulfilled for any reason.

Under canon 1310, §3, other cases must be referred to the Holy See, or the Congregations for Religious, Clergy, or Oriental Churches.

In respect to the case study at hand, as soon as Kathleen placed the cash money into Mary Ellen's hands, she accomplished a legal gift. Mary Ellen was under no obligation to use the gift for a trip to Ireland since Kathleen only expressed the hope that Mary Ellen would take the trip that she so wished she had taken. The archdiocese cannot void the gift since it was given and accepted

---

[36] In this canon, the reason needs only be "*congrua*" most often translated as suitable, proportionate or convenient.

[37] This canon treats the obligations that are not Masses.

[38] "*Reductio*" is in the sense of number, frequency, length, etc.

[39] The term "*moderatio*," in general, signifies a specific "*actio*" in the execution of a pious foundation, that is, a change in date, place, etc., along with the time and manner.

[40] The term "*commutatio*" indicates that changing the date, place, altar, etc., is an auxiliary or non-essential element of the will.

[41] The ordinary is still bound here by canon 1300 specifying "*diligentissime impleantur.*"

[42] This preservation of the intent of the founder is tantamount in civil law.

all before Kathleen's death. It was a gift inter vivos. Because of the proximity of the gift to death though, most states would require Mary Ellen to pay an inheritance tax on the money.

The bequest to the Shrine at Knock is legal both civilly and canonically. The Shrine is free to use it in any way it wishes. Because it is a gift to a charity, it is not subject to any inheritance tax whether state or federal.

The bequest to Saint Brendan's for the celebration of Masses in Irish, cannot be distributed. The specific condition upon which the gift is given, cannot be complied with. Under civil law, because this gift is given as part of the residuary, the other residuary legatees (recipients) have an interest in this gift failing. Since it is given as part of the residuary, if it fails, the other two residuary heirs will split that gift as well. Even if Mary Ellen, the executor, wanted to alter the gift, she would not be able to do so civilly without the agreement of the Shrine at Knock and Kathleen's home parish. With the rising construction costs of Imax theaters, the chances of that happening are simply not good.

If this gift had not been a residuary gift, but rather a gift with a set amount of money as a specific bequest, some states' civil laws would allow for some flexibility in satisfying the specific gift as long as the executor is in agreement. Many wills actually give the executor discretion on specific bequests with conditions to alter the condition as long as the spirit of the bequest is maintained. Scribers of wills with such bequests and conditions in the intent of the testator should be flexible in drafting such bequests.

The final gift is given specifically for the celebration of Masses for Kathleen and Andrew at the parish of Saint Bridget. With the addition of the failed residuary bequest for Masses in Gaelic, the parish has $375,000 in Mass offerings to be said at the rate of ten dollars per Mass in the parish. With two priests stationed at the parish, and assuming that the parish stops celebrating Mass for any other intention, it would take more than fifty-one years to satisfy this condition if two Masses are offered every day.

Civilly, the executor has some discretion in accepting the terms she deems satisfactory in fulfilling the condition of this residuary bequest. If she was of the mind that the celebration of one Mass was sufficient to insure salvation, this would be acceptable civilly. If she distributed the amount to a Mass guild of some kind, this would be another option for fulfillment of this conditional bequest. Any connection between the gift and the celebration of Mass, would most likely be acceptable in every state.

Canonically, there can be a reduction of Masses by the appropriate ordinary. Saint Bridget's must receive the permission of the ordinary in order to accept this gift. The ordinary is obligated to fulfill the conditions of the gift and the gift can only be accepted if he believes the intent of the testator can be satisfied. There is a general provision that the testator gives permission for a reduction or change in conditions. Canonically, the ordinary has the ability to reduce the Masses to be said; and civilly, Mary Ellen can accept this reduction. This can be done without great deviation from the condition set out, even though no provision for a deviation was outlined in the will itself or, the ordinary can establish a special program for Masses left in a will without specifying the number of Masses to be celebration.

CHAPTER TWENTY-TWO

INCORPORATED APOSTOLATES

MELANIE DiPIETRO, S.C.

INTRODUCTION AND CASE STUDY

This chapter is limited to a discussion of some fundamental concepts concerning the legal[1] structure of a public benefit or charitable nonprofit corporation[2] that are useful to protect the Church's interests as it carries out its charitable apostolates through the mechanism of a corporation. While the concepts discussed herein are common to all charitable, nonprofit corporations, the way in which they are used to protect canonical principles will vary according to the precise activity involved.

The application of both legal and canonical principles is very fact-specific. The application and the significance of the legal principles governing the fiduciary duties of trustees in a charitable, nonprofit corporation; the use and ultimate disposition of its property; and the access to revenue from government and private contracts for its services are each relevant to a determination of the canonical principles that may be operative in each situation. The actual governance structure that may work in a healthcare institution may not be as workable in a social service agency or in a college.

Too often, practitioners focus on discovering a model and replicating that model, without enough sensitivity to the specific facts and circumstances of the parties. Corporate models are solutions to identified canonical and legal interests.

---

[1] The use of "legal" structures or secular law in this paper is restricted to the context of American law. "Canonical" or "juridic" is restricted to the context of canon law.

[2] Charitable or religious corporations qualify as exempt corporations under Section 501(c)(3) of the Internal Revenue Code of 1986, as amended. The Model Nonprofit Corporation Act refers to these kinds of corporations as "public benefit or religious corporations." A corporation may have a non-profit structure in accord with state law without qualifying as a 501(c)(3) corporation, which are subject to trust law principles as well as corporate law. The 501(c)(3) public benefit, public charitable corporation is the topic of this chapter.

While some models may be more commonly useful, no one model, in precisely the same form, is appropriate for each situation.

The purpose of this chapter is to relate some fundamental principles of public charitable corporations to selected canonical principles that are relevant to the operation of incorporated apostolates. Hopefully, the discussion will enable those engaged in the apostolates to develop appropriate and workable structures tailored to their specific professional environment.

The discussion of the interrelationship of canonical and legal principles is preceded by three preliminary operational fact patterns. One, a description is given of the operational and structural distinctions between corporations and canonical entities.

Two, a distinction is made between church corporations and church-related corporations. The labeling of a church and church-related corporation as used in this chapter is not defined authoritatively in American statutes or case law. The factual distinctions are set forth by the author to assist the reader in following the author's analysis and thesis concerning the fact-specific application of canonical principles to corporations.

Three, a distinction is made between the autonomy of a freestanding corporation and the limitations resulting from participation of a church-related corporation in a joint venture such as the one illustrated in the case study. The case study presents a venture between a church-related community corporation and non-related corporation that unifies governance management. Through unified control over assets, but not transfer of ownership, an operational merger is effected.

The theory of the application of legal and canonical principles to the complex facts of a joint venture is the same as the application to freestanding corporation; it is just more difficult! The complex fact situation of the case study is used for several reasons. One, it is a situation currently facing many hospitals and diocesan charities agencies. Joint ventures are also being introduced in higher education. Two, addressing fundamental legal and canonical concepts in a complex situation reinforces the need to understand the underlying purpose for each of the governance structures of a corporation discussed later in the chapter. Three, the complex fact situation illustrates the need to understand the interrelationship between specific canonical concepts and the operation of law governing charitable corporations. Governance structures that may work in a freestanding corporation may not have the same effect in the life of a joint venture. Finally, the joint venture raises a fuller spectrum of issues than a simple freestanding corporation.

After the identification of the interrelationship of selected canonical principles with the fundamental legal principles, the chapter ends with some criteria for the application of these principles in the development of appropriate governance structures and the evaluation of changes to governance autonomy that may be necessitated by circumstances such as those described in the case study.

Distinctions between Canonical and Legal Entities

The appropriate application of canonical principles and the effective use of American law to protect canonical concerns in an incorporated apostolate requires a recognition of the factual and operational distinctions among the canonical entity, a church corporation and a church-related corporation.

The case study of this chapter involves the relationship between a canonical entity and church-related corporations. The church corporation, as defined in this section, is not involved in this case study. The diocese or the religious institute itself is the canonical entity. Throughout this chapter, the incorporated apostolate is referred to as the church-related corporation to distinguish it from a church corporation.

The corporation doing the business of the canonical entity, the diocese or the religious institute, is referred to in this chapter as a church corporation. Its purposes are very broad and may include the entire teaching, sanctifying and governing mission of the Church. It is funded primarily by its members, the faithful; its activities are primarily focused on its members; and its governance authority is vested only in those with ecclesiastical office. In American law, it usually enjoys the fullest protection from government laws and regulations granted by the First Amendment to Churches.

The church-related corporation is characterized by a narrower legal purpose and by a pluralism in funding, in governance and in the clientele served. Its funding may be through government and commercial insurance contract as well as contributions from the Church or faithful; it may be governed by representatives from the canonical entity who have *ex officio* positions as members or trustees and Catholic and non-Catholic trustees; and it serves all persons with no religious qualifications or intention to convert to the Roman Catholic Church.

Church-related corporations, such as hospitals, colleges and social services, do not enjoy the same scope of exemptions from the law. For example, they often are subject to federal and state laws controlling government grants and contracts, licensure, accreditation, labor management laws, employee laws, environmental regulations and so on.

Having the legal status of a public charitable, public benefit corporation, church-related corporations, like any other public charitable corporation, are subject to the jurisdiction of the state attorneys general, who represent the claims of the corporations' constituents and beneficiaries, donors and the public.

Because of their church affiliation, church-related corporations are also subject to challenges to their participation in government funding or to their adherence to their religious doctrines in the delivery of their services.[3]

The effective use of the American law of public charitable corporations to protect appropriate canonical interests requires clarity in the identity of the principal actor and the forum in which the activity is occurring. The canonical entity acts in the canonical forum when it is the primary actor engaged in sanctifying and governing the faithful and in teaching and preaching. The church corporation operates in the secular forum when it is the primary legal actor carrying on the business and property affairs of the canonical entity.

The focus of this chapter is on the church-related corporation operating in the secular legal forum. Therefore, it is necessary to be attentive both to the structure of the church-related corporation and to the operating relationship between the canonically responsible juridic entity[4] and the church-related corporation.

Autonomy: Freestanding vs. Partner in a Joint Venture

The development and evaluation of appropriate legal structures to protect church interests in the organization and operation of incorporated apostolates requires distinguishing the church-related corporation as a freestanding corporation from its participation as a partner in a joint venture as illustrated in the case study.

A freestanding corporation refers to a single corporation that enjoys a singularity and unity of legal purpose and governing authority. An example is a hospital, Catholic charities corporation or a Catholic college. While colleges may have various governance structures, most freestanding hospitals and charities agencies have a membership model of corporate governance. In this model, the appropriate governing authority of the canonically responsible juridic person or its designees are positioned as members who reserve certain powers in the corporation.[5] Through the members' unilateral reservation of control over the articles and bylaws of the corporation, the appointment of trustees, the approval of encumbrances and the sale of substantially all of the property of the corporation,

---

[3] *St. Agnes Hosp. of the City of Baltimore, Inc. v. Riddick*, 748 F. Supp. 319 (D. Md. 1990); Kendrick v. Sullivan, 766 F. Supp. 1180 (D.D.C. 1991).

[4] The canonically responsible juridic person, or juridic person, is the canonical entity responsible for the incorporated apostolate. It is either the religious institute or the diocese. The term "sponsor" is often used to refer to the responsible canonical entity.

[5] See Adam J. Maida and Nicholas P. Cafardi, *Church Property, Church Finances and Church-Related Corporations, A Canon Law Handbook* (Catholic Health Association of the United States, 1984) ch. 6 (hereafter referred to as Maida and Cafardi).

the approval of mergers or other corporate changes, and the approval of dissolution and the distribution of property upon the dissolution, American nonprofit corporation law is used to protect church interests in the incorporated apostolate. All of these powers are unified and in the exclusive control of the members, who are the representatives of the canonically responsible juridic person. This unilateral and initiating power allows the member to control the identity of the decision-makers in the corporation (trustees) and to establish the values which control both the process and the content of the decisions that are made in the corporation. There is one single duty of loyalty and obedience of the trustees to the single purpose and Catholic identity of the freestanding corporation.[6]

The joint operating company described in the case study is an example of a joint venture that integrates the governance, finances and management of two formerly unrelated freestanding corporations. There is such a unity of operations that they are often popularly referred to as "virtual mergers." The unity of purpose and power described above for the freestanding corporation is fragmented in a joint operating company. For example, the trustees of a joint operating company may have a fiduciary duty to both a Catholic hospital and a non-Catholic hospital, the joint venturers. The canonically responsible juridic person is usually distanced from immediate control of governance and management of the joint operating company, which controls its hospital. The duties of loyalty and obedience of the trustees are now to the general purposes of the joint operating company, not exclusively to the purposes of the church-related corporation or of any of the partners in the joint operating company.

The degree and scope of the canonically responsible juridic person's shared governing authority varies according to its political and economic strength in relationship to the partners in the joint venture. Therefore, the structure of each venture needs to be examined using the criteria of purpose and power, discussed later in the chapter, with the expectation that the model of each joint venture may differ according to what can be negotiated among the parties. There is no one model that can be replicated in every fact situation. Nor will every acceptable model satisfy all of the criteria.

The joint venture described herein is commonly referred to as a joint operating agreement. A joint operating agreement, often referred to as a "virtual merger" or a revenue sharing corporation is distinguishable from other joint ventures by its high level of governance and management integration. While not legally merged and while no assets may actually be legally conveyed initially, the opera-

---

[6]Daniel L. Kurtz, *Safeguarding the Mission: The Duties and Liabilities of Officers and Directors of Nonprofit Organizations*, ALI-ABA (American Law Institute, 1992) 726.

tional unification and the consolidation of services resulting from the intended maturation of the joint operating agreement is practically irrevocable. Therefore, the analysis of such a joint venture requires a technical and operational analysis of principles, legal and canonical, in the context of geographical, economic and political factors common to joint ventures among health and social service agencies as illustrated herein.

CASE 39

The religious institute, the Sisters of St. Lawrence, is the public juridic person canonically responsible in the church for St. Lawrence Community Hospital, which is two miles away from Ardmore Community Hospital in Ardmore, USA. The potential patient base of the service area of the two hospitals is expected to decline, causing a 30% loss of patient days to St. Lawrence and a similar loss to Ardmore. These decreasing occupancy levels create a number of vulnerabilities for St. Lawrence, including loss of market share, increased difficulty in managed care contracting and a more limited development of services, outreach activities and physician affiliations.

An analysis of future volume and capacity levels indicates that the two facilities should be combined into one. As a combined entity, they could offer more effective and efficient development of services for the residents of the area, more specialized acute care services and a broader continuum of services in the community.

If consolidation does not take place, the level of their competition will increase. Neither hospital has the capital resources to sustain such a competition contest. If Ardmore joined with another larger system, this would cause a severe drain on the limited resources of St. Lawrence since there would be intensified competition. St. Lawrence could risk bankruptcy by continued competition with a larger system. This, of course, increases the risk to bondholders and employees.

If the two hospitals joined together, they could achieve an initial savings of $50 million and devote continuing operating revenues to developing new and improved services.

St. Lawrence has done an exhaustive analysis of partnerships with Catholic facilities, and there is no Catholic hospital that can create an economic fit with St. Lawrence. However, St. Lawrence, if it collaborated with Catholic Charities, Inc., could be an attractive partner to Ardmore, and among them, they could create an integrated delivery service system for the residents of Ardmore. Since the diocese is the canonically responsible juridic person for Catholic Charities, Inc., the bishop expects the board and management of Catholic Charities to talk with

CASE 39: *continued*

the board of St. Lawrence Hospital. Since Catholic Charities is much smaller than St. Lawrence Hospital, its executive director is discussing a joint venture with a larger, non-church-related social agency so it can have more clout in negotiating with St. Lawrence.

St. Lawrence and Ardmore are talking but have not yet signed a letter of intent to create a revenue sharing, joint operating company.

Operational Effect of a Revenue-Sharing, Joint Operating Company

A joint operating company achieves many of the benefits of integration and centralized control that would result from a legal merger without an initial transfer of the title of the ownership of the assets. However, both corporations agree to place all of their operating assets under the control of the new joint operating company, wherein they share a permanent and substantial degree of governing authority. The Catholic partner, though still a corporation, loses the autonomy it had as a freestanding corporation. The new joint operating company determines the operating and capital budgets, the information system, the allocation of services between the healthcare sites and all management and contracting decisions. Governance powers reserved for unilateral exercise by the partners for their corporations is usually minimal. The partnering corporations share both the risks and rewards of the operation. Usually, there is a financial formula developed for the sharing of revenues generated by the partners to the joint operating agreement. Regardless of which corporation in the partnership generates the revenues, the formula allocates the split of risks and rewards between the partnering corporations. Often, it is foreseeable that two acute care corporations will be merged into one surviving acute care corporation. The parties agree to develop the network of services in their joint venture on objective economic and efficiency criteria. Therefore, theoretically, it is possible that the two existing provider corporations will remain. It is also possible that one campus will provide acute care services and another campus will provide other licensed healthcare or social services. It is also possible that the new company will be a licensed provider either in addition to the original licensed corporations or in place of the original licensed corporations. These kinds of decisions are vested in the newly created board of the joint operating company. Usually, no partner has any guarantees concerning future configurations of services or continued corporate existence.

In the typical shared governance arrangement of a joint operating company, the church-related corporation loses the power to initiate or to have exclusive control of any of the above decisions. These decisions constitute the unity of purpose and power described earlier in the discussion of a freestanding corporation. Usually, a joint concurring vote is required of both the church-related corporation and the non-church-related corporation to make fundamental and irrevocable decisions in the joint operating company. Such decisions may include the merger of the acute care facilities, the transfer of licenses or the admission of new members to the joint operating company. Legally, the consent of the church-related party may be necessary if the shared governance is based on an equal sharing of authority between the partners. In practice, however, once the services are consolidated, it will be operationally impossible to unravel the network. The sheer weight of economics may compel a later merger, which could result in the loss of a distinctive corporate church-related provider, even if the shell of a corporation can be maintained. The point of a joint operating company is to achieve precisely these efficiencies and unifications, without bias or control by the partners. The church-related corporation, over time, may not exist as a provider, but remain as an investment partner in non-Catholic provider or network. It is precisely this effect which necessitates a fact-specific operational and legal analysis over the life of the joint venture to determine the canonical issues in these types of ventures.

CANONICAL AND LEGAL PRINCIPLES

The canonical practice in the United States has been to discuss the application of the *Code of Canon Law* (code) to incorporated apostolates by focusing on the property issues in Book V of the code. This approach has been effective in focusing internal church attention to the development of the governance structures of freestanding corporations for the apostolates entrusted to one or more public juridic persons. The focus on property subject to Book V assumes the relationship to a public juridic person. The existence and relationship of a single responsible public juridic person to a freestanding corporation is present in the discussion of the unity of purpose and power described in the discussion of the typical membership model corporation. Since this singleness and unity of purpose exists in fact, the assumptions of the code and the principles of other canons relevant to the apostolates entrusted to public juridic persons, such as religious institutes, were and are operative. These principles and assumptions may not have needed to be explicitly identified in the discussion of governance structures for freestanding corporations related to single public juridic persons.

The advent of joint operating companies and the trend of religious institutes to seek greater collaboration with other juridic persons and the laity in the development of new canonical and legal structures requires a clearer articulation of the assumptions of the code. In addition to explicating the assumptions in Book V, it is necessary to identify the interrelationship of other canons, which are relevant in the application of the canons of Book V. These will include canons on the status of a public juridic person and its special role in acting "in the name of the Church." For religious institutes, it will include consideration of the importance of works entrusted to it by the Church. These canonical facts are relevant to the application of canons on the acquisition of property or property rights as well as the administration of property pertaining to a public juridic person for purposes authorized by the code and in compliance with standards defined by the code.

The following enumeration of the canonical principles to be protected through the various structures of a public charitable corporation attempts to describe the organic interrelationships of the canons of the code in regard to the public apostolate of the immediately responsible public juridic person for works entrusted to them and which they do in the name of the Church:

1. The proper objective of a church right or interest in property is the work of charity, which is essential to the Church's mission. The Church has the right and duty to perform works of charity or education and to acquire necessary resources to do them (c. 1254).

2. The Church has the right to use any just means for the acquisition of any type of, or right to, or interest in property for its objectives (cc. 1254 and 1259). This interest (whether it be a contract right, ownership, a trust obligation, a tangible or intangible legal right, etc.) and the objective of the property interest are to be protected in accord with the code and secular law (c. 1284).

3. The special status of a public juridic person enables it to act in the name of the Church (c. 116).

4. Religious institutes are entrusted with apostolic works which are, to each of them, "proper works" to be done in the name of the Church and in communion with the Church (cc. 578; 671; 675 and 677).

5. The public apostolate undertaken by a specific institute in its name is to be directed by the duly elected leadership (cc. 618; 622; 677 and 678) and in consultation with the diocesan bishop (c. 678) and subject to his coordination (c. 394).

6. The proper works of an institute constitute the patrimony and patrimonial condition of the institute (c. 578 and *Perfectae Caritatis*, pars. c. 2, 3 and 8).

7. The alienation of stable patrimony or any transaction worsening or jeopardizing the patrimonial condition of a religious institute (or of a diocese) is subject to the norms governing alienation (cc. 1291–1295).

8. In the use of property dedicated to a proper objective, the immediately responsible public juridic person must exercise prudential administration, preserving the capital, accounting for income and investments, protecting the intentions of donors and ensuring the availability of the safeguards of civil law and compliance with canon law (c. 1284).

9. In the use of property for proper objectives, administrators are to be vigilant in observing church teachings in regard to employees and the social life of the community (c. 1286).

Legal Principles of Public Charitable Corporations Relevant to the Above-Stated Canonical Principles

There are four fundamental legal concepts that provide the legal protection for the direction of the public apostolate by a responsible canonical entity and the administration of the property dedicated to an apostolate through the legal mechanism of a public charitable corporation.

1. Statement of Legal Purpose

The legal statement of purposes in the articles of incorporation and the bylaws needs to establish clearly the Catholic identity of the corporation in language appropriate to the specific activities and funding patterns of the corporation. The legal purpose clause addresses the canonical interests in numbers 1, 2, 3 and 6 above. The full significance of the legal purpose clause is explained in the discussion of criterion one below.

2. Governance Authority

The division and allocation of the governing authority in the corporation should provide for a position of effective legal control by, or effective accountability to, the juridic person. The legal position of control or of accountability, through whatever single mechanism or combination of legal mechanisms it is achieved, addresses the canonical interests in numbers 3, 4, 5, 6, 8 and 9 above.

3. Dissolution Clause

The articles of incorporation and the bylaws should provide that the juridic person determines the distribution of property upon dissolution. This addresses numbers 6 and 7 of the canonical principles.

4. Property in a Charitable Corporation

The canonical property interest of the Church in these corporations is not appropriately characterized as legal ownership. Corporations are legal fictions, "artificial persons." While one owns shares in a business corporation, the public benefit nature of a charitable corporation precludes ownership by a private person or entity, either of the corporation itself or of its assets. The more appropriate concept for charitable corporations is governance control. It is more useful to describe the nature of the church's property interest in the corporation by using the language of the powers of a corporation and the governance rights of incorporators that are secured through the legal act of incorporation.

The corporation is "more nearly a method than a thing." It is an association of persons which as a body politic exists separately from individual identities, and as a body politic, it is vested with certain powers such as (but not limited to) the following:

1. To have continuous legal existence, though membership changes;

2. To acquire, own, deal with and dispose of property, real and personal; and

3. To carry out authorized purposes and to develop procedures for carrying out those purposes.[7]

[7]Howard L. Oleck & Martha Stewart, *Nonprofit Corporations, Organizations and Associations* 6th ed. (New York; Prentice-Hall, 1994) 520.

This author proposes that these powers of a corporation are the "rights in relationship to property"[8] that constitute the "church property" interest to be protected. Through the act of incorporation, the juridic person stabilizes its apostolate in a civil law structure, which, through the operation of law, has the above-described powers. Through the structures and provisions of the nonprofit corporation law and the specific organizational documents of the corporation, the public juridic person ensures the perpetual dedication of the assets of the corporation to its apostolic purpose and gains the necessary legal relationship to the corporation and the property of the corporation to manage it in accord with the Church's teachings. The church property interest thus defined is the right of the public juridic person to create stability and continuous legal existence for a public work through the method of the corporation's legal purpose (1 above); the right of the corporation to receive assets dedicated to its legal purpose (2 above); and the right to determine the values, corporative culture of philosophy and procedures for the carrying out of the legal purpose of the corporation (3 above). This definition of church property interests encompasses all nine of the canonical principles stated above. This proposed definition maximizes the protection of the law sought in canon 1284 because it tracts American legal principles and does not involve canonical or legal discussions of "ownership" which could be misinterpreted to suggest a conflict between the canonical and legal systems. While the code may assume *dominium* which may include concepts similar to those implied in the common understanding of the English word, ownership, the notions of church property encompassed within Book V are not limited to a narrow concept of legal ownership as understood in American law or to notions of technical *dominium* as understood in canon law and Roman law.[9]

[8] For a discussion of the meaning and interpretation of temporal goods in Book V that supports the identification of legal rights and obligations in regard to material goods as church property, see Francis G. Morrisey, "New Canon Law on Temporal Goods Reflects Vatican II's Influence," in *The New Canon Law: Perspectives on the Law, Religious Life and the Laity* (Catholic Health Association, 1983) 49; Robert C. Becker, "Problems of Ecclesiastical and Religious Organizations: Canon Law Preliminary," *The Jurist* 44 (1984) 48–49; E. C. Clark, "History of Roman Private Law," pt. 2, *Jurisprudence* vol. 2, at (Bilvo and Tannen, 1965) 545–550.

[9] Maida and Cafardi, 215. For a fuller analysis of this thesis, see Melanie DiPietro, "The Interfacing of Canonical Principles and American Law in the Negotiation of Joint Ventures Between Church-Related and Non-Church-Related Corporations," in *Proceedings of the Colloquium on Public Ecclesiastical Juridic Persons and Their Civilly Incorporated Apostolates in the Catholic Church in the U.S.A.*, Pontifical University of St. Thomas in Rome, April, 1998. See also John J. Myers, "Book V The Temporal Goods of the Church." James Coriden, et al., eds. *The Code of Canon Law: A Text and Commentary* (New York/Mahwah: Paulist Press, 1985) 862–863.

APPLICATION OF CANONICAL AND LEGAL PRINCIPLES TO CORPORATIONS

Given the interrelationship of canonical and legal concepts described above and the variety of fact situations involving canonical entities and church-related corporations suggested in the case study, it is more useful, practically, to focus on the criteria to be used in creating new corporate structures or modifying existing structures than to focus on models. The bold statement of each criterion identifies the legal right to be retained "effectively" in the corporation by the juridic person or its designees. It is important to understand the underlying objective of each criterion. Whatever the legal model, mechanism or method used (for example, corporate structure, deeds, contracts), it should accomplish "effective legal control" for the underlying legal objectives identified in the discussion following each criterion.

Criterion One

The public juridic person should control the legal identity of the church-related corporation as set forth in the legal purpose clause of the corporate documents through legal authority over the articles and bylaws of the corporation. The "Catholic" denomination should be clearly stated in the purpose clause of the corporation. The enumeration of specific purposes should include the incorporation of the teachings of the Church.

In the situation of a joint operating company, it is important to analyze the legal purposes of all the existing corporations and the new joint operating company. Is it likely that the church-related corporation will not survive a foreseeable merger? If it is a reasonable expectation that the surviving corporation will not have a legal purpose protecting the Catholic purpose, provisions should be made in the agreement to protect the following underlying legal objectives for controlling the purposes of a public charitable corporation.

It is important to distinguish the control of the legal purpose statement in the legal organizational documents of the corporation from the power to approve philosophy and mission statements. While this power should be explicitly retained, it does not serve the legal function of the statement of legal purpose.

Legal Objectives of Criterion One

One of the critical reasons for controlling the authority to amend the articles of incorporation and bylaws of a corporation is to control the legal purpose clause of the corporation so that principles of charitable trust and nonprofit corporation law apply to protect the "Catholic dimension" of the corporation's activities.

Principles of charitable trust law impress a permanent legal obligation to use corporate assets of the church-related corporation in accord with the purposes set forth in the corporation's articles. Usually the purpose clause in church-related corporations explicitly incorporates the Catholic purpose in accord with church traditions and teachings. This religious identity incorporated in the purpose clause provides First Amendment protection for acting consistently with the Church's teaching, for example in hospitals, through adherence to the *Ethical and Religious Directives for Healthcare Services.* This is particularly important in the post-*Roe v. Wade*[10] environment (this Supreme Court case legalized abortion). Since *Roe v. Wade*, religious identity and conscience clauses have been used to protect hospitals in court challenges or legislative enactments seeking to compel Catholic hospitals to deliver all services and procedures regardless of their beliefs. This is also relevant to services of Catholic Charities. Challenges to compel the provision of all services legally permissible though morally unacceptable within a Catholic tradition have also come from accrediting bodies for medical education[11] and legal actions against Catholic Charities agencies.[12] As the provider and insurance functions become integrated in the managed care market of hospitals and social service agencies, the Ethical and Religious Directives[13] may become even more of a sensitive issue if legislation establishes a minimum level of services required for insurance licenses and these include prohibited services or allow exclusion of classes of persons based on criteria inconsistent with the preferential option for the poor. These issues will be relevant to both Catholic Charities agencies and hospitals as they develop integrated delivery networks such as initiated in the case study.

---

[10]*Roe v. Wade*, 410 U.S. 113, 93 S. Ct. 705, 35 L. Ed. 2d 147 (1973).

[11]*St. Agnes Hospital of City of Baltimore, Inc. v. Riddick*, 748 F. Supp. 319 (D. Md. 1990).

[12]*Kendrick v. Sullivan*, 766 F. Supp. 1180 (D.D.C. 1991).

[13]*The Ethical and Religious Directives for Catholic Health Care Services*, approved by the National Conference of Catholic Bishops, *Origins* 24:27 (December 15, 1994) 449, 451-461.

Sometimes the resulting joint operating corporation or the Catholic provider corporation may lose its Catholic purpose. The legal purpose is replaced by contractual agreements often entered into between Catholic and non-Catholic partners, wherein the resulting provider corporation agrees to adhere to the Ethical and Religious Directives. However, contractual rights, while necessary and acceptable in some situations, may not provide the same degree of legal protection as do principles of corporation law, constitutional law and charitable trust law for Catholic purposes which are specifically articulated in a corporate charter and create the religious identity of the corporation. The legal differences and enforceability between provisions in articles and bylaws of a provider corporation and those of contracts between providers need to be explicitly analyzed by the legal consultant to the Catholic party in the context of the state and federal laws controlling the corporation.

In hospitals and social service agencies, it is important to think about which corporation will hold licenses to provide services. The payment stream from government and insurers follows the licensed corporation. If all services are in one provider corporation whose charitable purposes are not Catholic, then the revenues flowing into that corporation are legally dedicated to the charitable purposes of that corporation and may not include a Catholic identity as described above. Since charitable corporation law limits the uses and transfers of charitable assets, it becomes necessary to examine both the likelihood and the effects of such a consolidation and the enforceability of rights of the Catholic corporation in the changing facts of new organization over the life of a joint venture. Any contractual obligation to transfer funds among the parties must be permitted by a charitable corporation's purpose clause; charitable trust law and nonprofit corporation law. This analysis needs to be done for the entire life of the joint venture. If the Catholic party is relying on contractual rights, these should be examined for the possibility of a challenge to their enforceability based on charitable trust law or nonprofit corporation law, either by future trustees or the attorney general or by a political adversary of the church-related corporation.

The nature and scope of fiduciary duties and responsibilities of members, trustees and officers are determined, in part, by the legal purposes. The *cy pres* doctrine means that the assets dedicated to a charitable purpose must continue to be used for that purpose or one very close to it as approved by a court or the Attorney General.

The use and the distribution of property, in the event of a sale or dissolution of the corporation, may be governed by *cy pres* principles, which in their application may direct distribution to the qualifying successor corporation with purposes most similar to those of the selling or dissolving corporation. In the case of a Catholic corporation, the *cy pres* doctrine is likely to be applied to direct distributions to other Catholic corporations with similar qualifying purposes.[14]

One of the statements of purpose should include support of a public juridic person's qualifying public charitable works. This purpose may be useful in supporting transfers of property in trust to a successor-controlled corporation. The successor corporation may use the assets for purposes permitted by the application of the cy pres doctrine if the event of a dissolution or even to permit gifts to qualifying corporations controlled by the juridic person.

Criterion Two

The public juridic person should have direct or indirect corporate authority to approve mergers, sales and other fundamental corporate reorganizations changing the purposes or identity of the surviving corporation.

Legal Objectives of Criterion Two

The analysis of the legal significance of the authority associated with a statement of corporate purposes also provides the underlying reason for the reserved power to approve mergers, sales of substantially all of the assets of the corporation and other fundamental corporate reorganizations. It applies, also, to control over the transfers or sales of substantially all of the assets of a corporation. It is important to trace the applicability of principles of charitable trust and nonprofit corporation law and constitutional law as they may be operative to the legal purpose statements of the surviving corporation or to the interrelationship of the

---

[14]The exercise of the *cy pres* power is described as follows:

Where property is given in trust for a particular charitable purpose, and it is impossible or impracticable to carry out that purpose, the trust does not fail if the testator has a more general intention to devote the property to charitable purposes. In such a case, the property will be applied under the direction of the court to some charitable purpose falling within the general intention of the testator. Austin Wakeman Scott and William Franklin Fratcher, *Scott on Trusts* vol. IVA, *The Law of Trusts* 4th ed. (Little, Brown and Company, 1989).

The term "qualifying purposes" means exempt purposes as defined in the federal income tax regulations. An organization may be exempt as an I.R.C. § 501(c)(3) organization if it is organized and operated for certain exempt purposes which include religious, charitable, scientific, literary and educational purposes. Treas. Reg. § 1.501(c)(3)–(d)(1)(i).

The principle of *cy pres* is often used in determining the identity of the corporation that may qualify to receive assets from the dissolving charitable corporation. Under this principle, the purposes of the receiving corporation should be as close as possible to the charitable purposes of the dissolving corporation.

network of providers as they will exist over the life of the proposed joint venture. Protections of the interests of the Church described in these criteria should not be lost inadvertently through transactions such as joint operating companies which may result in a future de facto or de jure merger. It is theoretically true that in a joint venture, joint approval of all partners may be needed to approve mergers and dissolutions. However, practically, the economics of the transaction may result in a de facto dissolution of the church-related corporation. In this situation, the church-related partner may have very little choice but to approve the merger or reorganization because of previous decisions or because of its minority position or for any number or reasons. Therefore, it is necessary to examine this criterion in the context of different scenarios that are possible in the life of the joint operating company.

This operational analysis may require supplemental contractual rights to protect the property interests of the church-related corporation in various scenarios.

Criterion Three

The church-related corporation should analyze the legal effect of the corporation's rights and its control over property transactions involving substantial changes and transfers of cash, the use of its assets in the operations of the joint venture and the distribution of assets upon sale or dissolution.

This analysis, which is more relevant to joint ventures than to freestanding corporations, should include a review of three separate property administration issues controlled by nonprofit corporation and trust law:

(i) Generation and use of revenues of the church-related corporation as a "going concern" and/or as a basis for valuations of the church-related corporation. These may be relevant if it is necessary to exercise the termination rights in the agreement among the joint venturers;

(ii) Control of any encumbrance of assets legally dedicated to "Catholic" purposes; and

(iii) Use and encumbrance of the land and buildings titled in the church-related corporation and the use of proceeds from sales or dissolutions.

Legal Objectives of Criterion Three

In a freestanding corporation, all of these property interests are unified. Therefore, the "going concern" value of the corporation is not at risk. In a joint operating agreement, each corporation continues to own its assets. However, control and use of the assets are usually transferred to the new joint operating corporation. In order for the joint operating company to achieve its purposes, the two corporations must operate as one, commingling the use of all of the parties' assets included in the joint venture. Therefore, it becomes necessary to examine, from a canonical perspective, the real economic value to the church-related corporation of "owning its own assets." It is necessary to trace what is owned and for how long.

Depending upon the facts and circumstances of each joint operating company, the operating value of the originating church-related corporation may lessen over time because of the transfer of equipment and services to a jointly owned non-church-related corporation. The originating corporation, having few provider functions, may have little or no value determined by any of the traditional methodologies used to determine the sale, exchange or dissolution value of the corporation itself.

While it may be reasonable to say that the future value of the land and buildings of the originating corporation may be ascertainable, single-purpose buildings may have little value now or in the future. It is commonly agreed that the real value of a provider corporation is in its licenses and contracting capacity, its "going concern" value.

The joint operating agreement's effective level of structural and financial integration that commingles the flow of revenues, transfers equipment, and consolidates services, literally has the potential to change the church-related corporation's role as a provider of service into an investor. This may be necessary to promote the ethical use of resources in a community. Because of the potential to render the corporation a shell organization with only a right to distributions of cash, it is necessary to examine these issues in detail. From the canonical perspective, joint ventures, including joint operating agreements and parent-subsidiary relationships, can result in a corporation having a right to revenues. It may not be a provider corporation. This raises a serious canonical issue since the purpose of any property right is its use to carry on an apostolate. The purpose of the criterion is to analyze this potential.

It is important to analyze what may happen during the life of the joint venture to the generation and use of revenues either by the church-related corporation itself as a "going concern" or, for its legally enforceable benefit. Joint operating agreements usually use financial formulae to determine each party's interests as the venture matures.

If the church-related corporation ultimately only has a right to receive cash payments through the revenue-sharing formula; or, in the event there is a de facto dissolution, a merger or consolidation of services, through the contribution/separation formula, the situation may give rise to a canon 1295 analysis.

The revenue-sharing formula is used to promote the greatest objectivity in the consolidation and allocation of services among the partners. Regardless of which site generates the revenues, each corporation has a percentage interest in the revenues, liabilities and distribution of profits generated during the operation of the joint venture. This formula replaces what may have been the service-generated revenues of the church-related corporation as a freestanding provider. The "contribution formula" is usually based on a market formula used to determine the value of each corporation and the assets it brings to the joint venture. If there is a termination, the parties use this formula to determine the distribution of assets among them. The contribution formula replaces what may have been the sales price for selling the property, plant and equipment of the church-related corporation as a freestanding corporation. Therefore, unlike the traditional methodology of looking to the single corporation for the valuation of the corporation, one now looks at the formulae in the agreement, which formulae have been developed by investment bankers to accommodate the purposes of the agreement. From the canonical perspective, these formulae should be within the norm of market methodologies used to evaluate similar corporations in the event of a sale or dissolution. The agreement should specifically identify the when, the how and the nature of the security of these potential payments to the church-related corporation if it becomes impossible for the church-related corporation to continue in the new joint venture.

One should also examine the conditions upon which the church-related corporation may withdraw from the joint venture. No financial penalties should attach to a withdrawal based upon the free exercise of the teaching authority of the bishop in regard to the Ethical and Religious Directives for Healthcare Services, specifically including Directives concerning future joint venture partners.

Practically, direct or indirect authority (which may only be a veto authority) over the following powers, at least for the assets attributable to the church-related corporation, usually accommodates the interests enunciated in (ii) and (iii) above:

♦ To approve of any sale, mortgage or encumbrance of assets and real property of the corporation;

- To merge, consolidate, dissolve or effect any fundamental corporate reorganization of the corporation; and

- To determine the distribution of assets upon dissolution or liquidation of the corporation.

In the future event of a withdrawal by the Catholic partner and the sale of its interests, the church-related corporation should be in a position to receive the value required by canons 1293, §2 and 1294. The church-related corporation should be in a position to receive a fair-market value for its liquidated corporation (based on the formulae discussed above) and should be able to assume complete and unilateral control of the direction of the proceeds from such a sale or withdrawal from the venture in accord with canon 1294, §2.

Criterion Four

In the freestanding corporation, the juridic person should have sufficient control to appoint and remove trustees and management.

In a joint operating company, the church-related corporation should have sufficient control and operational accountability for appropriate adherence to public church teachings in the business and clinical operations of the joint venture and/or the church-related corporations. This may be accomplished through traditional appointment of the trustees and management personnel or through new and alternative legal structures.

Legal Objectives Underlying Criterion Four

This issue is really concerned with ongoing control over the implementation of the philosophy and mission of the corporation. The structures should provide some level of accountability of trustees and management to the canonically responsible public juridic person or the church-related corporation for the affirmative implementation of church teachings in the management of its corporation or of the joint venture.

Philosophy and values or mission statements identify the content of a corporation's culture, while corporate purposes have those legal ramifications referenced above. In provider corporations such as healthcare and Catholic charities, specific inclusion of the social teachings of the Church and of the Ethical and Religious Directives into purpose and philosophy statements provide notice of the norms governing permissible clinical and business practices in a corporation publicly associated with the Church. The specific inclusion of the social teachings of the Church and of the Ethical and Religious Directives provides parameters for the exercise of discretion of the members and trustees. The incorporation of these teachings into the corporate documents coupled with the appointment of trustees and management are mechanisms in the corporation that help assure Catholic identity.

Unlike a self-perpetuating board in a non-church-related corporation, whose majority vote of sitting trustees determines the acceptable clinical and/or business practice in the corporation or the norms governing other morally significant behavior, the ethical parameters of the board in a Catholic facility are set by external official Church teachings such as the Ethical Directives for Healthcare and Catholic social teachings contained in encyclicals and pastoral letters. This is particularly significant for the public juridic person whose status creates a special relationship to the Church and which because of that status acts in the name of the Church.

Those persons enabled in secular law to exercise authority in the church-related corporation really do so, in a canonical sense, in the name of the juridic person. They need to be committed to and accountable for an appropriate level of responsiveness and care for the apostolate.

Traditionally, a "required"[15] reserved power provides for the retention of either direct or indirect control over the appointment of the board of trustees. Even in a membership model corporation, all control of the business and management of a corporation is normally vested by state corporation law in the board of trustees. Unlike clinical practices that can be specifically identified a priori, the affirmative implementation of the norms of the moral and social teachings of the Church in management policies, service delivery issues and business decisions cannot be specifically identified a priori, but are implemented by the informed and prudential judgment of a board exercising discretion in specific fact situations. The power of the juridic person, and of the church-related corporation to determine the identity of trustees assumes that persons specifically chosen by them are not only willing to be informed but are committed to the content of the Church's teachings, and will, as fiduciaries, exercise their corporate power and make prudential judgments in a way that affirmatively implements church teachings in clinical and business matters. They will also be disposed to collaborate with the efforts of the bishop and the public juridic person to coordinate the apostolates in the diocese expected by the code (cc. 394 and 678).

Because of the operational control of management in developing specific practices to implement policies, appointment of the president/chief executive officer

---

[15] Maida and Cafardi, 155–157.

has often been recommended to be retained, directly or indirectly, by the public juridic person (or the church-related corporation) for the same reason.[16] In fact, the degree to which there is a positive and discernible "Catholic identity" in a multi-million-dollar corporation is very dependent on the vision and choices of the chief executive officer and the board.

Shared governance arrangements such as most joint operating companies usually eliminate the public juridic person's initiating powers in the affairs of the corporation as well as the exclusive control of trustees. The public juridic person is often distanced from the authoritative decision-makers. Sometimes entities and trustees having no historical fidelity or even knowledge of the public juridic person are given complete governance and management control in the Catholic corporation. Therefore, it is necessary to examine the formal legal and operational mechanisms in the new organization that exist for the accountability of the decisional boards and management to the church-related corporation for the integrity of the apostolate. In a joint venture, neither party retains exclusive power over trustees and management unless one is economically dominant. It is very difficult to create acceptable or appropriate legal and managerial substitutes for the loss of unilateral control of the appointment and removal of governance and management. However, the loss of this unilateral power in a joint venture is usually unavoidable. Therefore, it is necessary to develop alternative legal mechanism(s) for ensuring some level of directive authority (albeit not unilateral and exclusive) over the affirmative determination of the interpretation and application of the values implemented in the policies and practices of the joint venture in order to substitute for the diminution of this strategic power to appoint and remove trustees and chief executive officers. It is this objective, the affirmative meaning of Catholic identity (and not just avoidance of prohibited clinical practices) that illustrates the meaning of an apostolate of a public juridic person in the name of the Church. This objective illustrates the limitations of focusing only on control of "alienation of stable patrimony."

[16] Maida and Cafardi, 162.

ILLUSTRATION OF THE APPLICATION OF THE CRITERIA TO SPECIFIC MODELS AND COMPONENTS OF THE CORPORATION

Corporate Models and the Division of Governing Authority

1. Membership Model: Freestanding Corporation

All of the underlying legal objectives of the criteria discussed in the preceeding section can be met in a freestanding corporation through variations of reserved powers held by Members in a freestanding corporation. The common practice is to create the canonical authority of the religious institute or of the diocese as Members in a corporation. They reserve the unilateral and exclusive powers to:

Amend the articles and bylaws of the corporation;

Appoint and remove trustees;

Approve encumbrances and sales of property;

Approve merges, dissolutions and fundamental reorganizations of the corporation; and

Determine the distribution of assets upon dissolutions.[17]

2. Non-Membership Model: Freestanding Corporation

If state law permits, the same effect can be achieved by creating two classes of trustees, one of, which is, *ex officio*, the canonical authority of the juridic person or its designees. The approval of the *ex officio* canonical trustees is needed for the above-enumerated actions of the corporation. Some juridic persons prefer this model because it operates in a more integrated way than the membership model.

Except for the unique issue of the "going concern value," which is an issue in the joint operating company, these five reserved powers are sufficient to address all of the criteria and, in fact, track the three powers that describe the church property interest defined in number 4 of Section Two.

---

[17] Maida and Cafardi, chs. 17, 18, 19.

3. Joint Operating Company

In a joint operating company, it is not possible for the immediately responsible public juridic person to retain these basic five powers unilaterally or exclusively. However, the church-related corporation should have "effective legal control." While a veto power may be acceptable under certain circumstances, it is preferable that the church-related corporation has at least a directive power. In this context, "effective directive control" means that the church-related corporation has legally enforceable rights. It also means that there is some level of accountability of management to the public juridic person or its designees for the operation of the corporation consistent with the purposes and values discussed in the criteria.

The difficult policy question in determining how credible the Catholic partner's identity is in a joint venture is in determining the acceptable degree of initiating or directive authority of the Catholic corporation over the substantive, value-laden decisions of the joint venture. This question focuses more on the canonical principles 1, 3, 4, 5 and 6 than on control of property. For some, a veto power seems sufficient. For others, the juridic person requires some greater affirmative, directive authority and accountability for value-laden decisions.

The legal remedies to enforce rights and the structures for management accountability should be practically useful. For example, many times in a joint venture the parties agree to arbitrate differences. Sometimes the remedies are injunctive relief. The actual successful use of injunctive remedies really needs to be examined in the context of the substantive procedural law governing injunctive relief. Legal counsel should be able to render an opinion that the structures used to address the criteria are protected by legally enforceable and efficient remedies. If the remedies are too cumbersome to use because they are disruptive to the corporations or too costly, they are not useful or efficient. Attention should also be paid to the source of payment for the exercise of legal remedies.

Purpose Statements

1. Church Corporations

The purpose statements of church corporations should be broad enough to include all of the activities of the canonical entity. There should also be a specific purpose statement to "support, promote and carry on" the specific activity of a sponsored church-related corporation. This purpose statement may be useful in the event of a distribution upon the dissolution of a church-related corporation.

2. Church-Related Corporations

The enumeration of purposes of the church-related corporation should also include a statement to "support, promote and advance" the public charitable works of the immediately responsible canonical entity. The presence of this purpose, though a secondary one, has provided the basis for gifts and transfers from one corporation to the other.

Dissolution Clauses

The dissolution clause in the articles of incorporation should be explicit in retaining the power to determine the distribution of assets upon dissolution to the canonically responsible juridic person. Or, in the alternative, there should be a statement that assets will be distributed to a qualifying similarly identified church-related corporation or to named qualifying corporations. The statement in the articles gives public notice and provides the basis for the application of the *cy pres* doctrine discussed above.

CONCLUSION

The environment of church-related corporations, whether colleges, healthcare or social services, is too complex to promote any one corporate model or even any one canonical theory or analysis. Rather, it is important to analyze both the legal and canonical facts. This author suggests attention both to the legal and operational facts as well as to canonical notions, which do not sever property interests from the status of a public juridic person who holds it for an apostolate.

Hopefully, the discussion and criteria presented herein will promote the protection of legitimate church interests and rights of participation in the public forum. The objective of the discussion has been to maximize the flexibility of those associated with incorporated apostolates to be faithful to principles of both canon law and the law governing public charitable corporations.

APPENDIX

NCCB COMPLEMENTARY NORMS, CANONS 1277; 1292, §1; 1297

CANON 1277: *Acts of Extraordinary Administration*

The diocesan bishop must hear the finance council and the college of consultors in order to perform the more important acts of administration in light of the economic situation of the diocese; he needs the consent of this council and that of the college of consultors in order to perform acts of extraordinary administration besides cases specifically mentioned in universal law or in the charter of a foundation. It is for the conference of bishops to define what is meant by acts of extraordinary administration.

Complementary Norm:

In accord with the norms of canon 1277, the National Conference of Catholic Bishops determines that the following are to be considered acts of extraordinary administration and therefore subject to the limits of canons that regulate such acts.

1. To alienate (in the strict sense, convey or transfer ownership) goods of the stable patrimony when the value exceeds the minimum limit (c. 1292, §1).

2. To alienate goods donated to the Church through a vow, or to alienate goods that are especially valuable due to their artistic or historical value regardless of the appraised value (c. 1292, §2).

3. To incur indebtedness (without corresponding increase in the assets of the diocese) that exceeds the minimum limit (c. 1295).

4. To encumber stable patrimony the value of which exceeds the minimum limit (c. 1295).

5. To lease church property when the annual lease income exceeds the minimum limit (c. 1297).

6. To lease church property when the value of the leased property exceeds the minimum and the lease is for more than nine (9) years (c. 1297).

Approved: *General Meeting, November 1985*

Promulgated: Memorandum to All Bishops, June 27, 1986

--------◆--------

CANON 1292, §1: *Sums for Alienation of Church Property*

With due regard for the prescription of canon 638, §3, when the value of the goods whose alienation is proposed is within the range of the minimum and maximum amounts which are to be determined by the conference of bishops for its region, the competent authority is determined in the group's own statutes when it is a question of juridic persons who are not subject to the diocesan bishop; otherwise, the competent authority is the diocesan bishop with the consent of the finance council, the college of consultors and the parties concerned. The diocesan bishop also needs their consent to alienate the goods of the diocese.

Complementary Norm: *Proposed Action:*

In accord with the prescriptions of canon 1292, §1, the National Conference of Catholic Bishops proposes that the maximum limit for alienation of church property be $1,000,000, or $5.00 per capita of the Catholic population, (whichever is the larger) up to a ceiling of $5,000,000. The minimum limit will be $500,000.

Approved: General Meeting, November 1985

Reviewed: Holy See (Congregation for Bishops in consultation with Congregation for Clergy)

Letter from the Apostolic Pro-Nuncio
(Prot. No. 1782/86/8) April 19, 1986

Final Decree: In accord with the prescriptions of canon 1292, §1, the National Conference of Catholic Bishops decrees that the maximum amount for the alienation of Church property is $1,000,000.[1] The minimum limit may be established according to canon 1292, §1.[2]

Promulgated: Memorandum to All Bishops June 27, 1986

Subsequent Action: The National Conference of Catholic Bishops approved two separate formulas for ascertaining the maximum amount for the alienation of church goods:

Proposal I: The maximum amount for a given diocese shall be calculated according to Catholic population (55.00 per person) between $1,000,000 and $5,000,000.

Proposal II: The maximum amount assigned to a diocese shall be one of three according to Catholic population:

1) Dioceses with a Catholic population of over 1,000,000 persons shall have a maximum amount of 55,000,000.

2) Dioceses with a population between 600,000 and 1,000,000 shall have a maximum of $4,000,000.

3) Dioceses with fewer than 600,000 persons shall have a maximum of $3,000,000.

Approved: General Meeting, November 1990

Reviewed: Holy See (Congregation for Clergy) Letter to NCCB President (Prot. No. 190357/I) April 16, 1991

---

[1] The maximum limit approved by the full body of bishops in November 1985 was subsequently not approved by the Holy See. The maximum amount of $1,000,000 was designated in the decree of April 19, 1986.

[2] The minimum limit approved in November 1985 was $500,000.

Interim Provision: The maximum limit established for the alienation of church property is $3,000,000 until the Episcopal conference establishes a single standard at its 1991 November General Meeting.[3]

Promulgated: Memorandum of the President, NCCB/USCC April 22,

———— ◆ ————

CANON 1297: *Norms for Leasing of Church Property*

After considering local circumstances, it is the responsibility of the conference of bishops to establish norms concerning the leasing of church goods, especially the permission to be obtained from competent ecclesiastical authority.

Action: See canon 1277: Acts of Extraordinary
Administration for reference to leasing of church property by the diocesan bishop.

1 The maximum limit approved by the full body of bishops in November 1985 was subsequently not approved by the Holy See. The maximum amount of $1,000,000 was designated in the decree of April 19, 1986.

2 The minimum limit approved in November 1985 was $500,000.

3 The two proposals approved by the bishops in November 1990 were not approved by the Holy See. The maximum limit of $3,000,000 was established as an interim provision in the Letter from Cardinal Innocenti, April 16, 1991.

---

[3] The two proposals approved by the bishops in November 1990 were not approved by the Holy See. The maximum limit of $3,000,000 was established as an interim provision in the Letter from Cardinal Innocenti, April 16, 1991.

GLOSSARY OF TERMS

Acquired right Right obtained in virtue of the legal consequences of a fact or act.

Administration The direction and management of goods, property, and activity of a juridic person for purposes befitting its mission.

Alienation The juridical transfer, with or without compensation, of the ownership or interest in real estate or other property to another.

Apostolic See (Holy See) Term which applies not only to the Roman Pontiff but also to the secretariat of state, the council for the public affairs of the church and other institutions of the roman curia, unless the nature of the matter of the context of the words makes the contrary evident.

Associations Christian faithful, either clergy or laity together, striving by common effort to promote a more perfect life or to foster public worship or Christian doctrine or to exercise other apostolic works, namely to engage in efforts of evangelization, to exercise works of piety or charity and to animate the temporal order with the Christian spirit.

Autonomous foundation See *pious foundation*

Bishops Through the Holy Spirit which has been given to them in ordination, bishops are the successors of the apostles by divine institution; they are constituted pastors within the church so they are teachers of doctrine, priests of sacred worship and ministers of governance.

Canonical equity Moderation and equilibrium of order according to the spirit of the gospels as well as the aspect of justice.

Catholic school One which ecclesiastical authority or a public ecclesiastical juridic person supervises or which ecclesiastical authority recognizes as such by means of a written document.

Chancellor Person appointed in every diocesan curia to see to it that the documents of the curia are gathered, arranged and safeguarded.

Christian faithful Those incorporated in Christ through baptism, constituted as the people of God, sharers in Christ's priestly, prophetic and royal office in their own manner and called to exercise the mission which God has entrusted to the Church.

Civil law The laws of a secular jurisdiction, as distinct from canon law.

Communicatio in sacris Participation in liturgical worship or in the administration of the sacraments by persons belonging to different Christian denominations that are not in full communion with the Catholic Church.

Components of a corporation Refers to the structures of a corporation such as members, trustees, reserved powers, voting procedures, dissolution clauses, etc.

Conference of bishops A permanent institution consisting of a grouping of bishops of a given nation or territory whereby, according to the norm of law they jointly exercise pastoral functions on behalf of the Christian faithful of their territory in view of promoting the greater good which the church offers to human kind, especially through forms and programs of the apostolate adapted to the circumstances of the time and place.

Contribution formula To determine the value of assets that each partner brings to a joint venture. Since assets may be sold and the proceeds stay available for use by the joint venture, one partner may not own assets as the venture matures. Its right to a distribution, upon termination or sale is then determined by a formula based on assets contributed to a joint venture.

Correptio A rebuke by the ordinary of a person who has caused scandal.

Cy pres Where property is given in trust for a particular charitable purpose, and it is impossible or impracticable to carry out that purpose, the trust does not fail if the testator has a more general intention to devote the property to charitable purposes. In such a case, the property will be applied under the direction of the court to some charitable purpose falling within the general intention of the testator.

Decree An administrative act issued by a competent executive authority in which a decision is given or a provision is made in a particular case in accord with the norms of law.

Delegated power That power which is granted to a person not by means of an office but by a particular authorization.

Delict Technical term for an external and morally imputable violation of a law or precept to which at least an unspecified sanction is attached.

Diocesan bishop Bishop with the care of a diocese.

Diocesan curia Those institutions and persons which furnish assistance to the bishop in the governance of the entire diocese, especially in directing pastoral activity, in providing for the administration of the diocese and in exercising judicial power.

Diocese A portion of the people of God which is entrusted for pastoral care to a bishop with the cooperation of the presbyterium so that, adhering to its pastor and gathered by him in the Holy Spirit through the gospel and the Eucharist, it constitutes a particular church in which the One, Holy, Catholic and Apostolic Church of Christ is truly present and operative.

Dispensation Relaxation of a merely ecclesiastical law in a particular case which can be granted by those who enjoy executive power within the limits of their competence as well as by those to whom the power of dispensing has been given explicitly or implicitly either by the law itself or by lawful delegation.

Domicile Acquired by residence within the territory of a certain parish or at least of a diocese, which is joined either with the intention of remaining there permanently unless called away or has been protracted for five complete years.

Ecclesiastical goods All temporal goods which belong to the universal church, the Apostolic See, or other public juridic persons within the church.

Eparch, eparchy Equivalent terms of the Eastern Catholic Churches for diocesan bishop and diocese in the Latin church.

Episcopal vicar A priest who possesses the same ordinary power which universal law gives the vicar general, either in a determined section of the diocese or in a certain type of business or over the faithful of a determined right or over certain groups of persons.

Equity Principle of adapting the law to the circumstances according to natural justice.

Extraordinary administration Actions which because of their nature, importance, or financial value, exceed the limits of the routine administration of the goods and activity of a juridic person. Such acts often require the permission of a higher authority.

Finance council A group of the faithful at the parish or diocesan level who assist the pastor or bishop by providing counsel in regards to financial matters of the parish or diocese.

Finance officer Appointed by the bishop after listening to the college of consultors and the finance council for a five-year renewable term. He administers the goods of the diocese under the authority of the bishop in accordance with the budget determined by the finance council, meets the expenditures which the bishop or others deputized by him have legitimately authorized.

Hierarch In the Eastern churches, the counterpart of the ordinary. See *ordinary*

Incorporated apostolate The works of health, education and charity activities that are carried on in public charitable corporations.

Indult Concession given for a certain period of time.

Injunctive relief A judicial process that requires a person to do or refrain from doing a particular thing.

Joint venture Activity of two or more persons entered jointly with shared liability.

Juridic person A subject of rights and obligations, constituted by the law itself or by a decree of a competent ecclesiastical superior. Juridic entity constituted by an act of a competent person and endowed with the capacity of acquiring and exercising rights as well as of contracting obligations, by the means and to the extent determined by the competent authority. See *public juridic persons*.

Law An ordinance of reason for the common good, made by one who has care for the community, and promulgated (Thomas Aquinas).

Lease Conveyance by an owner to a tenant of a right to possess the owner's property for a stated period of time, in exchange for a payment of rent.

License A permission to use a facility or property on a limited basis.

Local ordinary All mentioned under category of "ordinary" except superiors of religious institutes and societies of apostolic life.

Metropolitan Archbishop of a diocese; presides over an ecclesiastical province.

Monitio An admonishment by the ordinary of a person who has committed an offense.

More important acts of administration A category of acts of administration pertaining to the juridic person of a diocese. Such acts are the more significant ones and are determined by the diocesan bishop in light of the economic condition of the diocese (see c. 1277).

Ordinary In addition to the roman pontiff, diocesan bishops and others, who even if only on an interim basis, have been placed over a particular church or over a community which is equivalent to it, as well as those who possess ordinary general executive power in said churches and communities, namely vicars general and episcopal vicars; and likewise for their own members the major superiors of clerical religious institutes or pontifical right and of clerical societies of apostolic life of pontifical right, who possess at least ordinary executive power.

Ordinary administration Actions which are considered to be necessary for the daily operation and maintenance of the property and work of a juridic person.

Ordinary power (of governance) That which is joined to a certain office by the law itself.

Parish A definite community of the Christian faithful established on a stable basis within a particular church whose pastoral care is entrusted to a pastor as its own shepherd under the authority of the diocesan bishop.

Particular churches In which and from which exists the one and unique Catholic Church are first of all dioceses; to which, unless otherwise evident are likened a territorial prelature, a territorial abbacy, an apostolic vicariate, an apostolic prefecture, and an apostolic administration which has been erected on a stable basis.

Pastor The proper shepherd of a parish entrusted to him, exercising pastoral care under the authority of the diocesan bishop; in accord with the norm of law he carries out for this community the duties of teaching, sanctifying and governing, with the cooperation of other presbyters or deacons and the assistance of lay members of the Christian faithful.

Pastoral council Can be established to the extent that pastoral circumstances recommend it, to investigate under the authority of the bishop all those things that pertain to pastoral works, to ponder them and to propose practical conclusions about them.

Personalty Personal property as distinct from real estate.

Pious cause Anything done primarily in consideration of God and for a supernatural end and recognized as such by the Church.

Pious foundation Property given in any way to a juridic person in the church with a burden that is protracted of devoting some of the annual income of the celebration of a certain number of Masses, to the performance of other specified ecclesiastical functions, or to the carrying out of certain works of piety or charity. An *autonomous foundation* is a pious foundation that has been given its own status in virtue of an act by a competent ecclesiastical authority.

Pontifical religious institute A generic term for a religious order, congregation or a society with members who take public vows of poverty, chastity and obedience and live a common life. A *pontifical* institute is one in which the immediate ecclesiastical superior is the Holy See. A diocesan institute is established under the authority of a diocesan bishop.

Precept A decree directly and legitimately enjoining a determined person or persons to do or to omit something, especially concerning the urging of the observance of a law.

Presbyteral council A body of priests, like a senate of the bishop, representing the presbyterate who aid the bishop in the governance of the diocese according to the norm of law in order that the pastoral welfare of the portion of the people of God entrusted to him may be promoted as effectively as possible.

Prescription Operation of the law whereby rights may be acquired or extinguished. Legal recognition of rights acquired by actual use and corresponding extinction of rights after a set number of years and other conditions. In civil law operation of the law whereby rights might be established by long exercise of their corresponding powers (acquisitive prescription) or extinguished (extinctive prescription) by prolonged failure to exercise such powers.

Privilege A favor given by a special act for the benefit or certain persons; it can be granted by the legislator and by the executive authority to whom the legislator has given the authority.

Protopresbyter In Eastern churches the counterpart to a vicar forane. See *vicar forane.*

Protosyncellus In Eastern churches the equivalent to the vicar general. See *vicar general.*

Public association Grouping of Christian faithful erected by the decision of the competent authority acting in the name of the church according to the norms of law tending to the public good through charitable and religious ends.

Public juridic persons Aggregate of persons or things which are so constituted by the competent ecclesiastical authority that, within the limits set for them in the name of the church, they fulfill a proper function entrusted to them in view of the common good and in accord with the prescripts of law. Public juridic personality is given either through law itself or by special decree of the competent authority expressly granting it.

Quasi-domicile Acquired by residence within the territory of a certain parish or at least of a diocese which is either joined with the intention of remaining there at least three months, unless called away, or has in fact been protracted for three months.

Recognitio ("Review"), the act of a competent higher authority permitting the promulgation of the law of a lower-level authority. When specified by law, this prior review and confirmation by a superior authority is necessary before the act of the subordinate authority can have any legal force.

Responsible canonical juridic person The public juridic person of a religious institute or diocese accountable in canon law for an incorporated apostolate. Oftentimes this relationship is referred to as "sponsorship."

Revenue-sharing formula A mechanism often used in joint operating companies to determine how the total revenues of the joint operating agreement will be allocated among the parties. The purpose of the mechanism is to promote greater objectivity in consolidating and allocating services among the partners. Because of the formula, it is not as critical to control the identity of the corporation, which is the actual site of the service. The revenue is not to the site but to the joint venture.

Revoke General term for the power of law or any legitimate authority in some way to take away something, i.e., some right, privilege, or provision of law.

Roman curia Congregations or offices in Rome by which the supreme pontiff unusually conducts the business of the universal church which fulfills its duties in his name and by his authority for the good and service of the church. Their structure and competence are defined in special law.

Syncellus In Eastern churches, the counterpart of the episcopal vicar.

Vicar forane Sometimes referred to as "dean," a priest in charge of a grouping of parishes within a diocese.

Vicar general A priest who assists the diocesan bishop in the governance of the entire diocese and who is endowed with ordinary power.

BIBLIOGRAPHY

Abbo, John A. and Jerome D. Hannan. *The Sacred Canons: A Concise Presentation of the Current Disciplinary Norms of the Church*, vol. II. St. Louis: B. Herder Book Co., 1952.

Abbass, J. "The Temporal Goods of the Church" in *Two Codes in Comparison*, Kanonika, vol. 7 (Rome: Pontificio Istituto Orientale, 1997) 177-205.

Becker, Robert C. "Problems of Ecclesiastical and Religious Organizations: Canon Law Preliminary." *The Jurist* 44 (1984) 48–51.

Calvo, Randolph R. and Nevin J. Klinger, eds. *Clergy Procedural Handbook*. Washington: Canon Law Society of America, 1992.

Cafardi, Nicholas P. "Closing Churches, Merging Institutes and Dividing Dioceses: Developments in Church Property Since 1983." *CLSA Proceedings* (1990) 403-427.
    "Bequests for Masses: Doctrine, History and Legal Status." *Duquesne Law Review* 20 (1982) 403-427.

Capparos M. Ernest, Michel Thériault and Jean Thorn, eds. *Code of Canon Law Annotated*. Montreal: Wilson & Lafleur Limitée, 1993.

Code of Canons of the Eastern Churches. Latin-English Edition. Washington: Canon Law Society of America, 1992.

Congregation for the Clergy, et al. "General Instruction: De quibus quaestionibus circa fidelium laicorum cooperationem sacerdotum ministerium spectantem". *Acta Apostolicae Sedis* 89 (1997) 852-877.

Coriden, James, Thomas Green, and Donald E. Heintschel, eds. *The Code of Canon Law, a Text and Commentary*. New York, NY: Paulist Press, 1985.

Cusack, Barbara Anne and Therese Guerin Sullivan, *Pastoral Care in Parishes without a Pastor: Applications of Canon 517, §2*. Washington, DC: Canon Law Society of America, 1995.

Danagher, John J. "The New Code and Catholic Health Facilities: Fundamental Obligations of Administrators." *The Jurist* 44 (1984) 143-152.

DePaolis, Velasio "Temporal Goods of the Church in the New Code, With Particular Reference to the Institutes of Consecrated Life." *The Jurist* 43 (1983) 343-360.

"Questiones miscellaneae," *Periodica* 73 (1984) 462.

De Bonis Ecclesiae Temporalibus: Adnotatione in Codicem: Liber V. Rome: Pontificia Universitas Gregoriana, 1986.

"I beni temporali nel codice di diritto canonico." *Monitor Ecclesiasticus* 111(1986) 9-30.

"Excursus sui beni temporali nella Scrittura, nella Tradizione e nell'Insegnamento della Chiesa," in *Il codice del Vaticano II*. Bologna: Centro Edizione Dehoniane, 1995.

I beni temporali della chiesa. Bologna: Edizioni Dehoniame, 1995.

"Nota sul significato di bene ecclesiale." *Periodica* 84 (1995) 155-160.

DiPietro, Melanie. "The Interfacing of Canonical Principles and American Law in the Negotiation of Joint Ventures Between Church-Related and Non-Church-Related Corporations," *Proceedings of the Colloquium on Public Ecclesiastical Juridic Persons and Their Civilly Incorporated Apostolates in the Catholic Church in the USA* , Pontifical University of St. Thomas in Rome, April, 1998.

Farrelly, Adrian. "The Diocesan Finance Council: Functions and Duties According to the *Code of Canon Law*." *Studia Canonica* 23 (1989) 149-156.

Favergiotti, Anna. "Il Fondamento dell'Obbligazione Tributaria nello Stato Moderno e nel Diritto Canonico Latino ed Orientale. Note Comparative," in Raffaele Coppola, ed. *Incontro fra Canoni d'Oriente e d'Occidente* (Bari: Cacucci Editore, 1994) 571-582.

Fitzgerald, Michael. "The Canon Law Implications of the Physician/Hospital Organization in the United States of America." *Studia Canonica* 22 (1988) 27-65.

Frugé, Donald J. "Taxes in the Proposed Law." *CLSA Proceedings* 44 (1982) 274-288.

Fürst, C.G. *Canones-Synopse zum Codex Iuris Canonici und Codex Canonum Ecclesiarum Orientalium.* Freiburg im Breisgau: Herder, 1992.

Gauthier, Albert, O.P. "Juridical Persons in the *Code of Canon Law. Studia Canonica* 25(1991) 77-92.

Green, Thomas J. "Shepherding the Patrimony of the Poor: Diocesan and Parish Structures of Financial Administration." *The Jurist* 56 (1997) 706-734.

A Historical Essay on Tithes: A Collection of Sources and Texts. Rome: Terzo Natalini, 1973.

Kealy, Robert L. *Diocesan Financial Support: Its History and Canonical Status.* Rome: Gregorian University, 1986.
  "Methods of Diocesan Incorporation." *CLSA Proceedings* 48 (1986) 63-177.

Kennedy, Robert T. "McGrath, Maida, Michiels: Introduction to a Study of the Canonical and Civil-Law Status of Church-Related Institutions in the United States." *The Jurist* 50 (1990) 351-401.

Kurtz, Daniel L. *Safeguarding the Mission: The Duties and Liabilities of Officers and Directors of Nonprofit Organizations.* ALI-ABA (American Law Institute, 1992).

Maida, Adam J. and Nicholas P. Cafardi. *Church Property, Church Finances, and Church-Related Corporations: A Canon Law Handbook.* St. Louis: Catholic Health Association, 1994.

Manzanares, Julio. "De stipendio pro Missis ad intentionem 'collectivam' celebratis iuxta Decretum *Mos iugiter.*" *Periodica* 80 (1991) 579-608.

McDonough, Elizabeth. "A *Gloss* on Canon 1321." *Studia Canonica* 21 (1987) 381-390.

Metz, René. "Le Canons communs à l'Église latine et aux Églises orientales à la fin du XXe Siècle," in Raffaele Coppola, ed. *Incontro fra Canoni d'Oriente e d'Occidente.* Bari: Cacucci Editore, 1994.

Mitrofan, Ioan. "Les biens de l'Eglise selon le *Codex Canonum Ecclesiarum Orientalium.*" Kaslik, Lebanon: USEK, 1996, 415-446.

Misto, Luigi. "I beni temporali della Chiesa," in *Il Diritto nel Mistero della Chiesa*, Quaderni de Appollinaris 10. Rome: Pontificia Universita Laterraneses, 1992.

Modde, Margaret Mary. "Canonical Stewardship Responsibilities for Healthcare Facilities." *CLSA Proceedings* 51(1989) 83-94.

Morrisey, Francis G. "Book V: The Temporal Goods of the Church." In *The Canon Law: Letter and Spirit*. Eds. Gerard Sheehy, et al. 707-747. Collegeville, MN: Liturgical Press, 1995.

"Acquiring Temporal Goods for the Church's Mission." *The Jurist* 56 (1996) 586-603.

"The Conveyance of Ecclesiastical Goods." *CLSA Proceedings* 38 (1976) 123-137.

"New Canon Law on Temporal Goods Reflects Vatican II's Influence," in *The New Canon Law: Perspectives on the Law, Religious Life and the Laity*. Catholic Health Association, 1983.

"Ordinary and Extraordinary Administration: Canon 1277." *The Jurist* 48 (1988) 709-726.

"The Alienation of Temporal Goods in Contemporary Practice." *Studia Canonica* 29 (1995) 293-316.

Myers, John J. "The Diocesan Fiscal Officer and the Diocesan Finance Council." *CLSA Proceedings* 44 (1982) 181-188.

"The Temporal Goods of the Church," *The Code of Canon Law: A Text and Commentary*, ed. James A. Coriden et. al. NewYork/Mahwah: Paulist Press, 1985.

National Conference of Catholic Bishops. *Implementation of the 1983 Code of Canon Law: Complementary Norms*. Washington: United States Catholic Conference, 1991.

Stewardship: A Disciple's Response. Washington, DC: NCCB-USCC (bilingual edition) 1992.

Ochoa, Xaverius. *Index Verborum ac Locutionum Codicis iuris Canonici*. Città del Vaticano: Libreria Editrice Lateranense, 1984.

Oleck, Howard L., and Martha Stewart. *Nonprofit Corporations, Organizations and Associations,* 6th ed. Prentice-Hall, 1994.

Pontificia Commissio Codici Iuris Canonici. "De Iure Patrimoniali." *Communicationes* 5 (1973) 95.

Pontificia Commissio Codici Iuris Canonici Recognescendo. *Relatio: complectens synthesim animadversionum ab Em.mis atque Exc.mis Patribus commissionis ad novissimum schema Codicis Iuris Canonici exhibitarum, cum responsionibus a secretaria et consultoribus datis.* Vatican City: Typ. Polyglottis Vaticanis, 1981.

Pospishil, Victor J. *Eastern Catholic Church Law,* 2nd revised and augmented edition. Staten Island, NY, Saint Maron Publications, 1996.

Rincon-Perez, Tomas. "El Decrerto de la Congregacion para el Clero sobre accumulacion de estipendios (22-II-91)." *Ius Canonicum* 31 (1991) 627-656.

Roche, Garrett J. "The Poor and Temporal Goods in Book V of the Code." *The Jurist* 55 (1995) 299-348.

Sheehy, Gerard, et al., eds. *The Canon Law, Letter and Spirit.* Collegeville, MN: The Liturgical Press, 1995.

Ward, Daniel J. "Trust Management Under the New Code of Canon Law." *The Jurist* 44 (1984) 134-182.

Wrenn, Lawrence G. *Authentic Interpretations on the 1983 Code.* Washington, D C: Canon Law Society of America, 1993

Zielinski, Paul. "Pious Wills and Mass Stipends in Relation to Canons 1299-1310." *Studia Canonica* 19 (1985) 115-154.

Zuzek, I.. *Index Analyticus Codicis Canonum Ecclesiarum Orientalium,* Kanonika. Rome: Pontificium Institutum Orientalium Studiorum, 1992.

CONTRIBUTORS

JOHN R. AMOS is the Adjutant Judicial Vicar of the Archdiocese of Mobile; he received his doctorate in canon law from The Catholic University of America, Washington, DC in 1987.

NICHOLAS P. CAFARDI is Dean of the Duquesne University School of Law; he received his civil law degree from the University of Pittsburgh in 1975 and his licentiate in canon law from the Pontifical University of St. Thomas, Rome, in 1987.

WILLIAM P. DALY is the Director of Consultation Services for the National Association of Church Personnel Administrators; he received his M.S. in Political Science (Public Administration) from California State University, Los Angeles in 1981.

LAWRENCE A. DiNARDO is the Episcopal Vicar for Canonical Services for the Diocese of Pittsburgh; he received his licentiate in canon law from The Catholic University of America, Washington, DC in 1986.

MELANIE DiPIETRO, S.C. is a partner at the law firm of Buchanan Ingersoll, P.C.; she received her civil law degree from Duquesne University in 1975 and her licentiate in canon law from the Pontifical University of St. Thomas, Rome, in 1987.

PATRICIA M. DUGAN is a Defender of the Bond for the marriage tribunal of the Diocese of Camden, New Jersey and practicing civil attorney; she received her civil law degree from Villanova University, Villanova, Pennsylvania in 1980; and her licentiate in canon law from the Pontifical University of St. Thomas, Rome, in 1989.

FREDERICK C. EASTON is Judicial Vicar of the Archdiocese of Indianapolis; he received his licentiate in canon law from the Pontifical Lateran University, Rome, in 1969.

JOHN D. FARIS is the Assistant Secretary General of the Catholic Near East Welfare Association and received his doctorate in canon law from the Pontifical Oriental Institute, Rome, in 1980.

EUGENE J. FITZSIMMONS is pastor of St. Michael Parish in Gibbstown, New Jersey and Promotor of Justice for the Diocese of Camden, New Jersey; he received his doctorate in canon law from the Pontifical Lateran University, Rome, in 1971.

JOSEPH A. FRANK is Director of Risk Management and Insurance Services for the Archdiocese of Newark, New Jersey; he received his Master of Business Administration from Columbia University, New York, in 1978.

JORDAN F. HITE, T.O.R. is with the St. John the Baptist Catholic Church in Wagner, S.D. and serves as canonical counsel to two major healthcare systems; he received his civil law degree from the Georgetown University School of Law in 1963 and his licentiate in canon law from Saint Paul University, Ottawa in 1976.

MATTHEW P. HUBER is the pastor of Holy Family Parish in Missoula, Montana along with Spirit of Christ Mission in Lolo, Montana and is a judge for the marriage tribunal in Helena, Montana; he received his licentiate in canon law from The Catholic University of America, Washington, DC, in 1993.

ROBERT L. KEALY is the Judicial Vicar of the Court of Appeals of the Province of Chicago; he received his civil law degree from DePaul University College of Law, Chicago, Illinois, in 1976 and his doctorate in canon law from the Pontifical Gregorian University, Rome, in 1986.

ELIZABETH McDONOUGH, O.P. is canonical consultant for the Archdiocese of Washington and canonical counsel editor for *Review for Religious*; she received her doctorate in canon law from The Catholic University of America, Washington, DC, in 1982.

KEVIN M. McDONOUGH is the Vicar General and Moderator of the Curia for the Archdiocese of St. Paul and Minneapolis; he received his doctorate in canon law from the Pontifical University of St. Thomas, Rome, in 1987.

KEVIN E. McKENNA is the Chancellor and Director of Legal Services for the Diocese of Rochester; he received his doctorate in canon law from St. Paul University, Ottawa, in 1990.

FRANCIS G. MORRISEY, O.M.I. is the Titular Professor of Canon Law at St. Paul University, Ottawa; he received his doctorate in canon law from St. Paul University, Ottawa, in 1972.

THOMAS J. PAPROCKI is the Chancellor of the Archdiocese of Chicago; he received his civil law degree from DePaul University College of Law, Chicago, Illinois, in 1981 and his doctorate in canon law from the Pontifical Gregorian University, Rome, in 1991.

JOSEPH N. PERRY is an Auxiliary Bishop of Chicago, Illinois and instructor in Canon Law Studies at St. Mary of the Lake Seminary, Mundelein, Illinois; he received his licentiate in canon law from The Catholic University of America, Washington, DC, in 1981.

JOSEPH W. POKUSA is the Chancellor and Episcopal Vicar for Canonical Affairs for the Diocese of Camden; he received his doctorate in canon law from The Catholic University of America, Washington, DC, in 1979.

RICHARD B. SAUDIS is the Vice-Chancellor of the Archdiocese of Chicago; he received his licentiate in sacred theology from St Mary of the Lake Seminary, Mundelein, Illinois, in 1955.

ROYCE R. THOMAS is pastor of Christ the King Parish in Ft. Smith, Arkansas and has served on a number of committees of the Canon Law Society of America; he received his licentiate in canon law from The Catholic University of America, Washington, DC, in 1977.

WILLIAM A. VARVARO is pastor of St. Margaret's Parish in Middle Village, New York and has served as Judicial Vicar for the Diocese of Brooklyn; he received his doctorate in canon law from the Pontifical Gregorian University, Rome, in 1986.

DAVID J. WALKOWIAK is Associate Professor and Dean of Students at St. Mary Seminary and Graduate School of Theology, Wickliffe, Ohio and Vice Chancellor of the Diocese of Cleveland; he received his doctorate in canon law from The Catholic University of America, Washington, DC, in 1987.

INDEX

FORMULARIES: